Managing Distributed Databases

Building Bridges between Database Islands

Managing Distributed Databases

Building Bridges between Database Islands

Donald K. Burleson

A Wiley/QED Publication

John Wiley & Sons, Inc.

New York • Chichester • Brisbane • Toronto • Singapore

Publisher: Katherine Schowalter
Editor: Robert Elliott
Managing Editor: Mark Hayden
Text Design & Composition: Publishers' Design and Production Services

Designations used by companies to distinguish their products are often claimed as trademarks. In all instances where John Wiley & Sons, Inc. is aware of a claim, the product names appear in initial capital or all capital letters. Readers, however, should contact the appropriate companies for more complete information regarding trademarks and registration.

This text is printed on acid-free paper.

This publication is designed to provide accurate and authoritative information in regard to the subject matter covered. It is sold with the understanding that the publisher is not engaged in rendering legal, accounting, or other professional services. If legal advice or other expert assistance is required, the services of a competent professional person should be sought. FROM A DECLARATION OF PRINCIPLES JOINTLY ADOPTED BY A COMMITTEE OF THE AMERICAN BAR ASSOCIATION AND A COMMITTEE OF PUBLISHERS.

Library of Congress Cataloging-in-Publication Data

ISBN: 0-471-08623-1

Printed in the United States of America

10 9 8 7 6 5 4 3 2 1

For Maureen, Andy, and Jenny,
whose love and support made this book possible.

Special thanks to the following vendors for their assistance in producing this text:

ConQuest Software
Objectivity Incorporated
Object Management Group
Platform Computing Incorporated
Powersoft Incorporated
UniSQL Incorporated

Because so much of business now depends on getting and sending information, companies around the world have been rushing to link their employees through electronic networks. These networks form the key infrastructure of the 21st century, as critical to business success and national economic development as the railroads were in Morse's era.

Alvin Toffler,
from *Power Shift*

Contents

Preface

Due to the volatile nature of corporate computing in the 1990s, many corporations are faced with the challenges of managing widely distributed database systems, systems that span geographical areas, hardware platforms, and database architectures. This new way of managing systems has presented unique opportunities as businesses struggle to sort through the vast amount of hardware and software solutions. The benefits of open systems come with the curse of having an infinite number of configurations from which to choose.

While some managers deliberately plan distributed database networks, others are forced into distributed databases because of changes in corporate structure. Managers who are embracing "downsizing" and "rightsizing" migrations have created situations in which many diverse "islands" of information are spread across many computer networks.

"Open systems" has become one of the foremost buzzwords of the 1990s but very little has been written about the issues involved in managing a diverse network of databases and making disparate database systems behave as parts of an integrated enterprise. With the trend toward corporate acquisitions, many IS departments inherit new databases and must manage many diverse types of database systems, each with its own hardware platform, database architecture, and communications protocols.

As more companies continue to downsize their database systems, there is a whole new set of concerns for the systems manager. Regardless of whether a company finds itself in a distributed database environment by deliberate plan or as a result of corporate acquisitions, it is the responsibility of the manager to insure that all of the information resources within the organization communicate with each other. This "bridge-building" function is very foreign to the traditional manager who is accustomed to the centralized mainframe environment. The recent popularity of client/server tools has also affected the expectations of the end-user community. Users now expect systems that possess graphical interfaces, and they demand multiple windows that can simultaneously access information from many databases. This type of inter-database integration presents a challenge to the administrator, who must find a way for the hodgepodge of databases to act as if they were a single, integrated system.

There is more to distributed database management than mastering the technology. Successful managers are also aware of the psychological issues involved in distributing data resources. Just as the end-users feared loss of control when their data was merged into the centralized systems of the last decade, users today fear the loss of control as their information is spread across many systems. The savvy manager must be able to enforce control, building the confidence of the users while gaining their trust.

It is also the role of the systems manager to insure that all of the distributed databases remain intact, both from a physical and logical standpoint. A change to a PC database, for example, may have ramifications for the content of a mainframe system that resides on another continent. Managers must be able to insure the seamless connections and security that they were accustomed to in the mainframe days, and they must also insure that the system performs at acceptable levels.

Performance and tuning of these diverse systems is especially challenging. When users are running client/server applications against many distributed databases, there are many points of failure, and many subsystems that may contribute to slow performance. The manager must be able to view each of the individual databases as a component in a larger system, and to track performance across many platforms and database architectures.

With the recent push toward object-oriented architectures, the systems manager must also be able to integrate this new paradigm with legacy systems. These are only a few of the issues that managers face when they enter into distributed systems. This text addresses some of these issues and provides a detailed overview of the technological and human issues involved in creating and maintaining a successful distributed database.

1

History of Distributed Databases

1.1 INTRODUCTION

The philosopher George Santayana once said, "Those who cannot remember the past are condemned to repeat it." His statement is especially appropriate for understanding the evolution and future of client/server and distributed databases, which has had a profound impact on state-of-the-art technology. The foundations that were laid over the past 30 years will dictate the direction of future technology, and the savvy manager must be positioned to reap the benefits of this new technology.

This evolution is based on a very simple premise: Hardware advances always precede advances in software systems. This phenomenon dates from the first release of mainframe computers by IBM in the 1950s. At that time, the computer was a very mysterious commodity, and few people had actually seen one. The only understanding that the public had about computers was from Buck Rogers, and there was very little serious thought about any practical applications of computers to everyday life. The early adopters of mainframe computing were large corporations that purchased the behemoth computers more for prestige than for need. It was not until a few of these companies had installed the computers that the question arose, "What can we do with these things?"

The same events can be seen with the introduction of the first Altair personal computers in the 1970s. These early forerunners of the PC were very crude and had to be assembled from kits, requiring a detailed knowledge of electrical engineering, not to mention programming. The early pioneers developed the first operating systems, which evolved into DOS, and Kemeny and

Kurtz developed one of the first compilers for these machines, the BASIC compiler. Even with the availability of compilers, people still did not envision any commercial application for this emerging technology until the creation of VisiCalc, the first electronic spreadsheet. Only then was there a real product to justify the purchase of these machines. It is interesting to note that the development of electronic spreadsheets created a great deal of controversy, as even the most enlightened business schools struggled to find applications for this new tool. But once a need was identified and tools existed, the PC became generally accepted in the marketplace.

We also see this pattern in the introduction of supercomputer technology. When Seymour Cray was an engineer with Control Data Corporation (CDC), he proposed an architecture for a computer that could achieve speeds in excess of 100 MIPS (100 million instructions per second). The management at CDC rejected Cray's proposal, claiming, quite correctly, that there was no immediate need for such processors. Cray, who appears to have understood the principle that hardware advances precede commercial application, went off on his own and founded Cray Research. As he probably expected, his first product was greeted with skepticism, and the only immediate customers were the government research laboratories. After all, the detractors said, what good is a machine that can process 200 million operations per second? Fortunately, the government labs quickly recognized the potential of the new supercomputers for encryption and simulation, and software was developed that would exploit the power of these machines. Once the market was established, many companies that rely on simulations began to find justification for these machines. Today, many major oil companies have found that the powerful simulation capabilities of the supercomputers easily justify their price, saving millions of dollars in drilling costs.

1.2   THE EVOLUTION OF COMPUTER LANGUAGE

The most common way to describe the evolution of languages is to tie the language with the hardware that existed at the time it was introduced. The other major approach deals with the user's viewpoint and classifies the history of computing into three "waves": punch-card technology, video display technology, and graphical user interface (GUI) technology (Bloor 1993).

Language and Hardware

The first-generation technology was characterized by vacuum tube hardware. Languages that were developed during this period were designed to provide a handle on the generation of object code, the binary language that operates directly on the machine. These code *assembly languages* became very popular and added to the mystique of computing by requiring that programmers learn a very cryptic and unreadable language. Interestingly, until very recently, assembly languages were still used to write operating system and database software.

Second-generation systems were characterized by transistors, and gave rise to the first procedural languages that did not directly manipulate the computers' registers. This was the start of a trend toward "high-level" languages of the third and fourth generations.

The third generation of computing hardware was characterized by the integrated circuit (IC), and heralded the introduction of computer languages that could be called user friendly. Grace Hopper, the grand old lady of data processing, recognized that the existing computer languages were not as productive as they could become, and helped to develop a new language, designed for use by businesses. This language, the COmmon Business Oriented Language (COBOL), became an instant hit. Simultaneously, we find the development of Fortran (FORmula TRANslation language), and the real age of practical data processing had begun. During the third generation, a low-level language called C was developed by Brian Kernigan and Dennis Ritchie at Bell Laboratories. Its promise of portability and high performance have since catapulted it far beyond where anyone would have guessed.

Fourth-generation hardware was characterized by VLSI, very large-scale integration of processors, and the languages became even friendlier and easier to program. Fourth-generation languages (4GLs) took care of all of the low-level programming, and left it to the programmer to concentrate on high-level program implementations. For example, the 4GL programmer did not need to be concerned with the protocol interface to the video display monitor or the management of multiple screen displays. There was even discussion of development environments that could write the code on the behalf of the end-user, without any direct intervention from the programmer. Tools such as the "wizards" of Excel and Access are examples of end-user systems development.

The User's Environment and Language

Another way of looking at the evolution of computer systems is to look at the major changes in the characteristics of the user interface.

The first age of data processing was characterized by "batch" systems that were accessed via magnetic tape or punched cards. In these systems, all interaction with the database took place via "input decks" of punched cards. Interaction with the computer was performed through glass TTY devices, and the inaccessibility of these computers contributed to their mystery and appeal. When the first IBM 1401 computers began shipping, many company presidents purchased them long before they had identified a need for the computers, preferring to have the immediate right to brag about their glass-encased machine rooms and the gigantic computers that had a memory capacity of 64,000 characters and could perform 5000 calculations in a single second.

The creation of the first glass TTY terminals heralded the beginning of the age of online systems. Such systems interacted with ISAM or VSAM files, and used a teleprocessing (TP) monitor to manage transactions. The first major teleprocessing monitor was the Customer Information Control System (CICS) from IBM. CICS allowed programmers to create screens that the users could use for data query and input. Methods were devised to allow such screen structures as pop-up lists, scrolling screens, and menus. All actions were triggered by pressing function keys. The systems were written in *pseudo-conversational mode*. In this mode, the TP monitor goes to sleep after displaying the information to the user's screen. Only when the user specifies an action does the TP monitor wake up, capture the request, perform the action, and return to sleep.

It is interesting to note that "windows" were developed for online systems long before the general availability of PC-based windows systems. These early windows resided on mainframe computers and allowed the user to partition a section of the screen for the window, and view different subsets of information independently from the rest of the screen. While they did not have the benefit of a mouse or other Windows constructs such as push buttons, these systems allowed partial screens to be overlaid, one on top of another.

One must remember that the windows paradigm (on a single-processing PC) is really an illusion. What appears to be cascades of active windows is really an overlay of many pseudo-conversational screens that go to sleep when the window is switched or closed. (In fact, the only part of such an interface that is truly conversational is the software that was developed to track mouse movements.)

Of course, these early online systems were character-based. This limited the amount of information that could be displayed on a screen to an array of characters of 79 columns by 24 rows. Teleprocessing systems were incapable of displaying anything other than the standard character set, and nontraditional information such as bitmap pictures could not be displayed.

Characteristic of the online processing era were third-generation languages (3GLs) such as COBOL, Fortran, and C, and some fourth-generation languages (4GLs) such as Focus and ADS/Online. Databases of this era ranged from flat-file systems such as ISAM and VSAM, to hierarchical databases such as IMS, to the CODASYL network databases such as IDMS, to the relational databases such as Oracle, DB2, and Sybase.

The introduction of the mouse led to some new screen structures that were previously unavailable, such as the push button, radio button, and scrolling edit areas. Today, automatic voice recognition (ASR) is beginning to replace keystrokes and mouse movements.

The window-based *graphical user interfaces* (*GUIs*) that many end-users

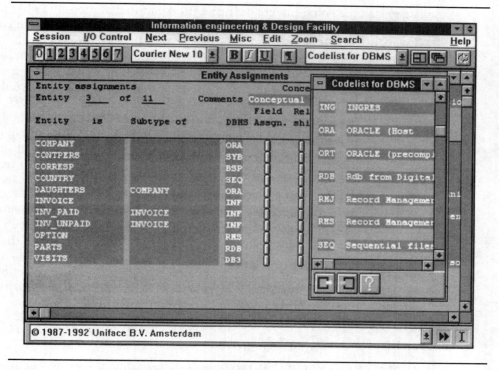

Figure 1.1   Window's-based interface.

have become accustomed to were only made possible after 1985. In terms of functionality, the graphical user interface was really not very different from a pseudo-conversational system (Figure 1.1). The other significant feature of a GUI is the ability to display textual information in any font size or font style.

As the new multiprocessing PC software becomes available (Windows NT), we will see that windows can become simultaneous—a true advance over the earlier pseudo-conversational systems.

1.3   WHERE WE ARE TODAY

The systems that were developed in the early 1990s were not as revolutionary as the demise of punched cards and the introduction of GUIs. Rather, the client/ server and distributed database movement is more invisible to the users.

A careful study of the evolution of online systems establishes a trend line that can give us some insight into the future of distributed and client/server systems. As processors continue to increase in speed and decrease in cost, the next revolution will exploit the inherent power of client/server and change the way information systems function, not just how they appear. For example, imagine high-speed processors on everyone's desk, with each machine having the power of an IBM 3090 mainframe. The client/server component would then become more of a data server than a shared processor, and corporate information could be extracted and manipulated freely within the information domain. The greatest challenges over the next decade will be the management of distributed data. Centralized corporate servers must be built and managed so that a user, regardless of geographical location or computer platform, can instantly access and manipulate data. These new servers will open up a new career field, with new jobs such as "object administrator."

The widespread acceptance of object technology will dramatically change the complexion of information systems programming. Just as Eli Whitney's idea of interchangeable parts changed the way that rifles were assembled in the 1700s, object technology will forever change the way that computer systems are constructed. Rather than being artists who create unique works, object-oriented programmers will take on the role of code "assemblers," choosing prewritten and tested code functions, and combining them in unique ways.

Cost-Effectiveness and Programming Languages

It is interesting to note that the object-oriented languages do not follow the pattern that we have seen in previous programming languages. If we take a look at people costs vs. CPU costs, we find that the procedural language of the day was suited to the economic situation at the time (Figure 1.2). The early second-generation languages were designed to be high in people resources but very efficient in CPU consumption. This is to be expected, because in the early 1960s people costs were less expensive than CPU cycles. Programming competitions in the 1960s judged the contestants by how efficient a program they could write, not by how fast they could write it. Processor cycles were precious, and the programmers were taught to carefully hand-execute each line of code before submitting it to the compiler.

As time passed, people costs remained constant while the costs of CPU time began to fall dramatically (Figure 1.3). Here we see the introduction of the third-generation languages such as COBOL and Fortran. These languages recognize the falling costs of CPU cycles relative to people costs, allowing programmers to become more productive, even if it meant more processing time to compile their programs. We still see carryovers from the earlier days, with features such as 66-level entries in COBOL, that served only to save a small amount of memory during execution time, but there is a clear trend to make procedural language programming more productive for the programmer.

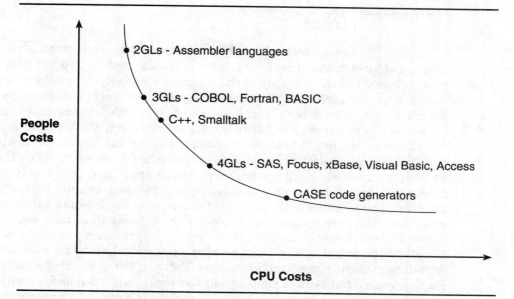

Figure 1.2   People costs vs. CPU costs.

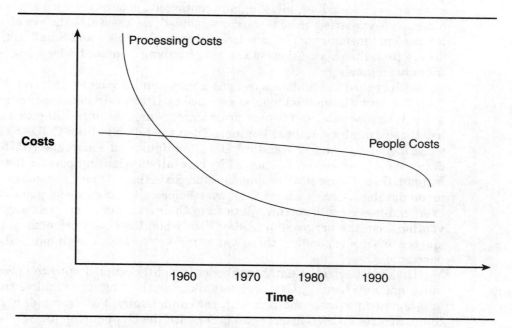

Figure 1.3   People costs vs. CPU costs over time.

Processing costs eventually fell by a factor of 100, and fourth-generation languages gave recognition to this new economic reality. Programmer costs now amounted to the majority of the manager's budget; the marketplace was demanding languages that could make programmers more productive. Here we see the introduction of high-level languages such as SAS, Focus, and "wizard"-based environments such as Microsoft Visual Basic and Microsoft Access.

However, the fall in processor costs cannot continue forever. As the potential of silicon technology is maximized—notice the flattening of the CPU curve in Figure 1.3—each marginal improvement in speed and power is becoming more expensive. When a new technology arrives—say, gallium arsenide—we may see another surge in the decline of processor costs. It is also interesting to note that computer programmers are worse off today than they were in the 1960s (in net-present value dollars). While programming skills have commanded high salaries, the programming profession has fallen victim to the friendliness of the procedural languages. Today, a ten-year-old can create and manipulate a database by using friendly tools with "wizards," and it is no longer necessary to have a master's degree in computer science to program a computer. Consequently, we see a trend away from the high salaries of the 1960s, when programming was a skill reserved for those who could afford the cost of many years of expensive training.

Given these trends, we might expect to see the next generation of languages as being even friendlier, allowing automatic code generation with a minimum of technical expertise. Here is the rub—instead, we are seeing the age of object-oriented programming. The new languages, such as C++ and Smalltalk, are a far cry from the expectations of the programming community for a high-level, friendly language.

With regard to databases, we see a very similar backward trend (Figure 1.4). The first commercial databases, such as IBM's IMS database, were very difficult to navigate, and it took programmers months of training to begin to use these complex database engines. Then the advent of the CODASYL network model provided a standard Data Manipulation Language (DML), but database access was still achieved by carefully navigating pointer lists. The introduction of the relational model (and Structured Query Language, SQL) made database access easier than ever before. SQL became so popular that even end-users could retrieve data from their own tables without any intervention from the programming staff. But when the object-oriented database started to become popular, there was a trend *away* from the simple SQL database access.

The object-oriented database model is tightly coupled with the programming language (usually C++ or Smalltalk), and the language requires that the programmer navigate the data structures manually. For example, here is a comparison of an SQL insert of an order with the C++ equivalent:

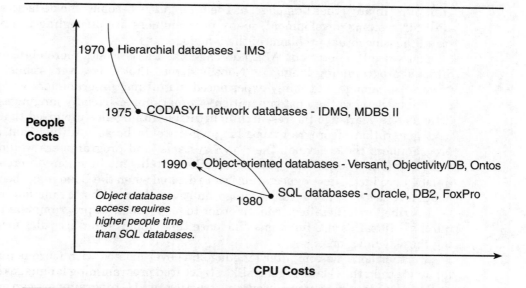

Figure 1.4 Database access—People costs vs. CPU costs.

SQL code:

```
INSERT INTO ORDER VALUES ("IBM", 123);
```

Object-oriented code:

```
order(customer &cust, int ordnum) { // order constructor
    cout << "\nCreating order " << ordnum << "\n";
    itemCount = 0;
    orderNum = ordnum;               // set the order number
    cust.orderList[cust.orderCount++] = this; // set cust -> order
    custOwner = &cust;               // set order-> customer pointer
};
```

1.4   A CLOSER LOOK: PROGRAMMING WITH C

Over the past several years the C language has become a very marketable language. Computer Careers sections of the want ads are full of C programmer positions with very attractive salaries, and those who understand the object-oriented extensions (C++) are in even greater demand. As a natural consequence, thousands of traditional mainframe programmers are rushing to add the C language to their skills. However, programming with C is unlike programming in any other language; as the C language becomes the de facto standard for systems development, many programmers are struggling to understand the conceptual problems of the language.

Not since the notorious APL language has there been a more obtuse and difficult programming language. Nobody denies that C is a very robust and powerful language, but many experienced mainframe programmers were expecting to go on to the next generation of programmer-friendly languages. As little as five years ago the research in artificial intelligence promised that the next generation of programming languages would be so intuitive that non-programmers could develop their own systems, and programmers would become "system assemblers," piecing together intelligent functions to create a finished product. These expectations were dashed when the C language became popular. C is a very low-level language, and even the most basic functions must be described with detailed code. In order to be productive, programmers must purchase libraries of C functions and learn the complex interface rules for calling these C functions.

Furthermore, no computer language has ever existed with more potential for abuse than the C language. Unlike structured programming languages such as Pascal, C does not enforce program structure, and C programmers can easily create applications that are unreadable, even by C experts.

The C language appears very cryptic to C novices, and the obtuse syntax of the language is compounded by professors who encourage their students to perform multiple functions within a single line of code. More than any other issue, the capability of C to deeply embed functions is one of the major obstacles to the readability of the language.

Function Nesting and Efficiency

Remember the early days of COBOL programming, when programmers were judged by how efficiently they could make a program run rather than on readability and maintainability? Today, most C and C++ programmers are taught to pursue efficiency with a nearly religious zeal, and this pursuit of efficiency has the undesirable side effect of making the programs very difficult to read and maintain. Compare the following code in COBOL and C:

COBOL code:

```
OPEN OUTPUT OUT-FILE.
WRITE OUT-REC FROM 'Hello World'.
```

C code:

```
char s[13]='72,101,108,108,111,32,87,111,114,108,100,33,0};
FILE* f; int i;
```

```
for(f=fopen("text.fil","w+"), i=0; s[i] && f != NULL;
fputc(s[i],f),i++);
```

Now I ask you, which code is easier to understand?

There is a natural trade-off between programming for readability and programming for efficiency. When a language is designed to be "programmer friendly" the syntax is easy to read and the programs are easily understood. This friendliness is at the expense of performance. Low-level languages such as assembler and C are designed to emphasize speed over programmer friendliness, and these languages are much harder to read and understand than the higher level languages (see Figure 1.1). C programmers are taught to make their programs efficient because C is often used to write system software such as databases. While efficiency is desirable in systems software, programming for efficiency can lead to major problems when writing application systems, such as payroll or inventory systems.

In order to fully exploit the power of C, you need to be able to nest functions so that you can reduce the number of variables that you need. Declaring and using many variables can detract from code readability just as much as nesting functions.

Some of the programming "purists" express great wonder at the ability of C to recursively nest functions within functions, and many university professors place emphasis on programming with a minimum amount of keystrokes. Clearly, the programming goal of "compact" coding is at odds with the management goal of maintainable code. Programming for elegance is not the same as programming for clarity.

With the emphasis on compact code, savvy C programmers can insure job security by nesting numerous functions within each other. Follow this method, and they can guarantee that nobody is able to decipher their work. Another benefit is prestige. Upon inspection of this type of coding, even self-professed C experts will never admit that they do not understand your code, and will make complimentary remarks about your ability to nest functions. The downside for programmers comes when they are asked to make modifications to the C program and discover that it takes many hours to understand what the code is doing before they have any hope of making changes to the program.

The answer to this efficiency/readability debate is moderation. Nobody advocates writing C like a COBOL program, where the code is carefully crafted to be readable. C++ has many powerful facilities such as encapsulation and information hiding, and we expect programmers to use these facilities.

The widespread acceptance of C as a de facto language standard is analogous to Eli Whitney's development of interchangeable parts. Before the introduction of C, systems were handcrafted and had few, if any, reusable parts. Today, vendors are marketing fully tested C and C++ libraries. Properly designed C programs are assembled from preexisting and pretested library routines, and the program itself becomes little more than a "shell" for the calls to the prewritten C functions. This dramatically changes the job of the programmer, who is no longer concerned with how a function works but with how to assemble functions into a cohesive program.

The Case for Element Nesting

There are some C experts who feel that deeply nested functions actually improve the maintainability of C code. For example, take the following code:

```
int fx(int a, int b) {
int c,d,e
c = max(a,b);
d= a + b;
e = 2*(d-c);      }
```

The code isn't any more readable than the following, which uses nesting:

```
int fx(int a, int b) {
int e;
e=2*((a+b)-max(a,b));   }
```

By placing multiple functions within a single statement, the programmer reduces the number of program variables, producing efficient, compact code with the minimum number of programming statements.

There is not going to be a simple resolution to the difference of opinion about coding style, but it does appear that C is here to stay and that "generally accepted" coding styles will eventually emerge. Until then, the industry will continue to evolve the C standard.

1.5   FUTURE TRENDS

The widespread acceptance of C and object-oriented programming is going to have broad ramifications for the database community. Whereas database languages have followed the procedural language trend of becoming friendlier, we see that the object technology paradigm is moving database programming back in time with respect to user friendliness. The speed of the language is important to system software such as a database management system where code may be called dozens of times each second. Conversely, application programmers want to enjoy a fast, simple data query language. To the writer of the database software, even the smallest performance improvement becomes important to the overall performance of the database, but it does not seem reasonable to expect application programmers to use the same language as the database software. Fortunately, vendors are recognizing that the obtuse "navigational" nature of C++ class structures can be bypassed by creating SQL-like interfaces into their object-oriented engines. This is very similar to the approach of Cullinet, which added SQL access to its popular IDMS database.

While object technology is going to change the fundamental way that programmers process information, there is still a trend to make the programming staff as productive as possible. As C and C++ class libraries become more widely available, we will see a movement into code reusability that will make up the differences in coding in a lower-level language such as C++.

REFERENCES

Batelle, J. et al. 1992. Planning for 1995: The future is now. *Corporate Computing*, December.

Bell, D. 1992. *Distributed database systems*. Addison-Wesley.

Blaser, A., ed. 1990. *Database systems of the 90s*. Berlin: International Symposium.

Bloor, R. 1993. The patterns of change: Are you ready for the third major computer technology wave? *DBMS Magazine* 6:1 (January).

Bobak, A. 1993. *Distributed and multidatabase systems*. Bantam Books.

Burleson, D. 1993. Distributed object technology. *First Class Magazine*, October.

———. 1994. C neophytes. *COMPUTERWORLD*, February 14.

———. 1994. Managing distributed databases—An enterprise view. *Database Programming & Design*, June.

———. 1994. An update on object-oriented databases. *Software Magazine*, November.

Chu, W., ed. 1986. *Distributed database systems*. Books on Demand.

Fiorio, T. 1992. Managing distributed applications. *DEC Professional*, December.

Hackathorn, R. 1993. *Enterprise database connectivity*. John Wiley.

Katzan, H. 1991. *Distributed information systems*. Petrocelli Books.

McFadden, F. 1994. *Modern Database Management*. 4th ed. Benjamin Cummings Publishing Company.

2

What Is a Database?

2.1 INTRODUCTION

The term "database" has been in use for many years and has come to mean just about any conceivable medium for the storage of information. There are relational databases, object-oriented databases, database machines—and it appears that the list of database-related terms is growing daily. So, what is a database?

The usage of the term "database" evolved from the definitions created by the Committee on Development of Applied Symbolic Languages (CODASYL) and its Data Base Task Group (DBTG). The CODASYL DBTG defined the characteristics that compose a database and included features such as backup and recovery, automatic recovery, and many of the other components that are found in most database offerings.

Generally, databases are categorized by the way they maintain data relationships. All database management software, regardless of its sophistication, is nothing more than a set of programs that store and manipulate data using a combination of basic data structures. The data structures are linked lists, tree structures, and hashing algorithms. Under the covers, all of the commercial databases use these basic data structures, and the configuration of these structures governs the type of architecture of the database.

The evolution of database architecture is shown in Figure 2.1. Note that up until the introduction of object-oriented databases, each architecture adds additional functionality. Here we see that easy data access (via SQL) had been lost in favor of the ability to store behaviors within the database. While many of the object database vendors are rushing to develop easy data access with software tools like SQL++ and ObjectSQL, there is still this divergence in database evolution.

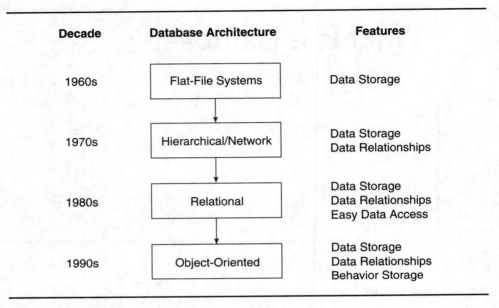

Decade	Database Architecture	Features
1960s	Flat-File Systems	Data Storage
1970s	Hierarchical/Network	Data Storage Data Relationships
1980s	Relational	Data Storage Data Relationships Easy Data Access
1990s	Object-Oriented	Data Storage Data Relationships Behavior Storage

Figure 2.1   Evolution of database architectures.

For the purpose of this text, the term "database" can mean any electronic storage of data, whether or not the information is stored in an electronic file form. Today, advances in independent access tools can make everything from e-mail to spreadsheets appear and function as traditional databases.

Over the past thirty years the number of transactions per second databases is increasing, irrespective of advances in the speeds of the processors (Figure 2.2). There has been a problem with some of the relational database offerings that sacrifice speed for improved flexibility, but many commercial relational databases can support hundreds of transactions per second and are fast enough for most business purposes.

The architecture, or type, of the database has a major impact on the implementation of the client/server system. There are databases that are designed to handle text data, databases that are good with numerical data, databases for high-volume transaction processing, and so on. As of this date, no one has developed a commercial database product that can handle all of the varied requirements of a large corporation. In some cases, the data requirements are mutually exclusive. For example, text-oriented database products are not designed for high-volume updating, and high-volume databases do not perform word searching effectively. Users with these dual requirements are forced to use two databases, one static database for the word searching, and another database for the high-

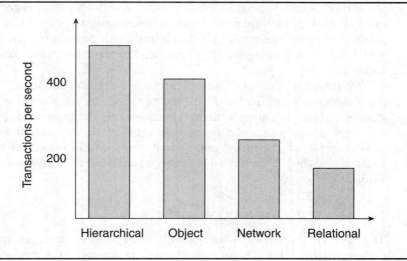

Figure 2.2   Relative speeds of the database architectures.

volume updating. These differing requirements have led to a plethora of customized databases, each with a specific market niche, for example:

Text searching: Oracle Book, Folio, Basis

High-speed processing: IMS/Fastpath, Teradata, MasPar, FoxPro

CAD/CAM: Objectivity/DB

Manufacturing: CA/IDMS

Multimedia: FoxPro, Folio

SGML text: Basis/SGML/Access, TechnoTeacher

Object-oriented: Objectivity/DB, Ontos, UniSQL, Versant

Relational: Oracle, Sybase, DB2, FoxPro

These incompatible data requirements have been the foremost reason for companies to embrace distributed databases. Remember, distribution can mean either geographical distribution or architectural distribution, and architectural distribution is often necessary for companies that have varied data requirements, and that also want a unified system.

Ignoring architectural issues for the moment, let's look at databases in terms of basic function. Functionally, we find three general types of databases.

Local, personal databases are probably the most popular databases today because of the advances in PC software. Every PC user, regardless of experience on data modeling, can create and manipulate data using these PC tools. Advanced functions such as table joining can be taken care of by "wizards," which embed the complex logic, freeing the user to create relatively sophisticated systems.

Distributed, shared databases are those that are commonly associated with data processing applications. These are multiuser databases with the ability to manage numerous simultaneous queries against the same data engine.

High-performance databases fall into two categories: those systems that must support thousands of concurrent users and hundreds of transactions per second, and those that have a very large volume of data and are computationally intensive.

2.2   DATABASE DESIGN CONCEPTS

The earliest databases were nothing more than electronic filing cabinets that served to store data. After commercial databases were introduced, organizations were able to store both data and the relationships between data items.

As data modeling became more sophisticated, rules were developed to allow for the efficient design of complex data models. The work of Dr. Peter Chen on the entity-relationship model and E. F. Codd's rules of data normalization are examples of some of the basic data modeling theories that have emerged during the past twenty years.

In their struggle to make database design a legitimate science, theoreticians began to publish papers that expanded on these early works and dealt with rare exceptions to basic data relationships. Examples include Boyce-Codd Normal Form (BCNF), fourth normal form (4NF), and fifth normal form (5NF). These theoreticians hoped that by applying mathematical rigor to their models, data modeling could gain the same legitimacy as the harder sciences.

Unfortunately, while theory is sometimes useful, many of the concepts had to be bent to accommodate practical considerations. Anyone who has attempted to design a relational database that is completely free of redundancy (third normal form) can attest that while the data is modeled correctly from a theoretical perspective, the performance of the database can be abysmal. Consequently, redundancy must be reintroduced into the design in order to achieve acceptable performance. Today, data modeling remains as much an art as a science, because the database administrator must decide what redundancy of data items to introduce into the model. While there are rules for the introduction of redundancy, the actual choices depend heavily upon the application, and cannot be quantified in a mathematical form.

The two factors that determine if a data item should be redundantly added are the size of the redundant data item and the volatility of the data item. For example, little harm could be done by introducing redundancy into a small, seldom-changing data item such as a SEX field. The field is usually one byte in length (M or F), and it will not change except in cases of surgical procedures. On the other hand, it would not be wise to redundantly introduce a data item that is both large and unstable. For example, STREET-ADDRESS might be 40 bytes long, and may change frequently. The redundant data item will be expensive to store on disk, and it will also require additional effort for the database to update the information in both places.

Data Relationships

There are five types of data relationships that must be considered when designing any database:

- One-to-one relationship
- One-to-many relationship
- Many-to-many relationship
- Recursive many-to-many relationship
- ISA relationship

In database modeling, a data item that has a *one-to-one relationship* with the primary key becomes an attribute of the table. For example, if the social security number has a one-to-one relationships with full_name in the PERSON entity, then social security number becomes an attribute of the PERSON entity.

In *one-to-many relationships*, a single occurrence of the owner entity may have several occurrences of the subordinate entity, but each subordinate entity will have only one owner (Figure 2.3).

Father to Son	One father may have many sons, but a son has only one father
Customer to Order	A customer places many orders, but an order is for only one customer

The *many-to-many relationship* implies that one entity has many of the other entity, and a converse relationship exists at the other entity (Figure 2.4):

Order to Item	Each order has many items, and an item participates in many orders.
Student to Classes	A student takes many classes, and a class has many students.

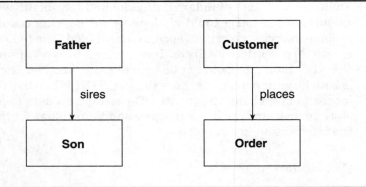

Figure 2.3   One-to-many relationships.

Note the introduction of the *junction* or intersection table in these relationships. The junction entity is required to create the many-to-many relationship between the data items. For relational implementations, junction entities must contain the primary keys of their owner entities. Object-oriented databases use

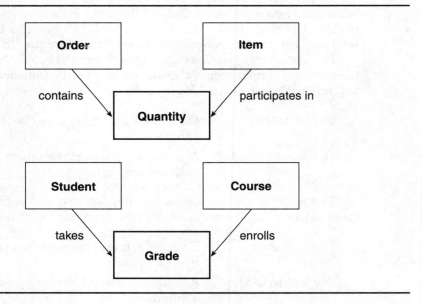

Figure 2.4   Many-to-many relationships.

pointers to link junction records, but the junction entities may contain additional data, such as GRADE or QUANTITY_ORDERED.

Recursive Data Relationships

In *recursive many-to-many relationships*, an object has a many-to-many relationship with other occurrences of the same object class. These relationships are sometimes called bill-of-materials (BOM) relationships, and the graphical representation of the recursive relationship is sometimes call a bill-of-materials explosion. These relationships are called recursive because a single query may make many passes through the tables to arrive at the solution.

As an example, a part may consist of other parts, and at the same time be a component in a larger assembly. A class at a university may have many prerequisites, and at the same time, be a prerequisite for another class. In the legal arena, a court case may cite other cases, and at the same, be cited by later cases (Figure 2.5).

A bill-of-material request for components of a Big Meal would show that a Big Meal consists of a hamburger, fries, and a Coke, a hamburger consists of two meat patties, a bun, and a pickle, a meat patty consists of meat and filler, and so on.

Consider the example of CLASS-PREREQUISITE. Figure 2.6 describes a course-prerequisite hierarchy for a university. Note that the is-a-prerequisite relationships are relatively straightforward, indicating which courses are required to take a course. For example, the prerequisites for Linear Equations 445 are Business 400, Accounting 305, and Multivariate Statistics 450. These courses also have prerequisites, which may, in turn, have prerequisites, and so on. We could "explode" the prerequisites for Linear Equations 445 as follows:

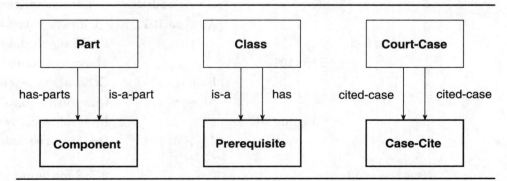

Figure 2.5   Recursive many-to-many relationships.

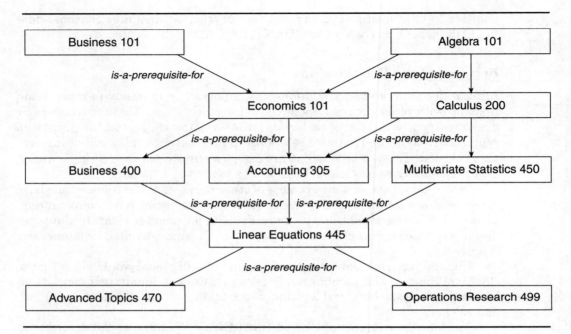

Figure 2.6   Recursive courses with prerequisites.

Prerequisite	Prerequisite	Prerequisite	Topic
Business 400			Financial management
	Econ 101		Macroeconomics
		Business 101	General management
		Algebra 101	Quadratic equations
Accounting 305			FASB regulations
	Econ 101		Macroeconomics
		Business 101	General management
		Algebra 101	Quadratic equations
	Calculus 200		Integral calculus
		Algebra 101	Quadratic equations
Multivariate Statistics 450			SPSS modeling
	Calculus 200		Integral calculus
		Algebra 101	Quadratic equations

Each occurrence of a COURSE object will have different topics, and an object-oriented implementation must be able to iterate through all courses until it reaches *terminus*, where the course has no further prerequisites.

Unfortunately, the recursive many-to-many relationship is very confusing and almost impossible to understand without the aid of a graphical representation. Students have suggested that these are called bill-of-material "explosions" because of what happens to their brain cells when they try to comprehend these relationships.

A nineteenth-century mathematician, Augustus De Morgan, described the recursive many-to-many relationship with a very entertaining poem:

> Great fleas have little fleas upon their backs to bite 'em,
> And little fleas have lesser fleas, and so ad infinitum.
> The great fleas themselves, in turn, have greater fleas to go on,
> While these, in turn, have greater still, and greater still, and so on.

It is helpful to visualize the recursive many-to-many relationship as an ordinary many-to-many relationship with the owner entity "pulled apart" into owner1 and owner2. Figure 2.7 shows how the junction entity is used to establish the relationship.

There is no substitute for a picture to help conceptualize a recursive many-to-many relationship. In the CODASYL model, these are called "set occurrence" diagrams, and they show the *pointer chains* that are used to link the relationships. For relational databases, table sketches are used to show the junction table that contains both an implosion and an explosion column. Students find that the set occurrence diagram is very helpful for understanding data relationships.

In Figure 2.8, it is easy to see how the database would be navigated to determine the components for a Big Meal. To navigate this diagram, start at the object Big_Meal and follow the has-parts link to the bubble containing the number 1. This is the quantity for the item, and following this bubble's is-a-part link tells us that one order of fries is included in a Big Meal. Now we return to the has-parts link for Big Meal, and find the next bubble, whose is-a-part link tells us that one soda participates in a Big Meal. We continue this process until we do not find any more entities in the has-parts relationship. In sum, the has-parts relationships indicate that a Big Meal consists of one order of fries, one soda, and one hamburger. We also see that the hamburger consists of two meat patties and one bun.

You can also see how the database can be navigated to determine which parts use a specific component. For example, start at the hamburger bubble, and navigate the is-a-part relationships to see that one hamburger participates in a Value Meal and one in the Big Meal.

Recursive relationships are also indicated. For example, if we were listing the components of a Big Meal, all components would also be displayed in the bill-of-material explosion:

The relationship:

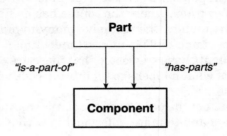

Is equivalent to:

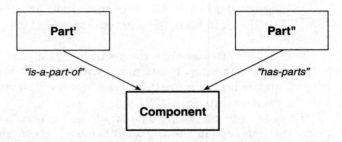

Figure 2.7 A recursive many-to-many relationship may be viewed as a many-to-many relationship.

PART1	PART2	PART3	Quantity
Hamburger			1
	Meat Patty		2
		Oatmeal	4 oz.
		Beef lips	3 oz.
	Bun		1
Fries			1 order
	Potato		1
	Grease		1 cup
Soda			1
	Ice		1/2 cup
	Drink		1/3 cup

Conversely, the recursion association could be applied to any item to see which items it participates in.

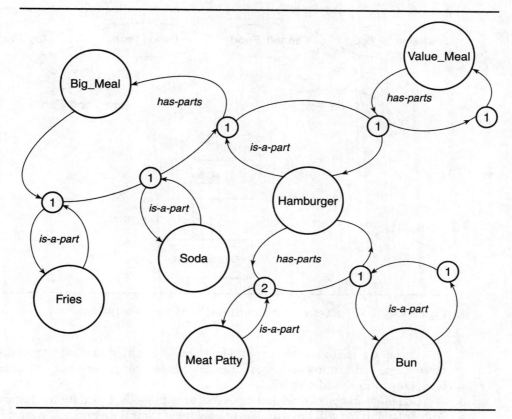

Figure 2.8   Set occurrence diagram: recursive relationship.

PART1	PART2	PART3
Fries		
		Big Meal
		Value Meal
Meat Patty		
	Hamburger	
		Big Meal
		Value Meal
	Cheeseburger	
	Big Zac	
Fried Pies		
		Value Meal

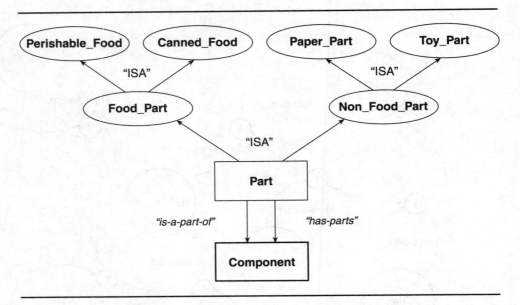

Figure 2.9   Recursive many-to-many relationships with ISA hierarchy.

These are quite simple examples; there are many database systems that have items with many subassemblies, and these recursions may go dozens of levels down in the hierarchy.

Consider an object-oriented database to manage fast food items (Figure 2.9). All nonfood items will have a class to hold all of their data and behaviors. This is an example of an "abstract" class, because no object of NON_FOOD_PART would ever be created. NON_FOOD_PART does include ordering behaviors, and the names of suppliers, but these will be inherited by the lower level classes, namely the TOY_PART and PAPER_PART objects. Next in the class hierarchy we would find the TOY_PART class, which also has data and behaviors; unlike the NON_FOOD_PART "abstract" class, TOY_PART is a "concrete" class. As we know, a concrete class will have objects, and all objects of the TOY_PART class will inherit the data and behaviors from the NON_FOOD_PART class.

The ISA relationship defines a subset of items within a hierarchy. For example, a sedan "ISA" subset of Car, which in turn "ISA" subset of the Vehicle class.

2.3   FROM MAINFRAME TO DISTRIBUTED SYSTEMS

The progression from the "glass house" environment to the open system did not happen overnight. One must remember that the ideas that developed into open systems were the very same ideas that were used to create the centralized database systems. These features of open, distributed database systems include scalability, ease of maintenance, and faster reaction time to changes. The following history will show that many of the features we seek in distributed databases have evolved as a steady progression.

The following pages are a historical review of database evolution, showing each of the enhancements that were introduced with each new architecture. It is important to review the problems that each database architecture solved as well as those new problems that were introduced. As you will see, there are striking similarities between object-oriented databases and earlier database architectures. By understanding the historical reason that object-oriented databases have evolved into their present form, we can gain insight into the future trend and directions of databases.

Flat-File Systems: c. 2200 BC–AD 1965

Prior to the development of the early commercial databases such as IMS, many "database" systems were a conglomeration of flat-file storage methods. The term "flat-file" includes physical-sequential storage (Figure 2.10) as well as the indexed sequential access method (ISAM) and virtual sequential access method

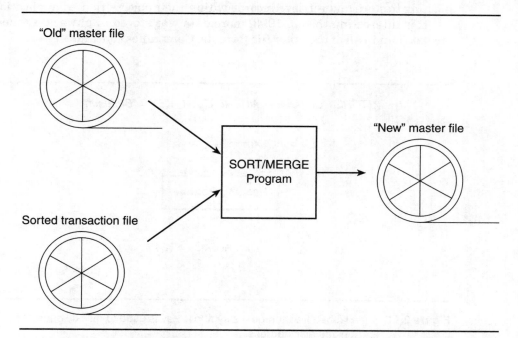

Figure 2.10   Physical sequential files are updated by the creation of a "new" file.

(VSAM). For physical-sequential file systems, updates were performed by re-writing the master file, and data access could only be performed sequentially. Other flat-file systems such as ISAM and VSAM were physical-sequential files with indexes, and were stored on disks or drums.

The data access methods used by these systems were very primitive. The BDAM (basic direct access method) was used for fast access and retrieval of information. BDAM uses a "hashing algorithm," which takes a symbolic key and converts it into a location address on disk (a disk address), as shown in Figure 2.11. Unfortunately, the range of addresses generated by these algorithms requires careful management. Because a hashing algorithm produces the same key each time it reads an input value, duplicate keys have to be avoided. BDAM file structures also consume a large amount of disk storage. Because records are randomly distributed across the disk device, it is common to see hashed files with more unused space than occupied space. In most cases, a BDAM file is considered "logically" full if more than 70 percent of the space contains data records.

Despite these problems, hashing remains one of the fastest ways to store and retrieve information. Most mainframe systems can take a symbolic key and convert it into a disk address in as little as 50 milliseconds. Although hashing is a very old technique, it is still a very powerful method. Many C++ programmers use hashing to store and retrieve records within their object-oriented applications.

It is interesting that in 1993, more data was stored in physical-sequential format than in all of the other file formats. Companies continue to use a flat-file

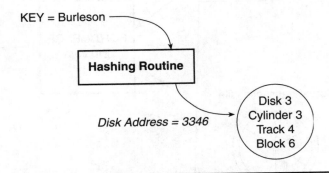

Figure 2.11   Hashed file storage—a symbolic key is used to quickly generate a unique disk address.

architecture because of systems that contain large amounts of unchanging, infrequently used data. Magnetic tapes, which are 10,000 times cheaper than disk, are still the most economical way to store large volumes of data.

Overall, online systems using ISAM and VSAM data structures were very difficult to create. Programmers were forced to write all of the details of the pseudo-conversational tasks, and it was very difficult to create complex transaction processing systems. The problems inherent in these systems were very serious:

Data relationships could not be maintained. Early flat-file systems could not easily recognize and manage the natural relationships between data items. One-to-many and many-to-many data relationships were often ignored, and widespread denormalization of the data occurred.

"Islands of information" developed within organizations, as different departments developed independent flat-file systems. These departmental "islands" were often written in different programming languages, with different file structures, and it was very difficult for departments to share information (Figure 2.12).

Widespread data redundancy developed. Departments within the corporate database often duplicated information, leading to the increased costs of data storage, and the possibility of update anomalies when a item was changed within one department but not within another.

Maintenance nightmares ensued. Because these systems had no repository of "metadata," program changes became very cumbersome. Whenever a file changed in structure, the programs that referred to the file could not readily be identified, and every program that referenced that file had to be modified and recompiled.

Tightly coupled data and programs led to maintenance problems. Because many application programs defined and maintained their own data structures, there was a problem as all new programs were forced to adhere to the calling procedures of the existing programs. The same communications problems exist within object-oriented systems. The CORBA standard for object-oriented systems was designed to insure that this problem would not resurface in the 1990s.

There was no concurrency control or recovery mechanism. Systems had no method for simultaneous updating of information, and no way to roll forward information in case of disk failure.

There was no method for establishing relationships between data items. The relationships between data items were generally lost, or had to be introduced with cumbersome data structures such as repeating fields within the records.

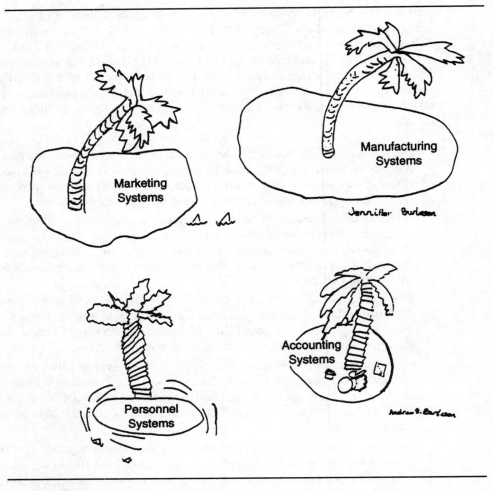

Figure 2.12   Islands of information.

The Hierarchical Database: c. AD 1965–1993

The problems associated with flat-file systems led to development of the first commercial database offering, IMS (Information Management System) from IBM. IMS is considered a hierarchical database, and is well suited for modeling systems in which the entities are composed of descending one-to-many relationships. Relationships are established with "child" and "twin" pointers, and these pointers are embedded into the prefix of every record in the database (Figure 2.13).

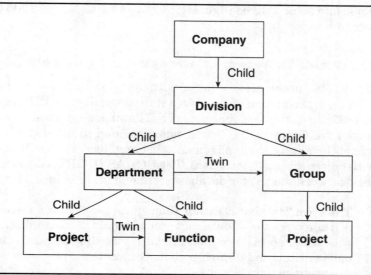

Figure 2.13   Hierarchical database architecture: child/twin pointers establish relationships.

IMS has concurrency control, and a backup and recovery mechanism. The recovery mechanism stores "before" and "after" images of each record that has changed, and these images can be used to "roll back" the database if a transaction fails to complete, or "rolled forward" in case of a disk failure. IMS could be used with CICS, and with its introduction developers began to create the first online database systems for the mainframe. But IMS has several major drawbacks. While it is very good at modeling hierarchical data relationships, complex data relationships such as many-to-many and recursive many-to-many (bill-of-material) relationships have to be implemented in a very clumsy fashion, with the use of phantom records. The IMS database also suffers from its complexity. Learning to program and administer an IMS database requires months of training, and consequently, IMS development remains very slow and cumbersome.

Who Has the "Fastest" Database? While IMS is considered a dinosaur by today's standards, IBM continues to sell new copies, and it is still used by hundreds of corporations. While some of these are "legacy systems" not easily converted to modern technology, many continue to use IMS because of its high speed. A hybrid of IMS, called IMS/FASTPATH, is one of the fastest commercial databases available, even by today's standards. IMS/FASTPATH is used at companies that may have hundreds or even thousands of concurrent transactions, and some IMS configurations have surpassed the 1000 transactions-per-second barrier.

The CODASYL Network Database: c. AD 1970–1980

Many of the problems associated with flat-file systems were partially addressed with the introduction of the IMS database product by IBM, but there remained no published standard for commercial database systems. The CODASYL Database Task Group (DBTG) was commissioned to develop a set of "rules," or a model for database management systems, just as the ODMG group is doing with object-oriented databases. The CODASYL DBTG developed what is called the "network model" for databases. Among other things, the group decided:

- The term "database" rather than "data base" would be used.
- A framework for a "data dictionary" would be created. The data dictionary was designed to store all metadata, including information about the database entities, relationships between entities, and information about how programs use the database.
- A standard architecture for database systems would be created, based on a combination of the BDAM (direct access) and linked-list data structures.
- There should be a separation of the logical structure of the data from the physical access methods. For example, a programmer could state OBTAIN CALC CUSTOMER WHERE CUST-ID = "IBM", without having to worry about where the record was physically stored on the disk.
- Procedures for concurrency control and database recovery would be established. Databases would manage record locks, preventing information overlaying, and databases could be rolled forward or rolled back, thereby insuring data integrity (Figure 2.14).
- A conceptual "schema" was described. The purpose of a schema is to govern the definition of the data and relationships. This was called DDL (data definition language), and was used to describe the business model. DDL included the constructs of files, areas, records, sets, and indexes. The term "set" was used to name a data relationship, and to describe the owner and member records in the relationship. Another construct was the subschema. Subschemas were used as a method for creating "user views" of the overall database and were also used to enforce system security.
- A standard data interface, called DML (data manipulation language), was developed to cover all selection and update operations that could be performed. DML verbs include:

Retrieval	GET, FIND, OBTAIN
Update	STORE, MODIFY, DELETE

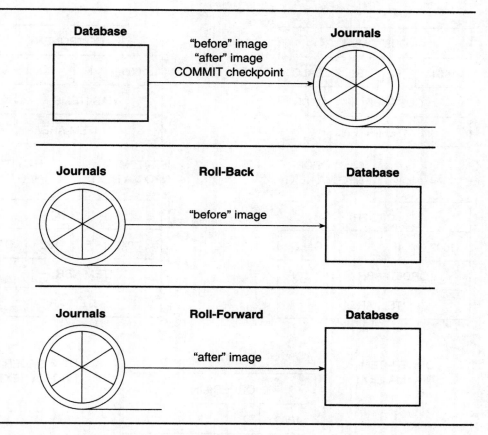

Figure 2.14 Journals allow data integrity.

Currency   DISCONNECT, CONNECT, FIND CURRENT OR
             RECORD-TYPE

The CODASYL model became the framework for new commercial database systems such as the IDMS database from Cullinane, and the MDBS2 database.

While the network model was very good at representing complex data relationships, it had one major drawback. The internal data structures were not transparent to the programmer, and the programmers were required to "navigate" the database structure to extract their information. Unlike when using a declarative language like SQL, a network database programmer would be required to specify the "access path," describing all of the records and the "sets" that would be used to satisfy the request.

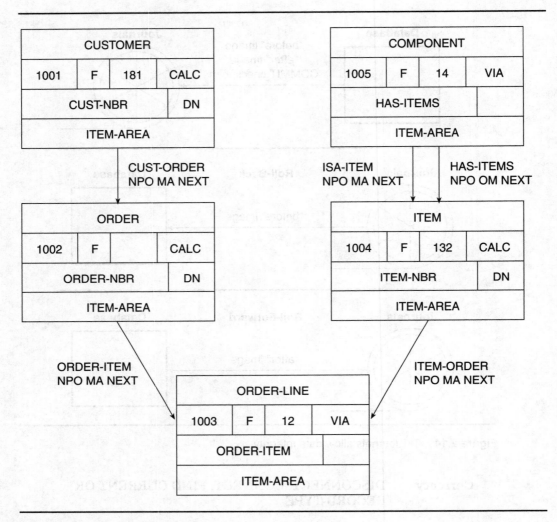

Figure 2.15   Bachman diagram.

A diagram tool to represent the data structures required by the CODASYL model was popularized by Charles Bachman, and his graphical depiction of the database schema became known as the Bachman diagram, or data structure diagram. In the Bachman diagram, records are represented as boxes and relationships, as arrows (Figure 2.15).

The CODASYL model combines two data storage methods to create an engine that can process hundreds of transactions per second. The model uses the basic direct access method (BDAM), which utilizes a hashing algorithm (sometimes called a CALC algorithm) to quickly store and retrieve records. CODASYL also employs linked-list data structures, which create embedded pointers in the prefix of each occurrence of a record. These pointers are used to establish relationships between data items. These pointers are called NEXT, PRIOR, and OWNER and are referenced in the data manipulation language (DML). For example, the DML command OBTAIN NEXT ORDER WITHIN CUSTOMER-ORDER would direct the CODASYL database to look in the prefix of the current ORDER record, and find the NEXT pointer for the CUSTOMER-ORDER set. The database would then access the record the address of which was found at this location.

The Bachman diagram describes the physical constructs of all record types in the database, including the location modes for all records (CALC or VIA), and all of the linked-list options. Some records are stored using hashing techniques, and records that are stored "CALC" use a symbolic key to determine the physical location of the record. CODASYL databases also allow for records to be clustered. Records with "VIA" indicate that they are stored on the same physical data blocks as their owner records. Data relationships are established with sets, which link the relationships together. For example, the ORDER-LINE records are physically clustered near their ITEM records. This is indicated on the Bachman diagram where the ORDER-LINE box shows VIA as the location mode, and the ORDER-ITEM relationship as the cluster set.

There were several advantages to the CODASYL approach, primarily in performance and the ability to represent complex data relationships.

For example, to navigate a one-to-many relationship, (e.g., to get all of the orders for a customer), a CODASYL programmer would enter:

```
MOVE 'IBM' to CUST-ID.
OBTAIN CALC CUSTOMER.
PERFORM ORDER-LOOP UNTIL END-OF-SET.

ORDER-LOOP.
   OBTAIN NEXT ORDER WITHIN CUSTOMER-ORDER.
   MOVE ORDER-NO TO OUT-REC.
   WRITE OUT-REC.
```

In this example, BDAM is invoked for the OBTAIN CALC CUSTOMER statement, and linked lists are used in the statement OBTAIN NEXT CUSTOMER WITHIN CUSTOMER-ORDER.

As a visual tool, the set occurrence diagram has great potential for use in object-oriented databases. The relationships between the objects are readily apparent, and the programmer can easily visualize the navigation paths. For example, in Figure 2.16 you can easily see that order 123 is for 19 pads, 3

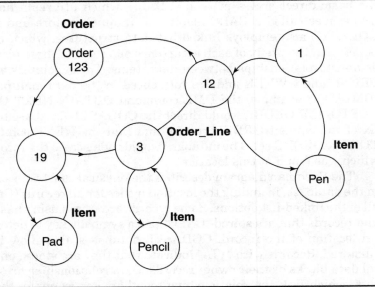

Figure 2.16   Set occurrence diagram: customer database.

pencils, and 12 pens. Cross over to the "item" side of the diagram, and you can easily see that pencils participate in order 123. For systems that physically link objects, the set occurrence diagram is an extremely useful visual tool.

Although the design of the CODASYL network model is very elegant, there were serious problems with implementation. Network databases, much like hierarchical databases, are very difficult to navigate. Using DML, especially for complex navigation, is a skill requiring many months of training.

Structural changes to network databases are a nightmare. Because the data relationships are "hard linked" with embedded pointers, the addition of an index or a new relationship requires special utility programs to "sweep" each and every affected record in the database. As each record is located, the prefix is restructured to accommodate the new pointers. Object-oriented databases encounter this same problem when a class hierarchy requires modification.

CODASYL databases were still far superior to any other technology of the day, and thousands of corporations began to implement their mission-critical systems on IDMS platforms. Even the Air Force used the IDMS database at the North American Air Defense Command (NORAD) to track incoming Soviet missiles (and, of course, Santa Claus at Christmastime). However, as soon as relational databases became fast and stable enough to support mission-critical systems, the cumbersome and inflexible CODASYL systems were abandoned.

Is the CODASYL Network Data Model Returning? One feature of the object-oriented paradigm is support for recursion. In order to be recursive, a data model must support the ability to reference a record without having to refer to a primary key value. Some researchers have proposed a method for assigning object IDs, but relational models cannot address the high overhead and potential problems involved in generating object IDs. Others have proposed a data model that allows a single field to contain multiple values, or even another table. In a procedural language such as C++, the problem of recursion is addressed very elegantly with pointers to structures.

The ODMG standard for object-oriented databases requires unique object IDs to identify each object, and they have deliberately not addressed the ability to access a row based on the data contents of the row.

Many researchers have noted remarkable similarities between the CODASYL Network Model (NWM) and the requirements for object-oriented databases (Schek 1991). The CODASYL model supports the declaration of abstract "sets" to relate classes together, and CODASYL also supports the notion of "currency," whereby a record may be accessed without any reference to its data attributes. CODASYL databases provide currency tables that allow the programmer to "remember" the most recently accessed record of each type, and the most recently accessed record within a set.

Schek and Scholl state, "This shows that some of the essential features of the object model can be found in the NWM; NWM records are instances of abstract types manipulated by a limited set of functions (called FIND's), mostly for navigational access. CONNECT and DISCONNECT are used to add or remove objects to or from relationships. Finally, GET retrieves data about the objects into a pre-defined communications area."

Of all of the existing database models, the CODASYL network model most closely matches the requirements for object-oriented databases, and with some refinement (such as the support of "cyclic" data relationships), the CODASYL model may reemerge in a new form, as the standard data model for object-oriented modeling.

Some vendors are already using the CODASYL model as the architecture for object-oriented databases. For example, the C-Data Manager, from Database Technologies, is an object-oriented database and programming environment that is based on the CODASYL Network Data Model, and uses ISAM file structures to index its data records.

The Relational Database Model: c. AD 1980–1990

Dr. E. F. Codd, a researcher from IBM, developed a model for a "relational" database in which the data resided in "pointerless" tables called "relations." These could be navigated in a declarative fashion, without the need for any database navigation. Relations within his model were very simple to conceptualize, and could be viewed as two-dimensional arrays of columns and rows. Codd's relational model contained a set of relational criteria that must be met for a database to be truly "relational." Interestingly, Dr. Codd's model of relational characteristics is so stringent that no company has yet offered a commercial database meeting all of his criteria.

Relational databases provide the following improvements over earlier database architectures:

Data independence. The data resides in freestanding tables that are not hard-linked with other tables. Columns can be added to relational tables without any changes to application programs, and the addition of new data or data relationships to the data model seldom requires restructuring of the tables.

Declarative data access. Database navigation is hidden from the programmers. When compared to navigational languages such as CODASYL DML in which the programmer is required to know the details of the access paths, relational access is handled with an SQL optimizer, which takes care of all navigation on behalf of the user. Relational data access is a "state space" approach, whereby the user specifies the Boolean conditions for the retrieval, and the system returns the data that meets the selection criteria in the SQL statement.

Simple conceptual framework. The relational database is very easy to describe, and even naive users can understand the concept of tables. Complex network diagrams that are used to describe the structure of network and hierarchical databases are not needed to describe a relational database.

Referential integrity (RI). Relational systems allow for the control of business rules with "constraints." These RI rules are used to insure that one-to-many and many-to-many relationships are enforced within the relational tables. For example, RI would insure that a row in the CUSTOMER table could not be deleted if orders for that customer exist in the ORDER table (Figure 2.17).

One of the greatest benefits of the relational database is the concept of data independence. Because data relationships are no longer hard-linked with pointers, systems developers are able to design systems based upon business requirements, with far less time being spent on physical considerations.

Codd's tables (relations) consist of columns and rows. Dr. Codd chose to call a row a *tuple* (rhymes with "couple"), and he refers to many rows as "instantiations of tuples." Perhaps this obtuse terminology helped to insure that the relational model gained respect as a legitimate offering, and many professionals began to adopt Dr. Codd's confusing terminology.

RI Rule = ORDER.CUST_NAME REFERENCES CUSTOMER.CUST_NAME

Two Options:

ON DELETE RESTRICT — Customers may not be deleted if they have orders in the ORDER table.

ON DELETE CASCADE — Customer delection will cause all orders for the customer to delete.

	CUST_NAME	CUST_STUFF
CUSTOMER	IBM AT&T DEC	Big Blue No Identity Bad Credit

	ORDER_NBR	CUST_NAME	ORDER_DATE
ORDER	123 124 125 126	DEC IBM IBM AT&T	3-4-93 3-4-93 3-5-93 3-5-93

Figure 2.17   Referential integrity.

Dr. Codd also introduced the concept of the structured query language (SQL). One should note that SQL is *not* actually a query language. SQL performs much more than queries (SQL allows updates, deletes, and inserts), and SQL is also not a language (SQL is embedded within procedural languages such as COBOL or C). Consequently, "structured query language" seemed a logical name for Dr. Codd's new tool.

SQL offers three classes of operators. The SELECT operator serves to shrink the table vertically by eliminating unwanted rows (tuples). The PROJECT operator serves to shrink the table horizontally, removing unwanted columns. The JOIN operator allows the dynamic linking of two tables that share a common column value. Most commercial implementations of SQL do not support a PROJECT operation, and projections are achieved by specifying the columns that are desired in the output. The JOIN operation is achieved by stating the selection criteria for two tables, and equating them with their common columns.

The following example incorporates a SELECT, a PROJECT, and a JOIN:

```
SELECT CUST_NAME, ORDER_DATE                /*PROJECT columns*/
    FROM CUSTOMER, ORDER
    WHERE
    CUSTOMER.CUST_NBR = ORDER.CUST_NBR      /* JOIN tables */
    AND CUST_TYPE = 'NEW';                  /* SELECT rows */
```

The most important features of the relational database are the ability to isolate the data from the data relationships and to eliminate the pointers used by hierarchical and network databases to establish relationships. In a relational database, two tables that have a relationship are defined with a *primary key* and a *foreign key*. This key can be used at run time to dynamically join the tables. Consider the one-to-many relationship between a customer and his or her orders. A relational table declaration would look like this:

```
CREATE TABLE CUSTOMER
( CUST-NO          INTEGER PRIMARY KEY,
  CUST-NAME        CHAR(80),
  CUST-ADDRESS     CHAR(300))

CREATE TABLE ORDER
( ORDER-NO         INTEGER   PRIMARY KEY,
  CUST-NO          INTEGER REFERENCES CUSTOMER(CUST-NO)
                           ON DELETE RESTRICT,
  ORDER-DATE       DATE,
  ORDER-STUFF      CHAR(80))
```

Below is a sketch of what these tables might look like when populated with data.

CUSTOMER TABLE

CUST-#	CUST_NAME	CUST_ADDR
123	Jones, Sam	123 First St.
456	Smyth, Bill	200 Third St.
789	Burleson, Don	2100 33rd St.

ORDER TABLE

ORDER-#	CUST-#	ORDER-DATE	ORDER-TYPE
a100	123	3/25/93	prepaid
a101	456	3/26/93	COD
a102	123	3/26/93	COD
a103	789	3/27/93	prepaid

In this model, the "referential integrity" is used to establish the one-to-many relationship and to insure that no occurrences of the customer record will be deleted if orders exist for that customer. This referential linking method creates great tremendous flexibility within the database. The only requirement to join two tables (thereby establishing a one-to-many relationship) is that the fields in the tables share the same type definition. For example, the fields EMP_ID in the EMPLOYEE table and EMP_NBR in the SKILL table could be used in a relational join, provided that they have the same data definition (INTEGER). In a distributed database environment, two tables in completely different systems can be joined at any time, adding to the flexibility of the relational architecture. Object-oriented systems do not support this feature, because all data relationships must be rigorously predefined, and "ad hoc" queries are not supported.

The Object-Oriented Database Model: c. AD 1990–2000

The next progression of database architecture is toward object-oriented databases. Just as early file managers stored data, network databases stored data and relationships, and object-oriented databases store data, data relationships, and the behaviors of the data (Figure 2.18).

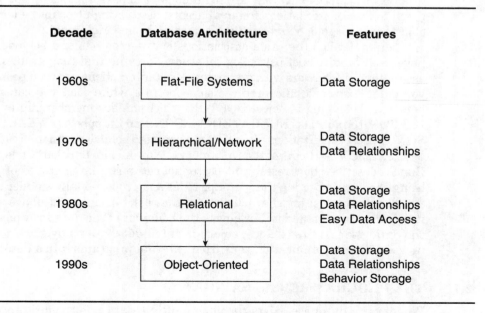

Decade	Database Architecture	Features
1960s	Flat-File Systems	Data Storage
1970s	Hierarchical/Network	Data Storage Data Relationships
1980s	Relational	Data Storage Data Relationships Easy Data Access
1990s	Object-Oriented	Data Storage Data Relationships Behavior Storage

Figure 2.18   Features of database architectures.

The object-oriented approach borrows heavily from the concepts of "intelligent databases" and "knowledgebases." Both of these concepts advocate storing behaviors within the database, such that data and business rules share a common repository.

With the properties of encapsulation, abstraction, and polymorphism, object technology systems are moving toward a unified data model that models the real world far more effectively than previous modeling techniques. Furthermore, a properly designed object-oriented model promises to be maintenance free, because all changes to data attributes and behaviors become database tasks, and not programming tasks.

Let's take a look at a human analogy to the object-oriented approach. It is very natural for humans to recognize objects, and to associate objects with their classes. It is also a very natural concept to associate an object with its expected behaviors. Even as very young children we learn to associate behaviors or characteristics with object classes. For example, it is not uncommon to visit the zoo and hear a three-year-old call all four-legged animals "doggies." The child has learned to associate an object class (dog) with a data attribute (four legs). Later a child refines this object-oriented paradigm and associates other data attributes with animal objects. A child also learns to associate behaviors (playing, having fun, pain) with different visual and auditory stimuli. Many young children learn to associate unpleasant behaviors (causing pain) with a visit to the grownup who wears a white lab coat (the doctor). McDonald's has spent millions of dollars exploiting this principle, much to the consternation of many parents, associating pleasant behaviors with objects such as golden arches, Big Meals, and Ronald McDonald.

Adults develop the same associations between objects and behaviors. There have been hundreds of psychological studies proving that "expectations," or the association of behaviors with attributes, affect interactions between people. When you enter a doctor's office and see someone in a white coat, you categorize the person as belonging to object DOCTOR, which implies membership in the class PERSON, the subclass EDUCATED PERSON, and the subclass WEALTHY PERSON. Object classifications also affect the expected behaviors. An interesting study by Professor Dick Harris of the University of New Mexico entitled "Cheaper by the Bunch" describes how restaurant personnel categorize large groups of people as being cheaper, expecting these groups to leave a proportionally smaller tip.

The distinguishing characteristic of the object-oriented database is its ability to store data behavior, but how is the behavior of the data incorporated into the database? At first glance, object-oriented databases may seem to be a vehicle for moving application code from external programs into a database.

2.4 THE PROGRAMMER AS NAVIGATOR

Whenever a database exists that has multiple data relationships, a programmer must navigate though the database in order to access the data. This navi-

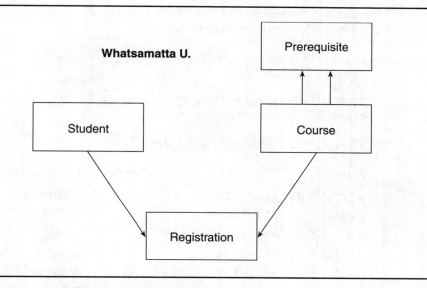

Whatsamatta U.

Figure 2.19   Entity/relation model.

gation requires the programmer to traverse through the data relationships to access the information.

For example, consider the entity/relation diagram for a university in Figure 2.19. In this model, a programmer might be asked to produce a grade report for all students at the university. The programmer must begin by creating a *loop*, or iterative process, that accesses all of the students in the proper order. In a relational database, the SQL command might look like this:

```
Select last_name, first_name
from STUDENT
order by last_name.
```

This might produce the following list:

ARCANGEL,	ALBERTA
BURLESON,	ANDREW
BURLESON,	JENNIFER
D'ARCANGELO,	MICHAEL
THAYER,	BILL

The next navigation step is to retrieve all of the courses for each student. Note that the course record is not directly connected to the student record.

Therefore, it is necessary to navigate through the GRADE record. The SQL statement can be expanded to include:

```
Select last_name, first_name, grade, course_ID
from STUDENT, GRADE
where
STUDENT.student_ID = GRADE.student_ID
order by last_name, course_ID
```

The solution set now looks like this:

Name	Grade	Course_ID
ARCANGEL, ALBERTA	A	CS101
ARCANGEL, ALBERTA	B	CS203
ARCANGEL, ALBERTA	A	CS405
BURLESON, ANDREW	A	MA450
BURLESON, ANDREW	A-	MA443
BURLESON, JENNIFER	C++	CS450
BURLESON, JENNIFER	A+	CS982
D'ARCANGELO, MICHAEL	B	MG455
D'ARCANGELO, MICHAEL	B+	MG230
THAYER, BILL	C	EN654
THAYER, BILL	A	PS101
THAYER, BILL	B+	EN235

At this point, we have most of the information that is required for the report card, but we are missing the course name and the credit hours for each course. To navigate to the COURSE record, the SQL is expanded again to include another relational JOIN. Note that the sort order has added course_level so that all courses are listed in their proper order:

```
Select    last_name, first_name, grade, course_ID,
          course_name, credit_hours
from STUDENT, GRADE, COURSE
where
STUDENT.student_ID     = GRADE.student_ID and
GRADE.course_ID        = COURSE.course_ID
order by last_name, course_level
```

The solution set now looks like this:

Name	Grade	Course_ID	Course_name	Credit
ARCANGEL, ALBERTA	A	Pascal	Pascal	3
ARCANGEL, ALBERTA	B	CS203	Fortran	3
ARCANGEL, ALBERTA	A	CS405	C++	4
BURLESON, ANDREW	A	MA450	Calculus	4
BURLESON, ANDREW	A-	MA443	Statistics	4
BURLESON, JENNIFER	C++	CS450	OODBs	4
BURLESON, JENNIFER	A+	CS982	Analysis	4
D'ARCANGELO, MICHAEL	B	MG455	Management	3
D'ARCANGELO, MICHAEL	B+	MG230	Marketing	4
THAYER, BILL	C	EN654	English	4
THAYER, BILL	A	PS101	Phys Ed	3
THAYER, BILL	B+	EN235	Speling	3

Now the only remaining navigation is to get the instructor name from the instructor record. The final expansion of the SQL would be like this:

```
Select       last_name, first_name, grade, course_ID,
             course_name, credit_hours, instructor
from STUDENT, GRADE, COURSE, INSTRUCTOR
where
STUDENT.student_ID        = GRADE.student_ID and
GRADE.course_ID           = COURSE.course_ID and
INSTRUCTOR.instructor_ID  = COURSE.instructor_ID
order by last_name, course_level
```

The solution set now looks like this:

Name	Grade	Course_ID	Course_name	Credit	Inst.
ARCANGEL, ALBERTA	A	Pascal	Pascal	3	Jones
ARCANGEL, ALBERTA	B	CS203	Fortran	3	Smith
ARCANGEL, ALBERTA	A	CS405	C++	4	Able
BURLESON, ANDREW	A	MA450	Calculus	4	Able
BURLESON, ANDREW	A-	MA443	Statistics	4	Jones
BURLESON, JENNIFER	C++	CS450	OODBs	4	Baker
BURLESON, JENNIFER	A+	CS982	Analysis	4	Smyth
D'ARCANGELO, MICHAEL	B	MG455	Management	3	Able

D'ARCANGELO, MICHAEL	B+	MG230	Marketing	4	Jones
THAYER, BILL	C	EN654	English	4	Baker
THAYER, BILL	A	PS101	Phys Ed	3	Smyth
THAYER, BILL	B+	EN235	Speling	3	Jones

We now have all of the information to produce the grade report cards, and all of the information has been sorted into the proper order. The final steps for the programmer are to reformat the information, removing redundant data items such as the student name, and to compute any totals that may be desired, such as the grade point average.

From this example we can see that there is a great deal of navigation that a programmer must perform, especially for complex queries.

The relative ease in generating this query attests to the declarative nature of the SQL language. In SQL, one only needs to specify the desired data items, the table that owns the data items, the join criteria, and the desired sorting order. The SQL language contains a software tool called an *optimizer* that interrogates the SQL request and determines the most efficient method for getting the solution set. The optimizer compares the SQL request with the state of the database. For example, the optimizer may choose to use an index if there are millions of rows in the grade table, or it may access the grade table without an index if there are not very many rows.

This example uses SQL—note that the only real navigation that had to be performed was the specification of the join criteria and the sorting order. Even though the final SQL might look complex, it is really quite simple compared to navigation in a database that does not support a declarative access language.

Even more complex navigation must take place if the programmer is using a nonrelational database. In a nonrelational database the programmer must navigate one record at a time. Here is a sample COBOL navigation that would produce the same result against a network database architecture:

```
COBOL-MAIN.

      OBTAIN FIRST STUDENT WITHIN STUDENT-IX.
      PERFORM STUDENT-SWEEP UNTIL DB-END-OF-INDEX.

SWEEP-STUDENT.

      MOVE LAST_NAME TO LAST_HOLD.
      MOVE FIRST_NAME TO FIRST_HOLD.
      OBTAIN FIRST GRADE WITHIN STUDENT-GRADE.
      PERFORM GRADE-SWEEP UNTIL DB-END-OF-SET.
      OBTAIN NEXT STUDENT WITHIN STUDENT-IX.
```

```
GRADE-SWEEP.

    MOVE GRADE TO GRADE_HOLD.
    OBTAIN OWNER WITHIN COURSE-GRADE.
    MOVE COURSE_ID TO COURSE_ID_HOLD.
    MOVE CREDIT TO CREDIT_HOLD.
    MOVE COURSE_NAME TO COURSE_NAME_HOLD.
    OBTAIN OWNER WITHIN INSTRUCTOR-COURSE.
    MOVE INSTRUCTOR_NAME TO INSTRUCTOR_HOLD.
    WRITE PRINT-REC FROM HOLD-AREA.
    OBTAIN CURRENT GRADE.
    OBTAIN NEXT GRADE WITHIN COURSE_GRADE.
```

As you can see, navigation in a nonrelational database can be far more complicated than relational navigation.

REFERENCES:

Bell, D. 1992. *Distributed database systems*. Addison-Wesley.

Blaser, A., ed. 1990. *Database systems of the 90s*. Berlin: International Symposium.

Bobak, A. 1993. *Distributed and multidatabase systems*. Bantam Books.

Burleson, D. 1990. *Practical application of object-oriented techniques to relational databases*. Wiley\QED.

———. 1993. Distributed object technology. *First Class Magazine*, October.

———. 1994. Mapping object-oriented applications to relational databases. *Object Magazine*, January.

———. 1994. Managing distributed databases—an enterprise view. *Database Programming & Design*, June.

Chivvis, A., and J. Geyer. 1993. Think again: face the facts. These misconceptions about downsizing are just lame excuses for procrastination. *Corporate Computing*, March.

Chorafas, D. 1989. *Handbook of database management and distributed relational databases*. TAB Books.

Chu, W., ed. 1986. *Distributed database systems*. Books on Demand.

Date, C. 1987. What is a distributed database? *InfoDB* 2:7.

Gray, B. 1993. Database/file servers. *Computing Canada*, March.

Hackathorn, R. 1993. *Enterprise database connectivity*. Wiley.

Katzan, H. 1991. *Distributed information systems*. Petrocelli Books.

Korzeniowski, P. 1992. Gateways link legacy, distributed databases. *Software Magazine*, November.

McFadden, F. 1994. *Modern database management*. 4th edition. Benjamin Cummings Publishing Company.

Mulqueen, J. 1993. Distributed database: a dream? *Communications Week*, March.

Ozsu, M. and P. Valdurez. 1992. Distributed database systems, where are we now? *Database Programming & Design*, March.

———. 1993. *Principles of distributed database systems*. Prentice-Hall.

Ricciuti, M. 1992. Terabytes of data—how to get at them? *Datamation*, August.

Stein, J. 1992. Distributed databases: What they are, what are they good for? *Journal of Object-oriented Programming*, July–August.

Stodder, D. 1992. Return of the process: client/server computing forces us to reexamine the data-centric approach. *Database Programming & Design*, March.

Weitz, L. 1992. Desperately seeking database independence: options for accessing diverse corporate data. *Software Magazine*, December.

Overview of Distributed Databases

3.1 INTRODUCTION

Five major developmental trends have impacted the current nature of distributed databases. While these trends overlapped, each was the natural successor to the one it followed and improved in some manner over the earlier technology:

1950s	Monolithic databases
1970s	Distributed databases
1980s	Personal databases
1980s	Networks of databases
1990s	Networked networks of databases

It is important to understand the differences between distributed databases and centralized databases. The benefits of centralized data were first described in the 1970s, and many of these benefits remain compelling today. In a centralized database, the database software maintains tight control over the data, both in terms of security and access. The system can be backed up and recovered as a single unit, and most important of all, the business relationships between the data items are controlled and maintained. Unfortunately, no vendor has yet been able to deliver a database engine that is robust enough to meet all of the data needs of a corporation. If a single database could support ad hoc queries (SQL), high-speed online transaction processing, and complex text searching, then there would be no incentive to distribute the database.

Centralized databases have been criticized for having a single point of failure. It is argued that a centralized data repository is at the mercy of the processor that drives the database; a failure of the central processor could put the entire enterprise off the air. Advocates of *distributed databases* point to the "safer" distributed approach whereby a failure on one network node will leave the remaining database nodes intact and running.

The widespread availability of the personal computer has also had an influence on the overall evolution of database systems. Once thought to be a toy, the personal computer has become powerful enough to support selected replications of corporate information. Products such as Microsoft's FoxPro have demonstrated such blistering performance that users routinely refresh local FoxPro databases from their mainframes and enjoy complete freedom and control of their private query databases. Some argue that the widespread demand for client/server is a direct result of the end-user's infatuation with the push-button, pop-up, GUI world of personal computers.

The newest frontier, networks of networked computers, is also another evolution of the personal computer revolution. As personal computers appeared on everyone's desk, LAN managers were created to link them together, and with gateways to the midrange and mainframe systems, the desktop workstation has become a vehicle for exploring cyberspace. This is most dramatically demonstrated with the Internet. With tens of thousand of participating computers, and new nodes being added at a rate of 200 each day, the Internet is the ultimate in distributed databases. In their quest for information, voyagers routinely cross diverse networking protocols, continents, and data architectures, all in a seamless fashion. Gophers, vacuums, WAIS products, and "bots" now allow a user to navigate through cyberspace with more confidence than ever before.

3.2　THE FACTORS THAT CREATE DISTRIBUTED DATABASES

There are four main reasons that companies adopt distributed database systems: advances in "specialized" database architectures, corporate "rightsizing" movements, corporate acquisitions, and ostensibly, improvements in performance and reliability. While all of these factors may influence corporate decision, a close inspection indicates that some factors are far more legitimate than others.

Specialized Databases

As little as five years ago, database vendors touted their products as corporate panaceas, appropriate for all types of data and application systems. DB2 was marketed as an all-purpose engine that was suitable for any application regardless of the size or performance requirements. With time, however, it became clear that DB2 was not suitable for systems that required thousands of transac-

Table 3.1   Samples of specialized database products.

Text databases	Oracle Book, Basis Plus, Folio
High-speed databases	CA-IDMS, IMS, Teradata
Object databases	Objectivity/DB Ontos, Versant

tions per second, and IBM began recommending IMS for very large, high-speed databases. At this point, other vendors began to embrace the concept of "the right database for the right application." Systems that required flexibility and ad hoc query were implemented with relational databases, and systems that had a lot of complex data relationships and high performance requirements were implemented with network or hierarchical database architectures. New types of specialized database products began to appear: special word-searchable databases for textual data, databases designed especially for CAD/CAM systems, and so on (Table 3.1). Database systems began their long march away from corporate repositories and into specialized niche markets.

Because of the failure of a single database vendor to create an architecture that meets their complete processing needs, many companies have no choice but to create distributed database systems.

Rightsizing

There has always been a strong economic incentive for companies to explore the new and powerful midrange and personal computers. With mainframe data centers costing millions of dollars each year, many companies have undertaken the shift to distributed database systems in the hopes of reducing their overall costs. In some cases this downsizing has paid off handsomely both in monetary savings and increased productivity. In other cases, the hidden costs of downsizing have mired management in a morass of expensive client/server tools. Client/server software can often cost thousands of dollars per PC, and the anticipated savings quickly evaporate when management faces the reality that distributed database systems require far more human resources than a centralized database. Companies must hire people to manage the PC LAN networks, communications experts to maintain the connectivity between platforms, DBAs to maintain each of the database products, and additional security experts to insure that access controls are maintained across all of the hardware platforms. These hidden costs have made rightsizing indefensible on purely economic grounds, and today most managers justify rightsizing by emphasizing the less tangible benefits of increased productivity.

Advances in database technology have also played a role in the spontaneous distribution of data. When PC-based database products such as Microsoft's

FoxPro proved that they could handle dozens of concurrent users on a PC LAN, many companies began to move parts of their centralized databases directly to PC networks. In fact, FoxPro has performed so well that many companies have been able to downsize directly from their mainframes to FoxPro databases. FoxPro can support multiuser databases with multimillions-row tables and up to 50 concurrent update sessions in a PC environment. A direct migration to FoxPro removes the need for client/server processing, and the users enjoy a GUI environment complete with Microsoft's distributed data exchange (DDE) and object linking and embedding (OLE).

Object technology databases are also becoming more popular, primarily because of the benefits of code reusability, fast systems development, and distributed data capabilities. Industrial-strength object-oriented databases now offer features such as data recovery, 24X7 availability, and client/server capability. The area of object-oriented database (OODB) is growing at a phenomenal rate. In 1992 the revenue from object-oriented databases was approximately $10 million, but International Data Corporation (IDC) estimates that the market for object-oriented databases may be as high as $446 million by 1996.

Corporate Acquisitions

Corporate acquisitions have also played a role in the distribution of corporate data. One of the reasons a company acquires a new subsidiary is to take advantage of the synergy that can result from the melding of the companies. Companies achieve power through information, and the rationale is that the melding of the information capabilities of the two companies will result in a single information entity that will exceed the sum of the information power of each individual unit. This is the main motivation for many corporate mergers. MIS managers must be ready to quickly incorporate a new database into their federation.

The problem of creating a unified federation out of diverse databases and platforms is aggravated of the misleading claims of our own industry. Vendors and researchers alike are calling the 1990s the "age of open systems," and users are being led to believe that integrating distributed databases has become a trivial task. Anyone who has tried to make a distributed database system can attest that the process is very cumbersome and time consuming.

Regardless of the reasons behind adopting a distributed database, companies are faced with trying to create a federated system from databases that are distributed geographically, architecturally, and by hardware platform.

3.3   ESSENTIALS OF DISTRIBUTED DATABASES

"Distributed database" means different things to different people. To the database vendors, a distributed database is a geographically distributed system composed entirely of their products. To the GUI/tools vendors, a distributed database is a system that is distributed architecturally, comprising systems with different architectures and access methods. To the hardware vendors, a distributed database is a system composed of different databases all running on the same hardware platforms. In fact, each of these descriptions fits the overall model, but there are some distinctions between a real distributed database and a loosely coupled system. The best definition of distributed database has been developed by C. J. Date, who stated 12 specifications for an ideal distributed database:

1. Local autonomy
2. No reliance on a central site
3. Continuous operation
4. Location independence
5. Fragmentation independence
6. Replication independence
7. Distributed query processing
8. Distributed transaction management (update processing)
9. Hardware independence
10. Operating system independence
11. Network independence
12. Database independence

1. Local autonomy

Local autonomy means that all of the data in the distributed network is owned and managed locally. For example, a site in New York would have a remote database that participates in a national distributed system. While functioning as a part of the distributed network, the New York database continues to process local operations independently of the overall distributed system, and the New York database does not rely on the distributed system to function.

2. No reliance on a central site

Ideally, all sites are equally "remote," and no one site has governing authority over another node. Each site retains its own data dictionary and security.

3. Continuous operation

While each site maintains its own unique identity and control, it functions as a part of a unified federation such that other remote sites may access information from the site in a seamless fashion. Each node is available to the overall system 24 hours per day, seven days per week. To accomplish this goal, remote sites may have "flying dump" or "hot backup" utilities to back up the database while it remains available for update.

4. Location independence

End-users do not necessarily know, or care, about the physical location of the databases that comprise the system. Data is retrieved without any specific reference to the physical sites.

5. Fragmentation independence

Fragmentation independence refers to the ability of the end-users to store logically related information at different physical locations. There are two types of fragmentation independence: vertical partitioning and horizontal partitioning (Figure 3.1). Horizontal partitioning allows for different rows of the same table to be stored at different remote sites. This is commonly used by organizations that maintain several branch offices, each with an identical set of table struc-

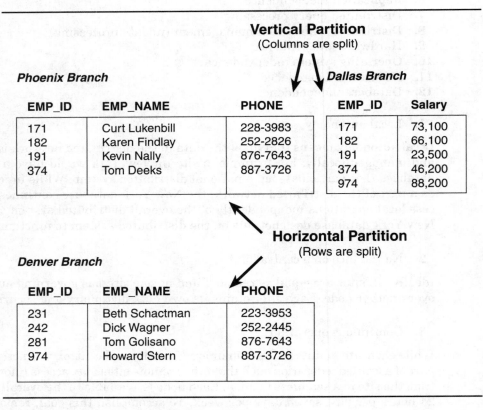

Figure 3.1   Horizontal and vertical partitioning.

tures. Vertical partitioning refers to the ability of a distributed system to fragment information such that the data columns from the same logical tables are maintained across the network.

Distributed SQL can be issued to cross the horizontal partition and treat the Phoenix and Denver tables as if they were a single entity:

```
SELECT *
FROM  employee@phoenix, employee@denver
ORDER BY EMP_ID;
```

For the vertical partition, the tables can also be treated as a single entity:

```
SELECT employee.EMP_ID, EMP_NAME, PHONE, SALARY
from employee@denver, employee@phoenix, salary@dallas
ORDER BY EMP_ID;
```

While vertical and horizontal partitioning are helpful for branch office distributed databases, both methods suffer some problems. Since each database continues to maintain two identities, one at the branch office and another for the overall federation, response time can vary widely depending upon the local demands on the tables. There is also the problem of data dependence: A failure at any one of the remote nodes makes a part of the overall system unavailable. This is not the case for a replicated distributed database.

6. Replication independence

Replication is the ability of a database to create copies of a master database at remote sites. These copies, sometimes called *snapshots*, may contain the whole database or any component of it. In relational databases, a CUSTOMER table may be snapped to many remote sites for read-only query. Subsets of the table may be requested, containing only specified rows and columns, and these replications are refreshed on a periodic basis.

7. Distributed query processing

Distributed query processing is more than the ability to execute a query against more than one database. In some database engines, the query is executed at the node that the user is signed on to, while other databases partition a distributed query into subqueries, executing each subquery on the host processor. In relational databases it is possible to query data items from widely distributed databases in a single distributed query. For example:

```
SELECT     customer.name,     customer.address,
order.order_number,
```

```
order.order_date
  from customer@tokoyo, order@paris
     where
     customer.customer_number = order.customer_number;
```

8. Distributed transaction management (update processing)

Distributed transaction management refers to a system that can manage an update, insert, or delete to multiple databases from a single query. Most database vendors use the *two-phase commit* to implement this process. The two-phase commit insures that all of the remote databases have successfully completed their sub-updates before the entire transaction is committed to the database. A failure at one of the remote databases will cause the entire transaction to fail; however, some new techniques allow partial commits, storing the unavailable updates and applying them as soon as the unavailable database comes online.

Suppose a CUSTOMER table resides in New York, and an ORDER table resides in Paris. The control mechanisms of the database would insure that the business rules for the related tables are maintained even though the component data resides on different processors. If a user attempted to add a row to the ORDER table in Paris, the central manager would check the referential integrity to be sure that the customer existed in the CUSTOMER table in New York. Another way to partition a database is with horizontal partitioning. *Horizontal partitioning* refers to the ability of the system to store "similar" information at many sites while the information continues to maintain its "sameness" with other information in the network. In a relational database, this might mean that some rows from a CUSTOMER table may reside at PARIS while other rows of the CUSTOMER table reside at LONDON. From the viewpoint of the application, the CUSTOMER table appears as a unified table. Many vendors implement this feature by using remote update capabilities, stored procedures, or database triggers.

9. Hardware independence

This refers to the ability of a query to query and update information regardless of the hardware platform on which the data resides. A single query from a PC might retrieve information from an IBM 3090, a local database on the PC, and an HP-9000 in a single transaction.

10. Operating system independence

Again, a query should not be dependent upon an operating system. PC-based queries may be entered from either MS-DOS or OS/2 systems, and may access databases residing on MVS/ESA, UNIX, or any other operating system.

11. Network independence

Network protocols should not be an issue for distributed databases. Many database packages support multiprotocol tools that speak to different networks according to their protocols. Protocol conversion routines allow synchronous channels (such as those on IBM mainframes) to communicate with the asynchronous UNIX world. They also accommodate differences in topology so that LU6.2 can communicate with TCP/IP, and so on.

12. Database independence

With database independence, it is possible to retrieve and update information from many different databases and database architectures.

Data Integrity Management

Data integrity refers to the ability of the distributed database to manage concurrent updates to data in many physical locations and to insure that all of the data is physically and logically correct. While data integrity is managed very effectively within a single database with row locking, deadlock detection, and rollback features, distributed data integrity is far more complex. Recovery in a distributed database environment involves insuring that the entire transaction has been completed successfully before issuing a commit to each of the components in the overall transaction. This can often be a cumbersome chore. (The issue of the "two-phase commit" is addressed in detail later in this text.) Many distributed databases overcome the problem of the two-phase commit by replicating their information, and rely on asynchronous replication techniques to enforce data integrity. Asynchronous replications require a master-slave type of configuration whereby a master database "relays" updates to the slave database on a periodic basis. This approach makes sense when the overall system does not require instant integrity.

Transparency Features

Location transparency refers to the ability of the distributed database to function as a unified whole and to appear to the end-user as a single unfragmented system. The end-user of the distributed system should not care what type of database the data is located on, where the database resides, or the access method that the database requires. While many companies have achieved this type of transparency, it is not without cost. Even a distributed system composed of relational databases has to deal with variances in each database's "100 percent ANSI compliant" SQL.

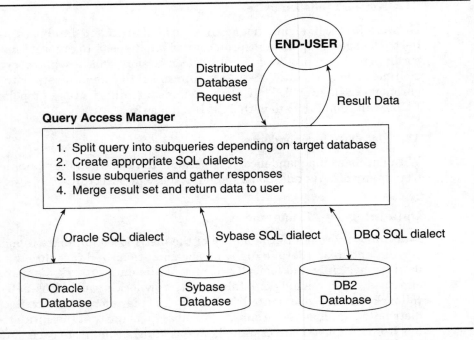

Figure 3.2   Single-architecture database queries and SQL dialects.

One of the most pressing problems of distributed databases is managing the various dialects of SQL (Figure 3.2). Each major database vendor, ostensibly to improve its implementation of SQL, adds "features" and extensions to its SQL. Consequently, any queries that use these features may fail in a distributed multivendor architecture.

These dialect problems are even more aggravating when the distributed database is composed of databases from nonrelational architectures. Sophisticated techniques must be used to interrogate the distributed query, identifying which data components reside in what architecture, and then decompose the subqueries into the appropriate access language (Figure 3.3).

Location Transparency

To understand transparency, assume that a business has a part inventory system with separate databases in Paris, Washington, New York, and Albuquerque. The manager wishes to know the level of widgets on hand in all of the

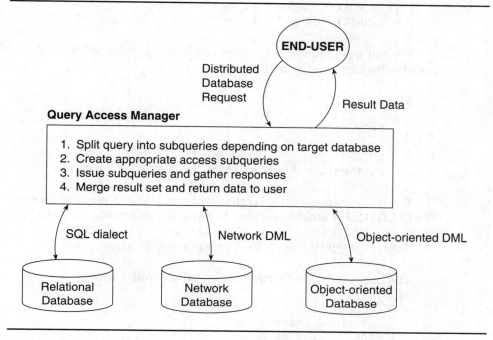

Figure 3.3   Multiarchitecture database queries.

locations, and issues the following SQL command to the distributed database manager:

```
SELECT count FROM INVENTORY WHERE partname = 'widget';
```

With transparency, the manager does not know or care what databases are interrogated to satisfy this request. For such a *global transaction*, it is the responsibility of the transaction manager to query all of the distributed INVENTORY tables and collect the counts from each table, merging them into a single result set.

In many relational databases such as Oracle with SQL*Net, transparency is achieved by creating "database links" to the remote database and then assigning a global synonym to the remote tables. Database links are created with a location suffix that is associated with a telnet name. The telnet name translated into an IP (Internal Protocol) address. In the following example, london_unix might translate into an IP address of 143.32.142.3.

```
CREATE PUBLIC DATABASE LINK london.com
    CONNECT TO london_unix USING oracle_user_ID;
```

We can now include any tables from the London sites by qualifying the remote site name in the SQL query.

```
SELECT  customer.customer_name,
        order.order_date
    FROM        customer@london.com,
            order
    WHERE
    customer.cust_number = order.customer_number;
```

But where is the location transparency? The DBA may assign synonyms for the CUSTOMER table in London to make the query appear to be local:

```
CREATE SYNONYM customer for customer@london.com;
```

The query can now be run with location transparency:

```
SELECT  customer.customer_name,
        order.order_date
    FROM        customer,
            order
    WHERE
    customer.cust_number = order.customer_number;
```

Procedures can also be defined for the remote table without any reference to its physical location. For example,

```
CREATE PROCEDURE add_customer ( cust_name char(8) ) AS
BEGIN
    INSERT ONTO CUSTOMER@LONDON.COM VALUES (cust_name);
END;
```

This procedure could be called with the statement

```
add_customer("Thayer")
```

Domains and Location Transparency

Many sites recognize the need to track the locations of remote databases while providing location transparency to the users and programmers. Domains are

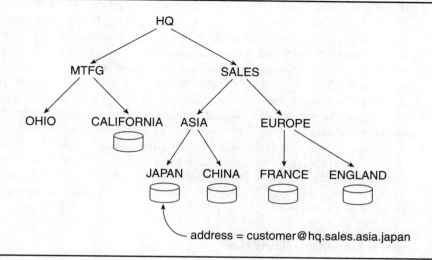

Figure 3.4   Hierarchy of database domains.

especially important in situations of horizontal partitioning, where tables with identical names are kept at numerous locations. Domains establish a logical hierarchy of physical locations for the enterprise (Figure 3.4). Each node in the network then assigns synonyms for all unique tables within the distributed network. For duplicate table structures that exist at many locations, abbreviated domains can be created. Assume that both Japan and Ohio have a customer table, identical in structure but containing different rows. We could assign Oracle synonyms as follows:

```
CREATE SYNONYM japan_customer FOR
    customer@hq.sales.asia.japan;

CREATE SYNONYM ohio_customer FOR
    customer@hq.mtfg.ohio;
```

Performance and Tuning Methods

The difficulty in identifying and correcting performance problems has plagued distributed systems since their earliest beginnings. Even within the context of a single transaction, distributed query optimization can be a formidable challenge. On a single database, query tuning takes place by running an SQL EXPLAIN and performing the appropriate tuning. However, when a query is "split" into distributed databases, the overall query tuning becomes much more complex. Many distributed database managers take a distributed query and partition it into subqueries, which are then independently optimized and run (sometimes simultaneously) on the distributed databases. The query is considered complete when the last subquery has completed successfully and the results are returned to the user. This approach is sometimes called "the weakest link" architecture, because if a distributed query partitions into, say, four subqueries, the longest running of the four subqueries determines the overall performance for the entire query, regardless of how fast the other three subqueries execute.

Clearly, tuning a distributed query must take into consideration the load on the network, the physical location of the database, and the availability of multiple CPUs. Today, tools are available to perform "load balancing" whereby a processor may borrow CPU cycles in order to balance the query and achieve maximum throughput.

Interoperability Facilities

Especially in volatile environments where hardware and network configurations may change frequently, it is very important for a distributed database to have the ability to address information regardless of the hardware platform or the architecture of the database. There are four types of interoperability that come into play with distributed databases: database, hardware, operating systems, and network factors.

Database interoperability refers to the ability of each database within a distributed database system to function autonomously, to allow the distributed database to access many different types of databases within the domain of a unified environment. Tools such as UniFace and PowerBuilder attempt to serve this market, providing mechanisms for subtasking database queries and merging result sets automatically.

Hardware interoperability refers to the ability of the distributed system to address resources at many locations on an as-needed basis. At the hardware level, it is possible for a single subquery of a distributed query to run on numerous processors, and load-balancing tools are available for assigning multiple processors to a single database.

For details on load-sharing products, see "A Closer Look: Platform Computing's Load-Sharing Facility" in Chapter 15.

3.4 REPLICATION AND RELIABILITY

In order to bypass many of the inherent problems with cross-database communications, data is copied and stored in multiple databases, often on different hardware platforms. The main reasons that companies replicate information are to improve reliability and to maximize access speed. In a client/server environment it is often difficult to get all of the data to all of the users who require the information. It is also difficult to balance processing requirements between light data users (e.g., online transaction processing systems) and heavy users (e.g., decision support systems for marketing).

Data replication is often a desirable choice where processing requirements demand that online systems get fast response even while researchers are performing I/O-intensive analysis against the same information. Should there be a failure with one of the component databases, the information remains available from the replicated database. This type of data replication is commonly called *data distribution*. Data distribution should not be confused with distributed databases. With data distribution, information is redundantly copied to another database, whereas in distributed databases the information is not replicated, even though the data may reside in many databases.

Master-Slave Replication

Some installations create "master-slave" replication, where a master database is used for updating, and multiple "query" databases are refreshed from the master each day. The master-slave method usually has a "change" database that keeps track of all changes to the master. When the time comes to propagate the changes to the slave databases, a background task is triggered to copy the data, and the change entry is then removed from the change database. To create a master-slave configuration, the following steps are required:

1. Define and populate the slave database, using copies of the table descriptions from the master catalog tables.
2. Create the propagation routines on the host database and establish host gateways into the slave databases.

While these steps appear straightforward, there are some problems that must be addressed. It is not uncommon for the master database to be a large, centralized database such as a DB2 database on a mainframe, while the slave databases may be smaller UNIX-based databases. The differences between the two databases is a major concern for the designers of replicated systems, especially in terms of SQL dialects. Table description in DB2/SQL is not the same as in Oracle/SQL (especially with referential integrity syntax), and it is impossible to maintain a single master catalog of table descriptions. Table changes to the master must be reviewed and rewritten to conform to the SQL CREATE dialect of the slave databases.

Another problem is timing. Database replication is used because a company cannot afford the overhead of instant database update (the two-phase commit issue), but then the database administrator must determine how long the time lag will be between the update to the master database and the updates to the slaves. Some choose to allow the updates to occur at a predefined time interval (say, each hour): the updates will all occur when the time interval is reached. Others base the updates to the slaves upon the level of activity in the slave databases. An activity threshold can be defined such that slave updates occur when all of the slave databases fall below this threshold. This method allows the slaves to be updated when they are not busy, but the end-users can never be sure about the currency of their slave database. A third approach has each slave database automatically poll the master when it is not busy to see if there are any updates awaiting propagation.

What if one of the slave databases becomes unavailable? Do we proceed to update only some of the slave databases, or wait until all of the slave databases are online and available for update? If we choose the simpler of the methods, requiring that all of the slaves be available, then we risk that a major failure of a slave database will affect the currency of the other slave databases.

On the other hand, if we choose to propagate changes regardless of availability, the change propagation subsystem must be able to track the changes to each slave. The most common approach for slave tracking is to have the propagator task reference a "change table" that keeps a list of all changes and a set of flags to indicate which slaves have been updated. Only if all of the slave databases are successfully updated is this row deleted from the change database. A change table might look like Figure 3.5. In this example, we see four transactions that were left over from the previous propagation cycle. These rows will

action	table	DataValues	AOK-DB1	AOK-DB2
insert	customer	('THAYER', 123)	N	N
update	order	(484, 'pen', 32)	N	N
update	customer	('SMITH')	N	
delete	order	(456)	N	

Figure 3.5   Sample change table.

continue to exist in the change table until database DB1 becomes available and the update propagates successfully.

If the distributed database uses replication such that business rules span physical databases, the maintenance of referential integrity (RI) becomes an issue. When business rules are enforced with referential integrity, the delay in propagation to the slave databases can create conditions in which the business rules are violated. Consider the simple business rule that no customers may be deleted if they still have outstanding orders in the order table. While this rule can easily be maintained in the master database, what happens when the dependent tables are replicated? If a local task on the slave database deletes the row for Jones, it does so without the knowledge that orders exist on the master database for Jones (Figure 3.6).

There are two solutions to this dilemma, neither of them elegant. The first is to run a query against the master order table to see if rows exist for the customer, and the second solution is to feed the slave task back to the master database so that the DBMS software will detect the RI violation.

Another alternative to periodic refreshing is to synchronize the master database with the slave database, and have all updates propagated to both databases. The choice between refreshing and synchronization depends upon the volatility of the data and the currency needs of the user community. For example, a static, nonchanging database can easily be refreshed daily, provided that the end-users understand that their data is only current to within 24 hours. For highly dynamic databases with constantly changing information, a synchronization scheme can be developed, but it is important to remember that there can be tremendous overhead when updating the replicated database. This overhead is especially noticeable when the system indexes are updated, and because indexes share a common root node, performance can degenerate if updates are being applied while the index tree is reconfiguring itself to accommodate the new data. It is also interesting to note that it is often faster to refresh a small database hourly than it is to incur the performance problems that accompany real-time updating.

Complete database refreshing is sometimes called the "snapshot approach," as a snapshot of the database is taken at a given time, and that snapshot is copied to the slave databases. In the popular Oracle database, snapshots are implemented as extensions to Oracle's SQL language. For example, the following Oracle snapshot retrieves customer and order information from London and Paris for all unfilled orders:

```
CREATE SNAPSHOT unfilled_orders
     REFRESH COMPLETE
     START WITH TO_DATE ('DD-MON-YY HH23:MI:55)
     NEXT SYSDATE + 7
```

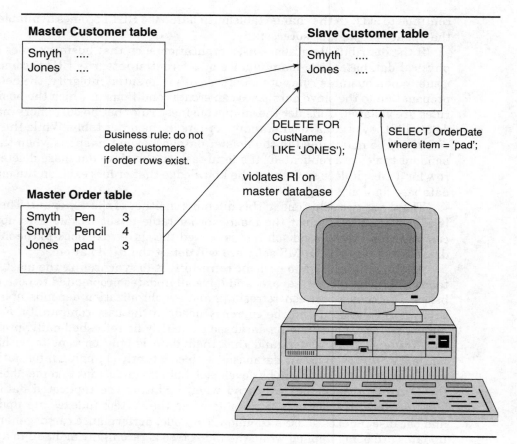

Figure 3.6 Referential integrity can be violated when updating slave databases.

```
AS
SELECT customer_name, customer_address, order_date
FROM customer@paris, order@london
WHERE
    customer.cust_number = order.customer_number
    AND
    order_complete_flag = "N";
```

Here we see that the snapshot will be taken at 11:55 P.M. and thereafter each seven days. The end-users will be told about the refreshing period, and the database software will automatically perform the extract. The DBA could also perform the extract manually by issuing the command

```
EXECUTE unfilled_orders.refresh_all;
```

Operating System Copy Replication

A popular alternative to master-slave replication is to use copy replication. Today's high-speed copy utilities can refresh an entire 20 MB database, including all of the system indexes, in less than 60 seconds. This can be scheduled to run each hour during the processing day, because it is so fast and simple to do a complete refresh that synchronization is only recommended for very large or very static databases.

Updating: Tight Consistency vs. Loose Consistency

With tight consistency, a two-phase commit architecture is used to insure that all copies of the replicated database are in sync at all times. In the loose consistency approach, a "primary" database is used as a master, and updates to the master are propagated to the slave replications. The propagation can happen in many ways. Updates may be propagated according to time or date, or may be triggered by a predefined database event, such as the addition of "critical" information. To summarize:

tight consistency

Plus: All databases are in sync in real time

Minus: Access can be lost with communications failure

loose consistency

Plus: Data can be reloaded from snapshots
              Asynchronous replication is possible

Minus: Slaves are not in exact sync with the master

The costs of data replication are not trivial. If the replicated data is to be updated instantly, a complex procedure must be installed to distribute the updates to all of the replicated databases. If the replicated data is not time-sensitive, then a method for refreshing the entire database is preferable, and the database is overlaid with fresh data on a periodic basis.

Replication: Improving Reliability

While there are advantages to database replication, what happens to update propagation when a network connection to a slave database is lost? Most technologies allow for the queuing of information until the communication has been reestablished, keeping a deferred list of updates.

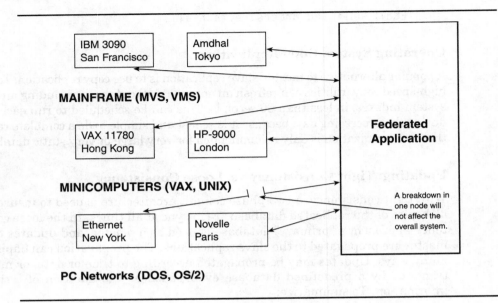

Figure 3.7   Multiple points of failure.

Some database vendors such as Sybase offer a replication server to insure that all of the databases remain synchronized. Another approach is to take a periodic snapshot of the master database and distribute it, as a whole, to all of the slave databases. The snapshot of the master database must be taken when the database is at a "quiesce," or quiet-state. For 24X7 databases, a method can be devised to perform a "flying dump," whereby an active database can be backed up while it is being updated, and this copy can be used to populate slave databases. In a flying dump, a "syncpoint" is established, and the backup is synchronized with the database journals. The journals keep the before and after images of all updated data. Because the backup and the system logs are in exact harmony, recovery is possible to any point in time.

The distributed processing that usually accompanies distributed database carries with it a certain benefit in terms of reliability: With each database engine on its own processor, a failure of a processor will only impact the users of that component in the federation (Figure 3.7).

Advantages of a Distributed Database System

DDS has some inherent advantages relative to the proximity of system components and the system's multitasking and multithreading capabilities. The most compelling argument for DDS has to do with "proximity," whereby a centralized database is segmented and thus moved closer to the users. For example, a user site in San Francisco may run its localized database on its own processor. San Francisco communicates directly with this local database, while other nodes of the federation access this database indirectly, via wide-area networks. Other users within the federation will still be able to access San Francisco's data in a seamless fashion, but they will remain dependent on the network and communications software to provide the seamless interface.

The second argument for improved performance are the multitasking and multithreading abilities that are sometimes found in distributed databases. The terms *multitasking* and *multithreading* sound very similar, but their methods for improving database performance are quite different.

Multithreading (sometimes called "interquery parallelism") refers to the ability of a database engine to split a query into subqueries and spawn subtasks to execute these subqueries. In order to support multithreading, the hardware must have multiprocessing capabilities, and the software must be able to "split" a request into components.

An alternative to multithreading is the use of "massively parallel" processors that have up to 16,000 individual CPUs. They use the "data decomposition" approach in which the query remains intact and the data is apportioned to many processors. Mark Tolliver, Vice President of Business Information Systems of MasPar, in Sunnyvale, California, markets such a system. "We believe that such data decomposition will allow us to effectively apply much larger computing capacity to complex queries because using more processors allows us to greatly increase the total communications capacity between the processors," says Tolliver. "Our approach requires the processors to communicate with each other, and we create enormous bandwidth communications between the processors, allowing the data to be decomposed and distributed. Conceptually, the array of processors is physically similar to a relational table, and each row of the table represents an individual processor."

Multitasking (sometimes called "intraquery parallelism") refers to the ability of the distributed database to query many databases at the same time. In a multitasking environment, the query is parsed and broken into components based upon the target database. These queries are then launched simultaneously, and the multitasking software waits patiently until all of the subqueries have been completed (Figure 3.8).

3.5 TYPES OF DATABASE DISTRIBUTION

There are three types of distributed databases that need to be considered. Each of these types has unique characteristics and unique solutions. While most companies have a hybrid of these types, a careful look at each type can shed light on the major issues of distributed database systems.

Geographical (horizontal) distribution refers to several databases that run

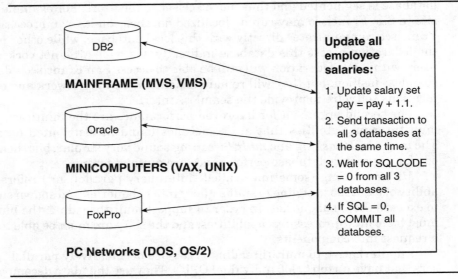

Figure 3.8   Multitasking databases.

under the control of different CPUs (Figure 3.9). It is irrelevant whether the databases are separated by several inches or by thousands of miles. In fact, it is possible to have a distributed database architecture within a single machine, as is the case with a quadratic processor. Machines such as the IBM 3090 have several CPUs contained within the box, and separate database systems can be run on each half of the CPU. Each database enjoys the benefit of an isolated

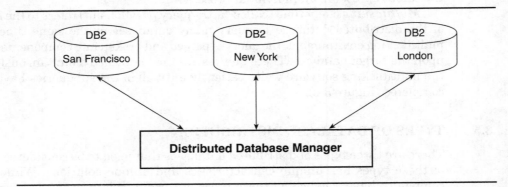

Figure 3.9   Geographical distribution.

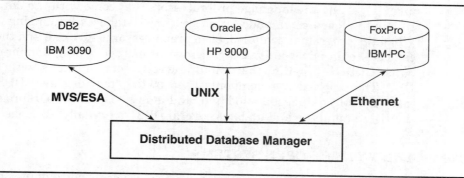

Figure 3.10   Platform distribution.

processor, but special distributed database communications are required to make the processors communicate with each other.

Platform (vertical) distribution refers to the existence of databases on diverse hardware platforms (Figure 3.10). Examples would be a FoxPro system on a PC LAN communicating with DB2 on a mainframe. Platform distribution is often used with client/server software so that a shared database can be distributed to PCs through a wide-area network.

Architectural distribution of the existence of distributed database that involve different architectures (Figure 3.11). An example would be an object-oriented database that communicates with a relational database, or a CA-IDMS database that communicates with a DB2 database.

Architectural distribution is the simplest type of DDS architecture to imple-

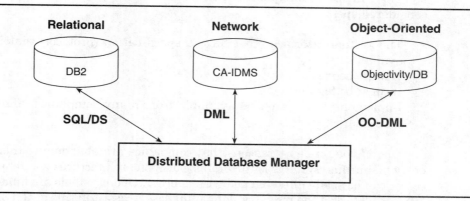

Figure 3.11   Architectural distribution.

ment. By using the language preprocessors that come with the database, it is simple to embed commands for each of the databases into a single program. When the program is compiled, each preprocessor is invoked, and the database calls are replaced by native calls. Using this method, a programmer can write a batch COBOL program that simultaneously communicates with IDMS and DB2. This approach is commonly used in the "master-slave" DDS, where a master IDMS database is updated, and a daily batch COBOL program reads the IDMS database and updates several DB2 "query-only" databases.

3.6   THE MYTH OF OPEN SYSTEMS

The term "open systems" has been used so often in the computer community that very few professionals seem to remember the goal of open systems. A fair definition of an open system would be a system that provides a mechanism to run applications transparently across heterogeneous environments. Open systems adhere to public domain standards. Systems written with these tools will thus be interoperable with other products, can be easily ported to new hardware platforms, and can be scaled according to the size of the system.

Standards are generally determined by committees, but do not become "real" standards until they are adopted by the user community. Many of the guidelines for open systems by IEEE, OSF, and OMG are not standards; they are endorsements. Endorsements do not become standards until they are widely accepted by the vendor community. In order to become widely accepted by many vendors, an endorsement must have a well-written and complete specification and an interface that is accessible. Only with these features will vendors be able to create multiple implementations of the endorsement, thereby moving toward a standard.

There are several requirements that must be met in order for a system to be considered open:

- The system interface must have a specification (protocol) that is openly available.
- It must be free.
- It must be legally clean.
- Implementations must be available from many companies, allowing the consumers a choice.

One of the foremost reasons that companies are abandoning their proprietary mainframe systems is the promise of open architectures whereby one processor can be easily interchanged with another. Open systems are hindered by a 30-year history of the industry's unwillingness to assist in this goal. IBM's early unwillingness to embrace the ASCII character set still haunts C programmers. And while C is touted as a portable language, it still suffers from characters that do not exist in IBM character sets. Each vendor has dual interests; on the one hand, to meet users' demands for open architectures, on the other hand, a selfish interest in keeping its architectures proprietary to enjoy continued usage.

There are five areas of standards that would be required for true open systems:

- Languages—Procedural languages (for example, C) would strictly adhere to standards, thereby making the systems that are written with these languages portable to other environments.
- Databases—Common access languages (for example, SQL) would be developed such that database access is independent of the database engine.
- Operating systems—Operating systems (for example, UNIX) would follow standard syntax such that entire environments could be moved to other platforms.
- Hardware—Computer hardware (for example, the IBM-PC) would adhere to standards, such that any processor could be replaced with another processor.
- Communications—Interoperable communication protocols (for example, CORBA) would be developed such that communications between hardware platforms is standard.

Today, there are no real open systems, and hardware and software vendors have an incentive to insure that true open systems are never available. Openness implies a nonproprietary implementation, and vendors are deeply afraid of developing products that can be instantly replaced by a competitor. SQL is a perfect example. Even though the ANSI committee developed a very rigorous definition for SQL, database vendors could not resist the temptation to "enhance" their implementations of SQL. The result is a series of dialects of SQL, none of which is completely interchangeable. These dialects have resulted in high overhead and interoperability problems for those attempting to deliver distributed SQL databases.

Even the IBM-PC standard is not truly an open system standard. The standard was initially developed by a vendor, without any input from the public at large, and the widespread acceptance of the architecture propelled the rest of the PC industry to copy this arbitrary standard. Consequently, the term "100 percent IBM compatible" has come to have many different meanings, as anyone knows who has ever experienced systems that behave differently depending upon which IBM-compatible PC is running the system.

In summary, the promises of portability, scalability, and interoperability have not been met by open systems, and there is some debate about whether the industry is truly motivated to achieve this goal.

SOLUTIONS FOR DISTRIBUTED DATABASE COMMUNICATION

There are many types of tools that organizations may use to make a distributed database function as a unified federation. There are many vendors that offer software solutions for communications between distributed databases, but none of the packages automatically enforces logical data integrity. For a complete federated database, one must create a "metaschema" to enforce all of the intra-system "rules." For example, referential integrity (RI) may be required so that rows from the customer table (residing in an Oracle database in Washington) cannot be deleted if rows exist in the order table (residing in a DB2 database in Chicago). This type of RI must be enforced procedurally, and it is the responsibility of the programmers to be sure that the business rules are maintained. There are no solutions for architecturally distributed databases that do not involve significant programmer intervention.

Essentially, IS managers must decide whether to purchase a distributed communications package or to create their own communications. The commercial packages that allow communications between different database architectures are often expensive, and some of the more sophisticated packages charge a fee for each run-time terminal that is connected to the interface. Examples of these tools include Uniface and EDA-SQL.

Consequently, some companies find that it is more economical to write their own communications interfaces. The most popular approach to "bridge building" uses remote procedural calls (RPCs) to establish communications between the systems. Collections of RPC calls may be incorporated into an application programming interface (API), and this API can be programmed with metaschema information to maintain distributed referential integrity and other business rules.

It is important to note that many of the commercial APIs may not meet the specific requirements of the distributed database. Many shops choose to use commercial APIs such as Microsoft's Open Database Connectivity (ODBC) product. ODBC allows distributed communications between relational databases, but does not possess an interface into nonrelational engines.

Another problem with commercial APIs is their speed. Virtually every database vendor has created its own dialect of SQL, and any commercial API must "generalize" the SQL request and translate it into the appropriate SQL dialect for the target database. The overhead incurred by these products when they "generalize" the SQL dialects consumes processing resources and often diminishes performance.

Many managers have noted that the exclusive dominion of relational database architectures is rapidly eroding. Relational access has been unsuitable for very large or very fast databases, and nonrelational databases such as IMS and Teradata have been used to fill this void. Object databases are also making rapid inroads into mainstream database processing. While some object databases offer an SQL interface (such as the UniSQL database), most of the others rely on nonrelational object-oriented data manipulation language (OO-DML) for data access.

There is an effort to create a new dialect of SQL called SQL3 that addresses the issues of distributed and object-oriented systems. Joe Chelko, a nationally recognized expert on SQL and a member of the development committee for SQL3, states that "the SQL3 standard is still in a state of flux, and is still several years away from being useful. At this time, SQL3 is elaborately confusing and baroque."

REFERENCES

Bacon, J. 1993. *Concurrent systems—an integration approach to operating systems, database and distributed systems*. Addison-Wesley.

Baum, D. 1993. Middleware: Unearthing the software treasure trove. *InfoWorld*, March.

Bell, D. 1992. *Distributed database systems*. Addison-Wesley.

Blaser, A., ed. 1990. *Database systems of the 90s*. Berlin: International Symposium.

Bobak, A. 1993. *Distributed and multidatabase systems*. Bantam Books.

Burleson, D. 1993. *Practical application of object-oriented techniques to relational databases*.   Wiley\QED.

———. 1993. Getting the GOOD GOOP on OOP. *COMPUTERWORLD*, April.

———. 1993. Distributed object technology. *First Class Magazine*, October.

———. 1994. Mapping object-oriented applications to relational databases. *Object Magazine*, January.

———. 1994. Managing distributed databases—an enterprise view. *Database Programming & Design*, June.

Chivvis, A. and J. Geyer. 1993. Think again: face the facts. These misconceptions about downsizing are just lame excuses for procrastination. *Corporate Computing*, March.

Chorafas D. 1989. *Handbook of database management and distributed relational databases*. TAB Books.

Chu, W., ed. 1986. *Distributed database systems*. Books on Demand.

Date, C. J. 1987. What is a distributed database? *InfoDB*, 2:7.

Goulde, M. 1992. Open systems: analysis, issues and opinions. *Open Information Systems*, December.

Gray, B. 1993. Database/file servers. *Computing Canada*, March.

Hackathorn, R. 1993. *Enterprise database connectivity*. Wiley.

Ozsu M. and P. Valdurez. 1992. Distributed database systems, where are we now? *Database Programming & Design*, March.

———. 1993. *Principles of distributed database systems*. Prentice-Hall.

Stein, J. 1992. Distributed databases: what they are, what are they good for? *Journal of Object-oriented Programming*, July–August.

Watt, P. and J. Celko. 1993. Hewlett-Packard's relational/object paradigm. *DBMS*, February.

Weitz, L. 1992. Desperately seeking database independence: options for accessing diverse corporate data. *Software Magazine*, December.

4

Basics of Client/Server Systems

4.1 INTRODUCTION

In the mainframe environments of the 1960s and 1970s, most online computer systems were characterized by "dumb terminals" that connected to a single data system. The terminals provided the user interface, while the application logic and database access were controlled by the mainframe.

Client/server, at its most basic, refers to the ability of a client, or requester, to make a request for services to another computer. The computer that receives the request, the server, interprets the request, and accesses the appropriate database, shipping the data as a response to the client. Another way to state this is that it is a computer architecture in which one system requests services from another system, and the other system satisfies the request for services. The requester is called the client and the provider is called the server.

Unlike the mainframe environment, client/server architectures allow the application code to reside in the client environment (Figure 4.1). Because the application code is tightly coupled with the user's environment, the user is free to manipulate information using any tool within that environment, and to request data access services from many databases on other computer systems.

As many companies began to downsize their systems to take advantage of the cheaper processors on smaller platforms, early client/server systems were developed to manage information across many diverse platforms.

Three terms came into vogue at this time: front-end software, back-end software, and middleware. Middleware is the software that establishes an application programming interface, or API, for distributed applications. Front-

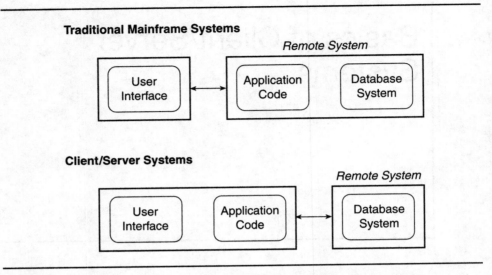

Figure 4.1   Client/server moves the application into the user environment.

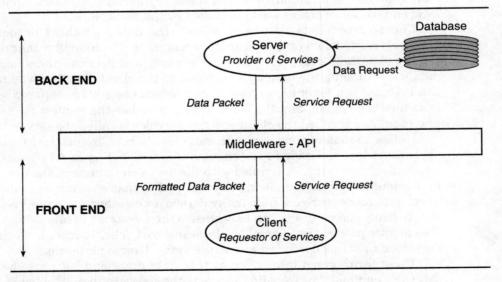

Figure 4.2   Client/server architecture.

end software is the client software, which sends requests for services, and back-end software generally is the server software, which receives and processes the request. In truly distributed processing, these terms are dynamic, because a front end for any transaction may also be the back end for another transaction (Figure 4.2).

4.2   FRONT-END SOFTWARE

Generally, front-end software falls into two categories:

- Reporting and query tools
- Program development software

Reporting and Query Tools

These systems provide one-way data transmission from the database server to the client. Because the systems are for retrieval only, the sophistication under-lying the data requests are hidden from the user. Examples of this type of software include Quest by Gupta and the Oracle database server. These tools allow the user to specify information requests in a friendly manner—for example, in terms of building a sample report or creating a graph. The front end then interrogates the request and generates SQL, which is sent to the server for processing. The requested information is delivered to the user and is formatted into the desired form, providing the user with spreadsheets and graphics.

Program Development Software

Most packages offered on multiple platforms fall into this category. They allow the programmer to develop a system on the PC and access information from a robust database server, such as DB2 on the mainframe or Oracle on a UNIX system. Products include Gupta's SQL Windows and Microsoft's Visual Basic, as well as some of the new graphical user interface (GUI) tools for PCs.

GUI ("Gooey") tools are among the hottest tools in client/server development software. Many of these tools promise to use object-oriented methods. Objectview tools from Matesys, SQLWindows version 4.0, and Powersoft's PowerBuilder are examples of object-oriented GUI tools.

Presentation managers are excellent examples of front-end software. Tools such as Microsoft Windows handle all of the processing on the client, including actions like mouse clicks and window scrolling.

Requests are passed to a data manager, which passes the requests to the API for processing on the host server. Many of the most sophisticated of these

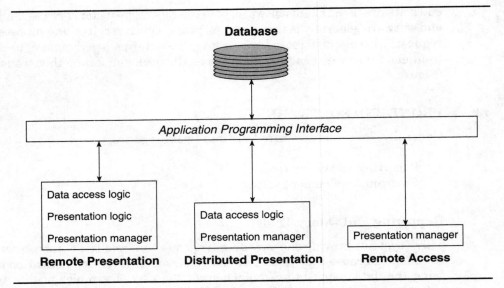

Figure 4.3   Three types of client front ends.

tools, such as Powersoft's PowerBuilder, manage all of the Windows and SQL formatting, leaving the user to develop an application without concern for the internals of the presentation manager or the workings of the data structures.

There are three levels of front-end client/server (Figure 4.3). The simplest is a presentation manager on the client, with all of the presentation logic and data access logic on the server. The middleground has the presentation manager and presentation logic on the client, with the data access logic on the server. In the third configuration, the presentation manager, presentation logic, and data logic are on the client.

4.3   BACK-END SOFTWARE

Back-end software is the software that manages requests from the client, retrieves the information from the database server, and passes it to the client front end. Most of these products only serve a single type of client, although multiple database back ends can be installed on a single data repository.

In most client/server environments, the server is a single database that interacts with the client. In distributed database environments, a back end may be a distributed database manager that manages multiple requests against many databases, collecting and formatting the requested information into a single packet for the client. A distributed database manager may deal with information that is in many different physical locations, and the manager maps this diverse data into a single logical package. As far as the client is concerned, the server appears to be a single database engine.

The back-end software interprets the request from the client and determines the physical access path to retrieve the desired data. The back-end system is also responsible for all database interface, and includes all database logic for rollback, error handling, and database commit processes. Because the back-end software is the only entity dealing directly with the databases, the back end is responsible for maintaining all transactions from the client.

Middleware is the interface layer between the client and the server. Middleware usually uses an application programming interface (API), a request language (SQL), and a local and remote "service layer" to manage the interaction between the platforms. Like an API, middleware is used to build commonality into applications by providing a common interface between the application and the operating system, but middleware includes additional code to assist in the management of the application across distributed database nodes. The goal of middleware is to encapsulate and hide the complexities of differing communications and operating system interfaces. The term *glue* has become a popular description of middleware, as middleware, as middleware provides the adhesive between the application and its operating environment, such that the application is free to be moved to other environments without requiring any changes.

Middleware can be divided into five major software areas: file transfer software, messaging products with an API and communications services for distributed networks, database/data access packages that link to various databases, online transaction processing systems, and remote procedure calls, with an API that works over multiple protocol stacks.

A standard middleware component is vital to developers of distributed applications because it shields them from the complexities and encapsulates the details of each operating environment behind a simple-to-use interface. With respect to distributed databases, the middleware can be used to provide a single view of multiple databases, such that end-users need only specify the view; all of the interdatabase communication, including two-phase commit processing, is taken care of on their behalf. When databases are added to the middleware equation, the system must take on another level of complexity, managing not only communication protocols and operating system interfaces, but the nuances of the database language dialects (SQL). Unlike the "gateway" style middle, where the developer chooses between databases of a single vendor, the true open middleware packages allow "uniform" access to different vendor databases and different database architectures. For example, the UniFace middleware tools allow access to relational databases such as Oracle, but also to pseudo-relational databases such as Basis-Plus. Because the open database middleware relies on "homogenizing" the dialects of database access, they are often criticized for poor performance.

There are many middleware products on the market, ranging from very complex systems such as DEC's NAS and IBM's SAA, to simple messaging packages. Here is a partial list of messaging products and vendors:

Product	Vendor
Communications Integrator	Covia Technologies
Focus	Information Builders
Network Application Services (NAS)	Digital Equipment
Message Express	Horizon Strategies
SmartStar Vision	SmartStar Corporation
Systems Application Architecture (SAA)	IBM
Pipes	Peerlogic Incorporated
PowerBuilder	Powersoft
UniFace	UniFace Corporation
X-IPC	Momentum Software

The term *middleware* is going out of vogue as a buzzword because of a recent decision by the U.S. Patent and Trademark Office, which has granted a registered trademark on the term *Middleware* to the software firm of TechGnosis Inc., on the basis of the company's early use of the term. TechGnosis now has exclusive rights to the word Middleware.

4.4   PARTITIONING THE APPLICATION PROCESSING

It is very important to understand that client/server does much more than distribute data across a network. One of the foremost reasons for using client/server is to share the processing load between the client and the server. There are two extremes that serve to illustrate this point. In the graph in Figure 4.4, we see several common approaches to the distribution of data and processing. All systems fall somewhere within this domain, depending on the amount of distributed processing and distributed databases.

Centralized data, centralized processing—This is the traditional approach to data processing in which all of the data resides in a common repository and all of the processing is performed by a centralized computer, usually a mainframe. This approach has the advantage of better control of the data and the processor, and has the main disadvantage of being subject to widespread performance degradation when the processor becomes overloaded. There is also a single point of failure; a CPU problem could cripple the entire system.

Centralized data, distributed processing—In this case, the data resides in a

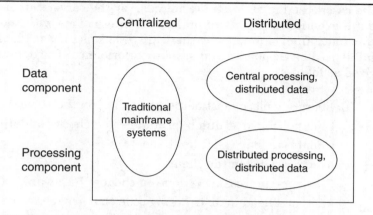

Figure 4.4   Distribution of data and processing.

central, controlled environment, but the processing is distributed across a network. The main advantage to this approach is the control over the data and the ability to use the cheaper processing on smaller platforms. The main disadvantage is that the database becomes a single point of failure, and a runaway task could bring the entire system to its knees. From an economic perspective this is one of the best approaches. The database resides on a single processor. This processor acts as a huge file server for the remote clients.

Distributed data, centralized processing—This is a common approach for geographically distributed systems. A centralized processor does all of the work, while remote data hubs access the data. The computers at the remote nodes act only as data servers, with all of the processing being done by a large central processor. The main advantage to this approach is the proximity of the data to the user in a distributed network, and the main disadvantage is the lack of centralized control over backup and recovery of the data.

Distributed data, distributed processing—This is the approach of many object technology systems, whereby both the data and the processing are distributed across a network. The primary advantage of this approach is the ability to assign both data and processors on an as-needed basis. The main disadvantage is the problem of coordinating backup and recovery of the data across all of the distributed nodes.

Client/Server Processing Issues

In a client/server environment, there is a large amount of flexibility in the configuration of processing. The processing can take place on the server, with the clients acting as "dumb terminals," or the server can exist solely to fetch data, leaving the clients to process all interactions with the database. Along this continuum of processing there are decisions to be made that are primarily influenced by economics and system performance. The options can be summarized as follows:

> Deliberately place most of the processing on the servers.
>> Clients behave as dumb terminals, and check out data from host.
>> Clients can have GUI front ends.
> Place processing on the client.
>> Cheaper—processing is done on cheaper hardware.
>> More overhead in distributing code changes to the clients.
>> May be slower for computationally intensive work.
> Allow the system to decide what processor to use.
>> Infinitely flexible.
>> Very scalable.
>> Not yet practical except with object-oriented systems and UNIX-to-UNIX clients.

One of the original promises of open systems was scalable architectures, in which just about any component of the computer system could be moved, increased in size, or reconfigured without interrupting the overall operation of the system. This scalability, by its very nature, gives the systems architect an almost infinite number of choices in how to store and process information.

In the good old days, it was always assumed that the server would be a large centralized computer such as an IBM mainframe, and the clients would be "dumb terminals" that served no other function than to allow the user to connect to the centralized system. The mainframe controlled every aspect of the application. From data collection to screen presentation, the data was usually managed by a centralized database (DB2), terminal communication was managed by a cohesive network manager (VTAM), and processing was under the complete control of a sophisticated time-sharing operating system (MVS/ESA).

There are advocates who say that the future will bring about a complete change in the processing paradigm. Rather than having a centralized processor, each client will do all of its own processing. These super-clients will have very large processors and will be able to perform even computationally intensive processing locally without straining the server. The server will change radically. Instead of serving data and processing, the server of the future will only act as data server, funneling and controlling the distribution of data to the intelligent clients from many data sources. Futurists argue that today's Pentium and RISC processors have processing power that was only available on large mainframes a few years ago, and that within a few more years there will be even more powerful processors.

Advocates of both extremes in architecture have taken to their arguments with an almost religious fervor. While even the centralized processing advocates recognize the value of sharing processing power, they point to the reality that any practical implementation of large distributed networks still use PCs connected to a mainframe, and the mainframe does all of the data access and processing. The 1994 Winter Olympics were a good example. Thousands of PCs were connected to an IBM mainframe, and the system was able to use the centralized facilities of the database to insure that all of the game information was controlled.

Another compelling argument for centralized processing is the fact that a change to an application is applied once, and all clients automatically grab and execute the correct version. When processing is distributed to many PC clients, code changes must be distributed to each of the clients. Imagine a network where 400 PCs are connected to a data server, and a complete set of the processing code resides on each PC. If a single PC is turned off, the new system code will not be copied to that PC. Thus human intervention would be required to insure that all of the PCs were using the correct versions of the application.

One solution to this dilemma is to implement a "code repository," so that the executable code is stored in a database on the server, and called for on an as-needed basis. Just as data can be centralized, source code repositories can allow the seamless distribution and control of different versions of processing code. If properly implemented, a scheme could be devised to allow the processor, on whatever platform it may be located, to access the desired code, already compiled. linked, and ready to execute. Of course, this on-demand approach to source code has drawbacks, the foremost of which is the increased demand on the network, which must now transfer both data and the programs that manipulate the data. A compromise approach is a method whereby the program code resides on the PC client, and is checked against the repository to see if it is the most current version. If the client code has become obsolete, then, and only then, is a new copy of the program transferred down to the client.

The advocates of centralized processing also point to the problems of managing security, data access, and data integrity across "open" systems. They state that it can be very difficult, if not impossible, to effectively distribute and control data across these networks; and considering that the existing mainframe control systems are the result of person-centuries of effort, it is foolhardy to undertake the rewriting of all of the control software.

The advocates of the "two-tiered" (decentralized) architecture argue that centralized processing systems are not scalable. For example, as more PCs are added to the network, the mainframe becomes increasingly burdened, and it is a constant challenge to keep enough horsepower on the mainframe. With the processors isolated on the individual clients, the system becomes infinitely scalable, and it does not matter to the server whether it is serving 10 or 10,000 clients. They also point out that processing on a PC is more than 10,000 times cheaper than processing on a mainframe, and that the distributed processing approach can be justified on purely economic grounds. They also point out that the smaller processors have software that is decades ahead of the mainframes. Imagine the effort it would take to create a mainframe processor that could duplicate Microsoft Windows, with a centralized processor tracking the mouse movements and GUI interfaces of thousands of simultaneous users.

In scientific environments the ability to distribute processing can be very important. If an analysis requires intense computation—for example, if a geologist wanted to compare two simultaneous simulations of earthquake activity—a new processor can be brought online and dedicated to the task without impacting the overall system. This ability to do "processor load balancing" gives the system the ability to choose and apply processing power on an as-needed basis, something that cannot easily be achieved with a large mainframe.

Of course, such load balancing requires human intervention. A human must determine the amount of processing power that the tasks require and manually assign the processor to the task. It would be nice to have a system that could dynamically draw processing resources on an as-needed basis, dedicating the horsepower to the processes that require the most service. There are some new client/server tools that are working on this type of dynamic partitioning. Forte Software, a California-based client/server developer, is creating a system that will allow processing power to be reallocated to the processes at run time.

There is also far less network traffic when each client does its own processing. The only network traffic is the transfer of data from the client to the server. This also gives the distributed processing system the ability to multithread an application. As recently as a few years ago, system designers argued that multithreading did not fit the way that most processing was performed, and therefore was of very little value to most corporate applications. They claimed that most of their processing was serial (do task A, then do task B, then do task C), and there were dependencies between processes such that simultaneous processing was not feasible.

However, designers are beginning to see merit in multithreading, even for the most mundane applications. For example, a text database may need to perform word-searching on a large document. If the document is partitioned, and each partition is assigned a processor, word searches can be split, with dozens or even hundreds of concurrent processes being spawned. This type of partitioning allows end-users to search trillions of bytes of textual information with subsecond response time.

Of course, the reality is that the systems designers must make a conscious decision about which tasks are most appropriate for the PC-client processing and which are better suited for the server's high-speed processors. There is a movement afoot that says that the best approach is to build the system on a standalone processor and defer the distributed processing issue until later in the implementation stage, when the processing requirements become more apparent. Personally, I feel that this is the better approach; it does not seem necessary to make the distributed processing decision early in the design process.

There are two "bases" for client/server: the client-based and the server-based architecture. The client-based approach has the GUI interface created and executed on the client, usually a PC. The server-based approach allows the GUI to be built and executed on the server, usually in a UNIX environment with windows.

For whatever reason, the most popular approaches today use a two-tiered client-based approach. The phenomenal success of Powersoft's PowerBuilder product and Microsoft's Visual Basic are testimony to this popularity. The client-based approach allows the developer to create a friendly GUI interface on the PC, but most, if not all, of the data access and computation is done on the server, using SQL calls to an interface such as ODBC. This tends to defeat the promise of scalability in a client/server model, as new clients place an increasing demand upon the data server.

4.5   TYPES OF CLIENT/SERVER

While client/server continues through its adolescence, standards are beginning to emerge, but there remain an almost infinite number of choices, in hardware, software, and presentation styles. With regard to client/server presentation styles, there are three general categories.

Distributed presentation (e.g., Easel, Motzart)—A character-based screen image that is generated on a mainframe or midrange computer is interrogated and re-presented on a PC GUI. The main advantages to the distributed presentation style is fast development, but in today's age of empowered end-users, character-based display has lost favor. However, many companies find distributed presentation to be an excellent short-term solution when the ultimate goal is a migration to client/server presentation.

Remote presentation (e.g., X-Windows)—Remote presentation styles offer dynamic distribution of logic, an emerging standard, and an open UNIX environment.

Client/server presentation (e.g., PowerBuilder, Visual Basic, Microsoft Access)—A remote client may access, manipulate, and return information to a host or a distributed network of host databases. This approach appears to be the most popular presentation style for distributed databases, and the flexibility of open database connectivity (ODBC) gateways has led many to adopt client/server for distributed databases.

Client Platforms

There are many platforms that are common to client/server systems. The most popular include MS-DOS, MS-Windows, Windows NT, HP/UNIX, SunOS, Macintosh, and OS/2. While some of the midrange client platforms remain popular, it has been a trend in the industry that most clients operate on PC platforms. The costs of midrange terminals such as Sun Sparc stations are prohibitive for many companies, and most end-users want to enjoy the ability to process information on the wide variety of PC programs.

When a shop attempts to deploy a very large client/server system—when the number of clients grows above 100—finding a common client platform becomes a concern. For example, some users may be using OS/2 while other use MS-Windows. It is usually impractical to write and maintain multiple copies of client software, so most IS shops require that clients adopt a standard environment for their PCs. This can cause great debates about the relative merits of, say, OS/2 vs. MS-Windows, but it is absolutely necessary for effective deployment of client/server that all of the clients reside on homogenous software.

Once the client platform and operating system have been determined, the GUI development tools can be determined. There are a great many GUI tools on the market, and all of the vendors claim that their tool is best suited to client/server development. A few of the most popular PC development tools include PowerBuilder, Visual Basic, Visual C++, MS-Access, ObjectView, and SQL/Windows.

At this time, there is a battle for market dominance between PowerBuilder and Visual Basic. There are those who believe that over the next several years one of these products will achieve market dominance and become a de facto standard, much as MS-Windows has become a standard for PC operating systems.

4.6 TIPS FOR INSURING SUCCESS

With so many shops entering client/server for the first time, shops often ask what they can do to insure their success and minimize heartache. While there is no magic formula, those companies that have been successful with client/server usually follow these guidelines.

1. Be prepared for setbacks.

Successful client/server developers plan time in the schedule to resolve problems. They take their most optimistic estimate of time for implementation and double it, and they do not underestimate the learning curve for the programming staff.

2. Train the programmers.

Many veteran programmers are threatened with the new tools of client/server and distributed database systems, and some harbor fears that they will not be able to learn the material quickly enough to remain valuable. Organizations that have been successful in their client/server development have created a nonthreatening environment for the programming staff.

3. Stick with industry leaders.

Even if an analysis shows that an obscure technology offers more robust features, there is a sound reason for sticking with one of the industry leaders. Training and technical support is more readily available, and pretrained development staff are available for consulting. Many companies choose their environments by simply looking for the most popular databases, hardware, and software packages.

4. Actively seek out potential performance bottlenecks.

A successful shop carefully probes for potential problems with data transmission, server response, and locking. Unlike a traditional architecture, client/server has many points of failure, and careful attention must be paid to tuning. A proactive approach to performance measurement can often make the difference between success and failure.

5. Design for flexibility.

From the inception of the project, design the client/server architecture such that you have the luxury of "swapping out" any component of the system that becomes obsolete or ineffective. A flexible design avoids any product or tool that even hints at a proprietary solution. Remember, the technology is changing rapidly, and your system must be able to keep pace with improvements in the environment.

REFERENCES

Bacon, J. 1993. *Concurrent systems, an integrated approach to operating systems, database and distributed systems.* Addison-Wesley.

Baum, D. 1993. Middleware: unearthing the software treasure trove. *InfoWorld*, March.

Blaser, A., ed. 1990. *Database systems of the 90s*. Berlin: International Symposium.

Bloomer, J. 1991. *Power programming with RPC*. O'Reilly & Associates.

Bobak, A. 1993. *Distributed and multidatabase systems*. Bantam Books.

Burleson, D. 1993. *Practical application of object-oriented techniques to relational databases*. Wiley\QED.

———. 1993. Distributed object technology. *First Class Magazine*, October.

———. 1994. Managing distributed databases—an enterprise view. *Database Programming & Design*, June.

Franklin, M. 1993. *Local disk caching for client/server database systems*. Dublin: Proceedings of the 19th VLDB conference.

Goulde, M. 1992. Open systems: analysis, issues and opinions. *Open Information Systems*, December.

Gray, B. 1993. Database/file servers. *Computing Canada*, March.

Hackathorn, R. 1993. *Enterprise database connectivity*. Wiley.

Lawton, G. 1993. Protecting integrity of distributed data. *Software Magazine*, January.

Ozsu, M. and P. Valdurez. 1992. Distributed database systems, where are we now? *Database Programming & Design*, March.

Stodder, D. 1992. Return of the process: client/server computing forces us to reexamine the data-centric approach. *Database Programming & Design*, March.

Weitz, L. 1992. Desperately seeking database independence: options for accessing diverse corporate data. *Software Magazine*, December.

Distributed Database Design

5.1 INTRODUCTION

While there are numerous books offering tips on the design of distributed systems, and CASE vendors who say that their tools are indispensible for distributed design, the only way to fully understand the issues involved in the design of a distributed database is to actually attempt a design. There is no substitute for experience.

It is critical to remember that database distribution is a design issue, not an analysis issue. It follows that any generally accepted analysis methodology will suffice for documenting the requirements of the system. Structured specifications with data flow diagrams (DeMarco style or Gane and Sarson style), along with a data dictionary and process logic specifications, are an excellent starting point for system design.

5.2 THE ECONOMICS OF DISTRIBUTED DATABASES

One of the primary reasons companies have for abandoning their mainframes is the promise of cheaper hardware and software. With the costs of an IBM mainframe data center approaching $500,000 per month, it is not surprising that many top IS managers force their organizations into the long march to open, distributed databases. The cost of database software also is dramatically more for mainframe systems. A large mainframe DBMS package can easily cost $250,000, while a good relational database for a UNIX-based midrange CPU can be had for as little as $10,000.

However, these savings must be balanced against the costs of maintaining the distributed systems. As processors are added to remote locations, human functions such as system administration, LAN management, and database administration must also be replicated. Also, while the costs of a database server may be quite low, when a company is ready to attach 1,000 PC workstations to the server, management is often shocked to find that the PC "seats" can range up to $2,000 per database desktop client. A PC workstation that uses a GUI with multiple database connections may cost more than $5,000, a figure that often makes managers question the economic justification for downsizing. A sound cost-benefit analysis must be performed that factors out all of the costs and savings for hardware, software, and human resources (Figure 5.1).

Many IS managers fail to realize that staff sizes may more than double depending upon the type of open system migration. The open system approach can have a tremendous initial cost, and the savings may not begin to accrue for several years. When a mainframe database is partitioned into 20 remote locations, you can expect to triple the database administration and system administration support staff.

But saving money is not the only reason for downsizing. Companies that rely on their competitive information are often forced onto the new midrange platforms in order to use the most advanced software. Object-oriented databases are found almost exclusively on midrange systems, and no company will be able to capitalize on object technology until it abandons its mainframe.

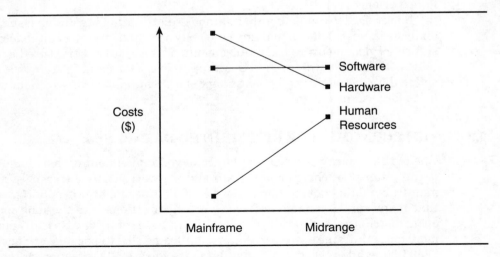

Figure 5.1   Downsizing cost factor analysis.

5.3   HUMAN FACTORS IN DISTRIBUTED DATABASE DESIGN

A good plan for downsizing must include the intangible factor of risk. While each individual hardware and software component may be fairly predictable and carry only low risk, the staff risks can be a major obstacle. The manager is forced to choose between retraining mainframe staff or replacing them with midrange programmers, database administrators, data center personnel, and so on.

Some companies opt for a slow migration into distributed systems. They introduce PCs with TCP/IP connections to the mainframe and give the end-users time to adjust to a GUI environment. The development staff can continue to develop applications using a PC version of their mainframe language while they are introduced to the C language. COBOL compilers, TSO, ISPF, and even job control language (JCL) are available for PCs, and mainframe programmers can immediately shift onto PC platforms. It is undisputed that program developers will be more productive on a PC workstation where they can instantly compile and test their programs. However, there is an additional burden on the DBA staff, since a scaled-down version of the database application must be replicated and maintained on each PC workstation.

Many companies understand that their downsizing adventure offers more than a chance to replace their legacy databases. It also offers the entire organization a chance to reassess its business processing goals and streamline and improve its overall method of doing business.

Some analysts advocate the business process reengineering (BPR) approach, while others follow the methods described by Michael Hammer for "reinventing the corporation." Hammer argues that the fundamental nature of business has changed, with customers having far more alternatives and demanding individual attention from their suppliers. Markets are also changing at a much more rapid pace than they have in the past, and information systems must be designed to be able to change as quickly as markets change.

Companies that are new to the marketplace and do not have the burden of legacy systems have found that they can accommodate the change to a distributed database environment far faster than their more "established" competitors, and that distributed databases allow them to provide faster, more accurate, and cheaper information processing. Many established and profitable companies suddenly find themselves losing market share to a small start-up competitor who can more effectively implement new technology.

5.4   DISTRIBUTED DESIGN EXAMPLE

The key to success is very simple: Start small. Companies that choose a very large or mission-critical system often become mired in technical problems and are never able to deliver a finished system.

Mastering distributed databases is something that one learns by doing, not by reading. If you really want to understand the issues firsthand, try the following exercise. It will take less than one week's effort, and you will completely appreciate the issues involved in distributing a database system. In order to do this exercise you will need the following:

- A small, well-tested system that resides on a midrange or mainframe
- A PC with connectivity software
- A distributed database connectivity tool such as ODBC
- A PC database such as FoxPro or Paradox
- Another database on the same platform as the source system

Begin with a small existing system that is not mission-critical to your company, and move part of the centralized data onto another platform. For example, let's assume that you have a customer-order system running on an Oracle database on a UNIX platform. This system is very old and in need of replacement, but all of the components have been fully tested and operational for years. We can see from Figure 5.2 that the database has five tables: a CUSTOMER table to store information about the customer, an ORDER table with order information, an

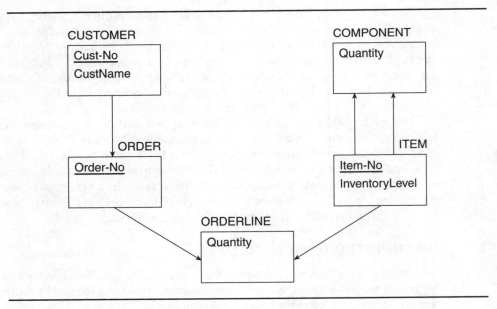

Figure 5.2   Sample database structure.

ITEM table for product information, a COMPONENT table, and an ORDERLINE table to store the quantity for each item that participates in an order.

Here you have many choices in distributing the system. You could move some tables to another relational database on the same platform, such as Sybase. You could move some tables to another relational database on a different platform, such as FoxPro on a PC LAN. Or you could move a table into another architecture on the same platform, such as Objectivity/DB on UNIX.

Depending upon the architecture of the target system, there is a great difference in the amount of effort that will be required to move the data (Figure 5.3). When the target system is a relational system, it is relatively simple to extract the data and reformat it for import into relational tables. Other architectures such as hierarchical or network databases will require complicated load programs, and the migration will be far more difficult.

In this example, we will export the CUSTOMER table from Oracle to a flat file on UNIX, and then massage the CREATE TABLE syntax for the dialect of the target relational database.

You can export the SQL syntax that was used to create the Oracle table to a flat file, but be prepared for the SQL syntax to fail when you attempt to run it against the Sybase compiler, especially if the Oracle table definition contains referential integrity rules. As you will see, there are many dialects of SQL, and it will be necessary to massage the table declaration syntax to conform to the target database.

If you are using referential integrity (RI), you will notice that the RI syntax

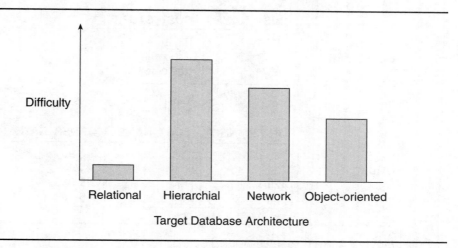

Figure 5.3   Difficulty of moving data to other architectures.

probably is very different in the new target database. Referential integrity is used to maintain business rules. Relational systems allow for the control of business rules with "constraints." These RI rules are used to insure that one-to-many and many-to-many relationships are enforced within the relational tables. For example, RI would insure that a row in the CUSTOMER table could not be deleted if orders for that customer exist in the ORDER table (Figure 5.4).

It should now be clear that it will be difficult to enforce this business rule in your new distributed environment. While it is relatively simple to tell an Oracle system not to delete a row from its CUSTOMER table if rows for that customer exist in the ORDER table, it is not simple to enforce this rule when the CUSTOMER table resides in Sybase and the ORDER table resides in Oracle. For now, remove the RI rules, and remember that you will need to manually replicate the RI rules in your application.

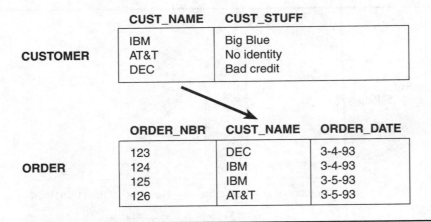

RI Rule = ORDER.CUST_NAME REFERENCES CUSTOMER.CUST_NAME

Two Options:

ON DELETE RESTRICT   Customers may not be deleted if they have orders in the ORDER table.

ON DELETE CASCADE   Customer delection will cause all orders for the customer to delete.

CUSTOMER	CUST_NAME	CUST_STUFF
	IBM	Big Blue
	AT&T	No identity
	DEC	Bad credit

ORDER	ORDER_NBR	CUST_NAME	ORDER_DATE
	123	DEC	3-4-93
	124	IBM	3-4-93
	125	IBM	3-5-93
	126	AT&T	3-5-93

Figure 5.4   Referential integrity.

The next step is to import the data into the newly defined table. This can be done in one of two ways. The easiest way is to massage the flat file that was created when you exported the CUSTOMER table into SQL INSERT statements. For example, the data could be massaged to state:

```
INSERT INTO CUSTOMER VALUES ('Burleson','1 Publishers
Parkway','Webster','NY')
INSERT INTO CUSTOMER VALUES ('Joe Chelko','123 4th St.','New
York','NY')
```

Another method is to use the target database's import facility to populate the table.

Now that the data has been partitioned, you can build an application that accesses the Sybase CUSTOMER table and the Oracle ORDER table. The big question is, how are you going to make these tables function as if they resided in a unified database? Whenever a distributed request is made to tables within different architectures, the query must be partitioned into separate subqueries to be executed against each database engine. The processor that governs the distributed request will act as the consolidator, merging the result sets and performing any post-retrieval processes such as ORDER BY or GROUP BY clauses.

For this example, all you really want to do is to join these tables for a customer, pulling the customer information from Sybase and the order information from Oracle. If it were possible to directly address SQL across different products, a query might look something like this:

```
SELECT SYBASE_CUSTOMER.customer_name,
     SYBASE_CUSTOMER.customer_address,
     ORACLE_ORDER.order_date
FROM
     SYBASE.CUSTOMER,
     ORACLE.ORDER,
WHERE
     SYBASE_CUSTOMER.cust_number=ORACLE_CUSTOMER.cust_number and
     SYBASE_CUSTOMER.customer_name like 'Burleson '
```

Notice that this SQL is using node names to identify the physical location of the tables. While this is not standard SQL syntax, it serves to illustrate the point that you need to join these diverse tables.

For a more realistic test, you would want to get information from all tables. The following SQL joins the CUSTOMER table with the ORDER table where customer_name = Burleson. It then joins the order_table entries with the order_line table, and order_line with the product table, to get the product information.

```
SELECT SYBASE_CUSTOMER.customer_name,
       SYBASE_CUSTOMER.customer_address,
       ORACLE_ORDER.order_date,
       ORACLE_PRODUCT.product_name,
       ORACLE_PRODUCT.product_cost,
       ORACLE_PRODUCT.product_name
FROM
       SYBASE.CUSTOMER,
       ORACLE.ORDER,
       ORACLE.ORDER_LINE,
       ORACLE.PRODUCT
WHERE
       SYBASE_CUSTOMER.cust_number=ORACLE_CUSTOMER.cust_number and
       ORACLE_ORDER.order_number = ORACLE_ORDER_LINE.order_number
       and
       ORACLE_ORDER_LINE.prod_number = ORACLE_PRODUCT.prod_number
       and
       SYBASE_CUSTOMER.customer_name like 'Burleson'
```

The easiest way to access these tables is to use a tool that has already defined the access protocols for each database, such as the popular Uniface tool.

If you wish to access a remote database node from a PC platform, the steps are similar in that you would punch the relational table to a flat file, and transfer this file to the PC using FTP or some other file transfer utility.

The steps for populating a relational table on a PC platform are somewhat different from those for a midrange database. Most PC databases do not support CREATE TABLE SQL, and the table must be defined using the online GUI screens. In order to define the table to FoxPro, you will need to choose File>New from the menu, and manually define a PRODUCT table with identical column names and field sizes. Fortunately, population of a FoxPro table is very simple. In your PC text editor, insert a delimiter character after each field in the flat file. Be sure to choose a character that does not exist in the data, such as the circumflex (^) or at sign (@). The massaged file would look something like this:

```
Don Burleson^121 Public Parkway^Fairport^NY
Joe Chelko^123 4th St.^New York, NY
```

This flat file can now easily be imported into FoxPro. From the FoxPro command menu prompt, issue the following commands:

```
CLOSE DATA
USE PRODUCT
APPEND from c:\myfile.dat TYPE SDF DELIMITED with '^'
```

This will take the data from your flat file and move it into the FoxPro table. Incidentally, even though FoxPro does not support SQL INSERT statements, it is one of the easiest databases for data migration.

Also, because FoxPro's "Rushmore" technology is so fast, many sites have moved systems directly from mainframes into FoxPro. It has been reported that systems can be moved directly from mainframes onto FoxPro data servers with improved response time. Personally, I have migrated three systems from an IBM 3090 to FoxPro, and each of these systems performed faster than its counterpart on the mainframe.

5.5 NETWORKING ISSUES

The concept of open network architectures is important to the function of distributed databases.

The Open Systems Interconnect Model (OSI)

OSI is the brainchild of the International Standards Organization (ISO) and was developed as a communications protocol model to provide a structure for designing protocol families.

OSI provides services at all levels, from the presentation to the end-user down to the physical message layer:

Layers				Layers	Function
Application	7	←→	7	Application	Network/User Services, NFS, ftp, rlogin
Presentation	6	←→	6	Presentation	Data Representation, XDR
Session	5	←→	5	Session	Opens Communication Link, RPC
Transport	4	←→	4	Transport	Connects Processes, TCP
Network	3	←→	3	Network	System Addressing, IP
Data Link	2	←→	2	Data Link	Groups data into frames for transmission
Physical	1	←→	1	Physical	Network Hardware, 802.3, 802.5, FDDI

Figure 5.5   Sample Open Systems Interconnect model.

Application	Provides all services directly comprehensible to application programs
Presentation	Transforms data to and from standardized formats
Session	Synchronizes and manages dialogs
Transport	Provides transparent, reliable data transfer from end-node to end-node
Network	Performs message routing for data transfer between nodes
Data Link	Detects errors for messages moved between nodes
Physical	Electronically encodes and physically transfers messages between nodes

Protocol vs. Topology

Many misunderstand the relationship between a topology and a protocol. At the most basic level, a topology is the physical layer (e.g., T1 lines, Ethernet) and the protocol is the software that runs on top of the topology (e.g., TCP/IP, DECNet). Figures 5.6, 5.7, and 5.8 show three topologies. Note that any protocol can be run against any topology.

System Protocols

The protocol is the software layer that resides on top of the topology. In theory, any of the following protocols can run under any topology. The most popular topologies include:

DNA—DEC's Distributed Networking Architecture
   Announced in 1975 by DEC for use in VMS.

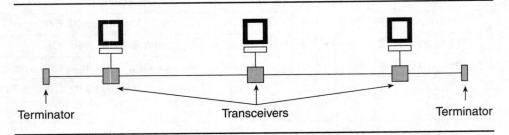

Terminator   Transceivers   Terminator

Figure 5.6   Ethernet—The dominant topology that was jointly developed by Xerox, Intel, and DEC.

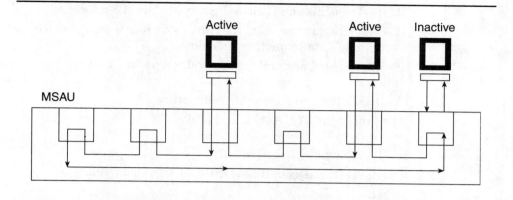

Figure 5.7   Token ring—A ring topology that uses a token-passing access method developed by IBM.

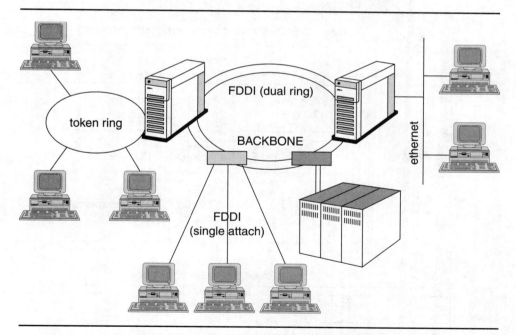

Figure 5.8   FDDI (fiber distributed data interface)—Basically a modification of the token ring topology. FDDI is a fiber optics implementation that utilizes dual, counterrotating rings that enable recovery in case of faults.

TCP/IP—Transmission Control Protocol/Internet Protocol

TCP—A standard protocol that allows a process on one machine to send a stream of data to another machine.

IP—A standard protocol that provides a packet delivery service across a network.

SNA—IBM's System Network Architecture

Announced in 1974. A standard protocol, the most commonly used protocol.

X.25—Developed by Bell Canada

The basis for ISDN and the OSI model for open systems.

Open Network Frameworks

Open network frameworks generally include several primary components, and are generally a large collection of many interacting components, for example:

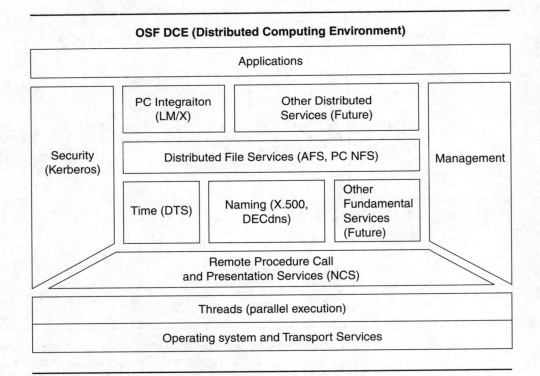

Figure 5.9   Sample open network framework.

- Transaction support services such as the X/open XTP model
- User interface support such as MIT's X11 protocol
- Security services such as Kerberos
- Messaging services such as X.400
- Naming services such as X.500

Examples of open network frameworks include:

DCE	Distributed Computing Environment
CORBA	The Common Request Broker Architecture by OMG
SAA	The System Application Architecture by IBM
OSI	The Open System Interconnection

The goal of open network frameworks is to provide a single system view for a widely disparate set of corporate, departmental, and local resources (Figure 5.9).

REFERENCES

Bacon, J. 1992. *Concurrent systems, an integration approach to operating systems, database and distributed systems.* Addison-Wesley.

Blaser, A., ed. 1990. *Database systems of the 90s.* Berlin: International Symposium.

Burleson, D. 1993. *Practical application of object-oriented techniques to relational databases.* Wiley\QED.

———. 1993. Distributed object technology. *First Class Magazine*, October.

———. 1994. Building your own SQL generator. *Database Programming & Design*, January.

———. 1994. Mapping object-oriented applications to relational databases. *Object Magazine*, January.

———. 1994. Managing distributed databases—An enterprise view. *Database Programming & Design*, June.

Chu, W., ed. 1986. *Distributed database systems.* Books on Demand.

Date, C. 1987. What is a distributed database? *InfoDB* 2:7.

Demers, R. et al. 1992. Inside IBM's distributed data management architecture. *IBM Systems Journal*, September.

Goulde, M. 1992. Open systems: analysis, issues and opinions. *Open Information Systems*, December.

Katzan, H. 1991. *Distributed information systems.* Petrocelli Books.

McFadden, F. 1994. *Modern database management*, 4th edition. Benjamin Cummings Publishing Company.

Ricciuti, M. 1992. Terabytes of data—how to get at them? *Datamation*, August.

Shinhyalov, I. and P. Bourne. 1992. The shape of database to come. *DEC Professional*, November.

Stein, J. 1992. Distributed databases: what they are, what are they good for? *Journal of Object-oriented Programming*, July–August.

Watt, P. and J. Celko. 1993. Hewlett-Packard's relational/object paradigm. *DBMS*, February.

Weitz, L. 1992. Desperately seeking database independence: options for accessing diverse corporate data. *Software Magazine*, December.

Enterprise Management of Distributed Databases

6.1 INTRODUCTION

In the 1970s, computer theorists touted the benefits of the "centralized data repository," and companies began the long and arduous task of moving all of their corporate data into one large and centralized database system. Centralized databases promised that all of the corporate information could be easily managed in a tightly controlled environment, and that all of the information could be shared with all of the end-users.

In the late 1980s, advances in midrange hardware and software made smaller hardware platforms attractive, and mainframe systems began to fall from favor as companies embraced the idea of downsizing, and started to shift their systems to the cheaper midrange computers. Newspapers and magazines were full of promises that these new midrange systems combined with client/server technology were making mainframe systems obsolete.

Downsizing concerns the distribution of processing, and not the distribution of data. Unfortunately, many companies confused the concept of distributed processing with distributed databases, and the downsizing efforts commonly resulted in the widespread fragmentation of the centralized data resource. Distributed database systems may now span many platforms, operating systems, communications protocols, and database architectures.

Historically, distributed database systems (DDSs) evolved from a need to distribute processing to improve database performance. Early distributed databases were implemented with each database having identical database software, and the data was tightly coupled with the application. In essence, these enterprise systems did nothing more than take advantage of the "multibrain" processors in the mainframe. A mainframe with a *dyadic* processor structure is able to support two databases, with a processor dedicated to each database. The more powerful mainframes with *quadratic* processors allowed all four individual processors to be logically partitioned to function as a single, dedicated processor. An example would be a DB2 system on a IBM 3090 with dyadic processors. The database would be logically partitioned such that one portion of the database would run on one of the 3090 CPUs while another partition would run on the other 3090 CPU. A distributed system results even though the databases are of identical configuration and are running on the same machine, and performance is enhanced because both of the CPUs within the 3090 are sharing the database workload.

Federated Databases

The federated approach to database management is very different from distributed database management. Whereas distributed databases are often carefully planned, federated databases often evolve as a result of external circumstances. As MIS shops began to inherit database systems from newly acquired companies, the federated approach was developed to cope with the challenge of creating a unified system from diverse architectures. Managing a federated database has been a reactive endeavor—trying to make the best of a bad situation. Unlike a true distributed database, a federated database is characterized by loosely coupled applications and diverse data models. Most distributed database systems use a combination of true distributed database and federated databases, and the term *distributed database* will be used to describe this hybrid.

The goals of distributed database are very noble: users anywhere in the organization can request information from their PCs without any regard for the storage method or the physical location of the data. A global schema maintains the integrity of all of the information and insures that all of the business rules are maintained within the distributed database network (Figure 6.1). With distributed database, the manager can take advantage of the benefits of different database architectures; data that is used for decision support can be kept in a relational database, while other data that requires high-speed access can be kept in a hierarchical database. A single, unified application can access all of the corporate information simultaneously, regardless of the target platform or the architecture of the database. The end-user has complete and instant access to all corporate data, and the system appears to be a unified federation. Because the distributed database architecture allows the manager to choose the best hardware platform for each of the data components, smaller midrange computers can replace the expensive mainframes. If this sounds almost too good to be true, read on.

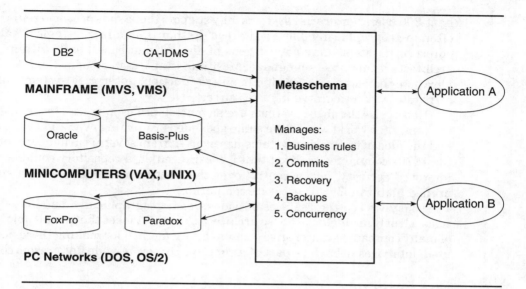

Figure 6.1   The federated database model.

Enterprise Databases

Enterprise computing differs from traditional data processing in several important ways (Figure 6.2). Instead of traditional "departmental" systems with per-

	Departmental systems	Enterprise systems
Database	Single architecture Small size (<20 GB) Central location	Multiple architecture Large size (> 500 GB) Geographically dispersed
Application	Freestanding application Dedication to functional area	Corporate-wide computing Entrie functional breadth
Network	Centralized processing Small numbers of users Centralized data	Distributed processing Large numbers of users Distributed data

Figure 6.2   Enterprise vs. departmental database systems.

haps 300 users, enterprise systems may support thousands of concurrent users, often in geographically dispersed areas. Rather than a large, single database, enterprise systems may have dozens of distinct databases, each with its own architecture and access language. Most important, instead of a standalone application dedicated to a specific business function, enterprise systems offer a corporate-wide integrated data resource.

Enterprise database systems are as much a philosophy as a technology. In the computer world we see the same good ideas returning over and over again, and the idea of enterprise systems has evolved from several earlier concepts. In the 1970s companies realized that a centralized data repository could provide improved security, better control over the distribution of data, and a single, unified platform for all corporate computing.

Today we see the realities of widespread, geographically distributed systems; clearly, a single database architecture cannot meet the overall objectives of many companies. Enterprise computing is a method for making these distributed databases behave as part of a cohesive corporate-wide data resource.

REFERENCES

Batelle, J. et al. 1992. Planning for 1995: the future is now. *Corporate Computing*, December.

Blaser, A., ed. 1990. *Database systems of the 90s*. Berlin: International Symposium.

Bobak, A. 1993. *Distributed and multidatabase systems*. Bantam Books.

Burleson, D. 1994. Mapping object-oriented applications to relational databases. *Object Magazine*, January.

———. 1994. Managing distributed databases—an enterprise view. *Database Programming & Design*, June.

Fiorio, T. 1992. Managing distributed applications. *DEC Professional*, December.

Hackathorn, R. 1993. *Enterprise database connectivity*. Wiley.

McFadden, F. 1994. *Modern database management*, 4th edition. Benjamin Cummings Publishing Company.

Mulqueen, J. 1993. Distributed database: a dream? *Communications Week*, March.

Shinhyalov, I. and P. Bourne. 1992. The shape of database to come. *DEC Professional*, November.

Object Technology and Distributed Databases

7.1   INTRODUCTION

The latest movement in the trendy database marketplace is to offer products that use object technology and also offer the popular SQL access language. On one side of this market we see the "pure" ODBMSs developing SQL interfaces to their object architectures, while the relational vendors are creating object layers for their table structures. While neither of these approaches is ideal from the perspective of the MIS manager, there has been great progress in both directions, and programmers who have mastered SQL will now need to understand the object-oriented dialects of SQL, including SQL++ by Objectivity Inc., Object SQL by Ontos, and SQL/X by UniSQL. Many proponents of the relational model state that the ad hoc query capability of SQL is inconsistent with the OO principle of encapsulation, but the sheer popularity of SQL has led to many attempts to reconcile it with object-oriented systems.

The object/relational hybrids promise to allow users to keep their existing relational technology while gaining object features. Unlike traditional relational databases, these hybrids allow cells within a table to contain multiple values or even another entire table. This nesting of tables within tables allows far more flexibility than in traditional database systems.

This chapter will explore how programmers must adapt their SQL programming to deal with objects. It will include comments from actual users of SQL++ and discuss how programmers can prepare for this new SQL paradigm.

7.2   A CLOSER LOOK: UNISQL

Courtesy of Dr. Won Kim, President and CEO, UniSQL Incorporated

Introduction

During the past three decades, file systems, navigational database systems (hierarchical and network systems), and relational database systems have been used as platforms for managing data for conventional transaction-oriented applications. The problems of developing applications that require access to heterogeneous data sources that are managed separately by different file systems and database systems have thus far been addressed in a few different ways.

One way has been to convert and transfer all data from one data management system to another. An installation can adopt this approach if it is sufficient to have data transferred from one system to another primarily to have the data read by the latter. An installation would also adopt this approach if it decides to replace its data management system (e.g., IMS or TOTAL) with a different data management system (e.g., DB2 or the UniSQL/DBMS). For example, the IMS EXTRACT facility is provided with IBM's relational database products, SQL/DS and DB2/MVS, to support conversion and transfer of data from an IMS database to a relational database. There are potentially serious problems with this approach. First, if the purpose of conversion and transfer of data from system A to system B is simply to make the data available for processing by B, reverse conversion and transfer of the part of the data that is updated by B can be necessary from B to A. Second, if system A is to be discarded after mass conversion and transfer of all data, there is still the issue of supporting the applications that have been written in A. The applications need to be converted to run in B, either manually or automatically; or an emulator of system A can be provided on top of system B to continue to run the applications. Supporting existing applications after a wholesale transfer of data and the data management system has proven to be a very difficult problem indeed.

Another solution that has been used, although not very successfully, is the so-called gateways for specific pairs of data management systems. For example, the INGRES line of database products includes gateways between the INGRES relational database system and the DEC RMS file system, and between INGRES relational database system and the DEC RMS file system, and between INGRES and PC-based dBase systems. There are gateways (called *CONNECT) between the ORACLE TM relational database system and IMS, between ORACLE and IMS, and between ORACLE and RMS. A gateway between system A and system B translates a query in A's language into an equivalent query in B's language, and submits the translated query to system B. The gateway solution has some serious limitations. First, the gateway approach does not support transaction management, even for a pair of systems. In other words, the gateway from system

A to system B is merely a switch-and-query translator; system A does not coordinate concurrency control and recovery of transactions that involve updates to both systems' databases. Second, the gateway approach is concerned only with the problem of translating a query expressed in one language into an equivalent expression in another language. As such, it does not address the issues of homogenizing the structural and representation differences between different schemas.

Today, the database research community has concluded that the most viable and general solution to the problems of interoperating heterogeneous data systems is the federated multidatabase system. Simply put, a multidatabase system (MDBS) is a database system that resides unobtrusively on top of existing database and file systems (called "local database systems") and presents a single database illusion to its users. In particular, an MDBS maintains a single "global" database schema against which its users will issue queries and updates; an MDBS maintains only the global schema, and the local database systems actually maintain all user data. The global schema is constructed by consolidating (integrating) the schemas of the local databases; the process of consolidating the local schemas in general requires neutralizing (homogenizing) the schematic differences (conflicts) among them. The MDBS translates the global queries and updates for dispatch to appropriate local database systems for actual processing, merges the results from them, and generates the final result for the user. Further, the MDBS coordinates the commit and abort of global transactions (queries and updates) by the local database systems that processed them to maintain consistency of data within the local databases. An MDBS actually controls multiple gateways (or drivers). It manages local databases through the gateways, one gateway for each local database.

The UniSQL/M MDBS is a multidatabase system for UniSQL, Inc. that integrates multiple UniSQL/M MDBS databases and multiple relational databases, as shown in Figure 7.1. The UniSQL/M MDBS currently offers drivers for ORACLE, SYBASE TM, and INGRES; UniSQL also offers a driver-generator product for generating a driver for any SQL-based relational database system. The following summarizes the objectives, database schema, architecture, and benefits of the UniSQL/M MDBS for application development.

UniSQL/M MDBS Objectives

The UniSQL/M/MDBS satisfies the following broad requirements for uniformly managing heterogeneous databases:

> Objective One: The UniSQL/M/MDBS obviates the need for a batch conversion and transfer of data from one source (e.g., an ORACLE database) to another (e.g., a UniSQL/X database).

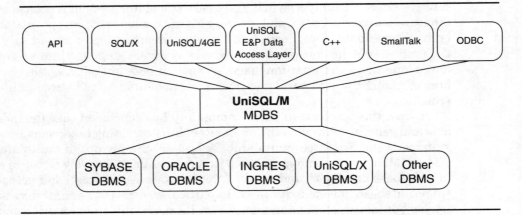

Figure 7.1   UniSQL/M multidatabase system.

Objective Two: The UniSQL/M MDBS requires absolutely no changes to the local database system (LDBS) software; this preserves what is known as "design autonomy." In other words, the UniSQL/M MDBS appears to any of the LDBSs as just another application or user.

Objective Three: The UniSQL/M MDBS does not prevent any of the LDBSs from being used in its native mode. In other words, users of an LDBS can continue to work with the system for transactions requiring access to only data managed by the system, while users will use the UniSQL/M MDBS to issue transactions that require access to more than one data source. In this way, applications written in any of the LDBSs are preserved, and new applications that require access to more than one data source can be developed using the UniSQL/M MDBS.

Objective Four: The UniSQL/M MDBS makes it possible for users and applications to program in one database language, namely SQL/M. In other words, the users and applications should not have to work with the different interface languages of the LDBSs.

Objective Five: The UniSQL/M MDBS shields the users and applications from the heterogeneity of the operating environments of the LDBSs, including the computer, operating system, and network protocol.

Objective Six: The UniSQL/M MDBS, unlike most previous attempts at allowing the interoperability of heterogeneous database systems, supports distributed transactions involving both reads and updates against different databases.

Objective Seven: The UniSQL/M MDBS is a full-blown database system, that is, it makes available to users all the facilities provided by standard database systems, including schema definition, nonprocedural queries, automatic query optimization updates, transaction management, concurrency control and recovery, integrity control, access authorization, both interactive and host-language application support, graphics application, development tools, and so forth.

Objective Eight: The UniSQL/M MDBS introduces virtually no changes to the operation and administration of any LDBSs.

Objective Nine: The UniSQL/M MDBS provides run-time performance that approaches that of a homogeneous distributed database system. This means that the UniSQL/M MDBS screens the heterogeneity of the LDBSs with minimal overhead.

Objective Ten: The UniSQL/M MDBS supports a data model that is rich enough to support object-oriented database design and application development, and that subsumes conventional data models (i.e., relational and hierarchical models).

Before the UniSQL/M MDBS can be used, a UniSQL/M global schema must be defined. Figure 7.2 illustrates how a UniSQL/M global schema is constructed from local schemas. The local schema is the schema of a local database. The export schema is the portion of the local schema that the administrator of a local database makes available (i.e., authorizes) for access by UniSQL/M MDBS users. The common schema is the export schema that is translated to an equivalent UniSQL/M schema. The integrated schema is the schema that is created by the UniSQL/M database administrator by combining all common schemas and resolving schematic differences among them. The external schema is a set of views that UniSQL/M users and the UniSQL/M database administrator get by combining all common schemas and resolving schematic differences among them. The external schema is a set of views that UniSQL/M users and the UniSQL/M database administrator can define on the integrated schema. The UniSQL/M global schema consists of the integrated schema and the external schema.

Figure 7.3 illustrates three exported local database (LDB) schemas; LDB1 and LDB2 are relational databases, and LDB3 is an object-oriented database. Note the schematic differences among the local schemas. The Faculty table in LDB1 has an attribute called Name, while the Faculty table in LDB2 has two attributes, LastName and FirstName. The Employee class in LDB3 has an attribute Supervisor, which is missing in the Employee tables in LDB1 and LDB2. Further, in LDB3, the class Faculty is defined as a subclass of Employee.

Figure 7.4 shows one possible integrated schema that can be created from

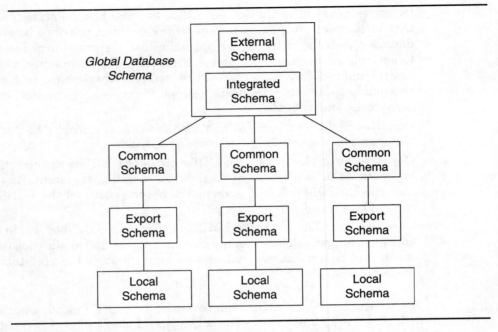

Figure 7.2   Constructing a global database schema.

these local schemas. The classes Employee and Faculty from LDB3 have been renamed to Employee-3 and Faculty-3, respectively. Employee-1-2 is the union of Employee from LDB1 and LDB2. Further, Faculty-1-2 is derived from the LastName and FirstName attributes in Faculty from LDB2. In other words, using the SQL/M schema definition facilities, the schematic differences between Faculty in LDB1 and LDB2 have been neutralized. UniSQL/M users can now issue SQL/M queries against the integrated schema.

The data model (and database language) of the UniSQL/M MDBS is an object-oriented data model that is a natural outgrowth of the popular relation data model (and ANSI SQL relational database language). This makes it possible for a UniSQL/M global schema to represent a consolidation of a heterogeneous mix or relational local schemas, but also a combination of relation and object-oriented local schemas. In the above example, the integrated schema contains an inheritance hierarchy consisting of the Employee-3 and Faculty-3 "virtual" classes defined over the Employee and Faculty classes in the object-oriented LDB3.

A UniSQL/M global schema can contain not only an inheritance hierarchy,

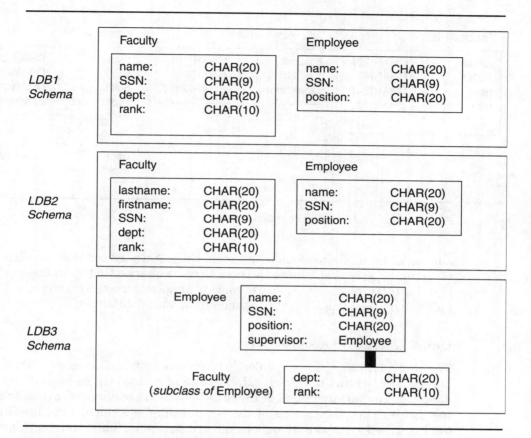

Figure 7.3   Example local database schemas.

but also methods and composition of relations (and classes). For example, a method named "Retirement Benefits" can be written and attached to Faculty-1-2 in the global schema as shown in Figure 7.4. Remember that Faculty-1-2 is a virtual class defined over relations Faculty in LDB1 and LDB2; but methods can be defined on it, and methods can be run against tuples retrieved from the local databases. The UniSQL/M MDBS makes this possible by automatically generating object identifiers (OIDS) for the tuples of the local databases that are retrieved for the corresponding virtual classes defined in the global database.

The object-oriented global scheme also allows the schema designer to construct a nested composition structure with the virtual classes defined against relations in local relational databases by having one virtual class appear as the

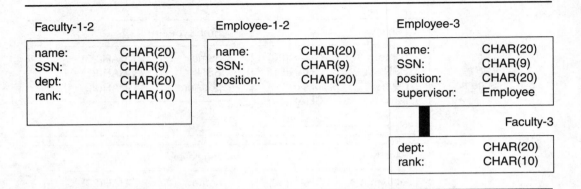

Figure 7.4   Example integrated schema.

domain of an attribute of another virtual class. A nested composition structure of virtual classes then allows the user to issue queries that span the compositional structure (known as "path queries") and to access, by navigation, each individual object (tuple) that is fetched from a local database.

UniSQL/M MDBS Architecture

The UniSQL/M MDBS is a full-fledged database system. It provides data definition facilities so that the global database can be defined on the basis of the local database. The data definition facilities include means to harmonize (homogenize) the different representations of the semantically equivalent data in different local databases, as well as query and update the virtual database (requiring query optimization and query processing mechanisms). Multiple UniSQL/M users can simultaneously query, update, and even populate the "virtual" database (requiring concurrency control mechanisms); the users can submit a collection of queries and updates as a single transaction against the virtual database (requiring transaction management mechanisms); the users can also grant and revoke authorizations on parts of the database to other users (requiring authorization mechanisms).

The architecture of the UniSQL/M MDBS, shown in Figure 7.5, has a single UniSQL/M site driving multiple local database sites. The UniSQL/M MDBS is itself a client/server architecture; multiple UniSQL/M clients interact with a single UniSQL/M server. UniSQL/M MDBS users can develop applications that access multiple local databases using a number of application development and database access tools that come with the UniSQL/M MDBS. Figure 7.5 shows an Interactive SQL/M processor—embedded SQL/M preprocessor for C, API

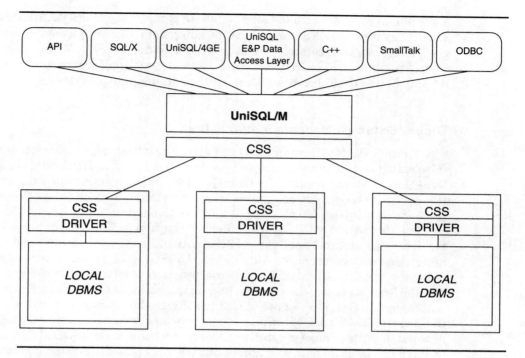

Figure 7.5   UniSQL/M client/server architecture.

(UniSQL's call level interface), C++ programmers, Smalltalk interface for Smalltalk programmers, Microsoft Open Database Connectivity (ODBC) interface for PC-based applications, and UniSQL/4GE graphical database tools. The UniSQL/4GE tools include VisualEditor for designing, browsing, and editing the schema and database contents; MediaMaster for designing report templates and generating reports using objects fetched from the database via SQL/M queries; and ObjectMaster for generating GUI front ends for database applications. The E&P Data Access layer interface is the database access language proposed by Petrotechnical Open Software Corporation, a consortium of major oil and gas companies formed to promote a standard for data access and exchange among next-generation database management systems to be used by oil and gas companies.

The UniSQL/M MDBS manages all global database control information, including the global schema, and submits and manages transactions that invoke one or more local database systems. There is one driver for each local database system communicating with the UniSQL/M MDBS. The driver resides on the same site (computer) with the local database system. The UniSQL/M MDBS and the drivers interact via a communication subsystem (CSS) implemented on top of the TCP/IP socket protocol. The architecture of the UniSQL/M MDBS is completely nonintrusive to local database systems, and applications and users can directly access their databases through their local database systems.

Global Database Schema Management

The UniSQL/M MDBS maintains the global database as a collection of views (also called *virtual classes*) defined over relations in local RDBs and classes in local UniSQL/X databases. The UniSQL/M MDBS also maintains a directory of the local database relations and classes, their attributes and data types, and methods that have been integrated into the global database.

The UniSQL/M MDBS global schema definition facilities allow mechanisms for neutralizing a full spectrum of schematic differences that can exist among heterogeneous local schemas. Although the UniSQL/4GE VisualEditor tool makes is easy for the UniSQL/M MDBS schema designers to visualize the global schema and the local schemas, the creation and maintenance of the global schema is not automated. In fact, it is not possible for a software tool to automatically generate the integrated schema, given the export schemas of local databases. The database administrator must create the integrated schema for UniSQL/M users. Similarly, the UniSQL/M database administrator must periodically update the global schema to reflect changes in export schemas. In general, it is impossible to automatically translate changes in export schemas to equivalent changes in the integrated schema.

Distributed Query Processing

Although the UniSQL/M MDBS maintains the global schema, the data of interest to the UniSQL/M MDBS users are all stored in local databases. In other words, the objects associated with the virtual classes defined in the UniSQL/M global schema reside in local databases; these objects materialize in the UniSQL/M MDBS when queries are run against the virtual classes.

Using the information in the global directory it maintains, the UniSQL/M MDBS translates the queries and updates to equivalent queries for processing by the local database systems that manage the data that the queries and updates need to access. The goal of UniSQL/M's query translation is to "put as much processing as possible" in the local database systems. This means that as much of the WHERE clause of a UniSQL/M query as possible is included in the query being dispatched to each local database system. In this way, the UniSQL/

M MDBS maximizes the selectivity of each query that is dispatched to a local database system; in other words, the UniSQL/M MDBS minimizes the size of the query result that is returned from each local database system.

The local database drivers pass the translated queries and updates to the local database systems, and pass the results to the UniSQL/M MDBS for format translation, merging, and any necessary postprocessing (e.g., for processing the ORDER BY or GROUP BY clauses in an SQL query, and also performing interdatabase joins).

Distributed Transaction Management

The UniSQL/M MDBS supports "distributed transaction management" over local databases, which means that all updates issued within one UniSQL/M transaction, even when they result in updates to multiple local databases, are simultaneously committed or aborted.

The UniSQL/M MDBS transaction management preserves the traditional atomicity and serializability properties of transactions. This means not only that the UniSQL/M MDBS users are able to issue queries and updates against LDBs but also that they will be able to group such queries and updates into transactions. The UniSQL/M MDBSs process multiple concurrent global transactions by interleaving them to maximize transactions throughput and to protect each transaction from interferences from other transactions. Further, the UniSQL/M MDBS guarantees that the effects of aborted global transactions are completely erased from the LDBs and the effects of committed global transactions are indeed committed in all LDBs involved.

The UniSQL/M MDBS transaction manager implements a pessimistic transaction scheduler that preserves the serializability criterion that is used in conventional centralized and homogeneous distributed database systems. In addition, it resolves global deadlocks (i.e., deadlocks among global transactions). Further, the transaction manager implements the distributed two-phase commit protocol over the LDBSs to preserve the atomicity property of transactions. An important assumption made is that each LDBS involved in processing global transactions that contain updates supports two-phase commit protocols or two-phase locking.

UniSQL/M MDBS Benefits

The UniSQL/M MDBS in the first full-fledged commercial multidatabase system and the first to use a full object-oriented data model (and database language) as the common global data model (and database language). It is also the first to support:

- Simultaneous updates to multiple local databases.
- Distributed transactions management over multiple local database systems.
- Neutralizing a full range of schematic differences among local schemas.

These technological accomplishments translate to the following benefits for the application developers:

One: The UniSQL/M MDBS offers a single database language. Application developers need not learn and use multiple local database interface languages to develop applications that need to access multiple local databases.

Two: The single database language supported is an object-oriented language that is a compatible extension to the ANSI SQL relation database language. Application developers can immediately become productive.

Three: The UniSQL/M MDBS is a full-fledged database system, quietly supporting queries, updates, authorization, and transaction management over the global database. Application developers need not implement these functions in their application—they need only make use of the facilities provided in the UniSQL/M MDBS. In particular, the distributed transaction management facilities supported in the UniSQL/M MDBS automate the maintenance of consistency across multiple local databases, in the presence of multiple simultaneous UniSQL/M users and even crashes of the UniSQL/M MDBS and/or local database systems.

Four: The UniSQL/M MDBS comes with a full range of application development tools and database access tools (shown in Figure 7.5), making application developers more productive.

Five: The UniSQL/M MDBS minimizes performance overhead due to distributed query processing by minimizing the size of the result of a query processed in each local database system. The UniSQL/M MDBS achieves this by maximizing the selectivity of a query to be processed in each local database system, that is, by pushing as much as possible of the WHERE clause of a UniSQL/M query to the query that is dispatched to each local database system.

Six: UniSQL's object-oriented data mode (and database language) is a natural outgrowth (extension) of the popular relational model and language. Application developers can take advantage of the object-oriented facilities of the UniSQL/M MDBS to be even more productive. The UniSQL/M MDBS in effect extends local relational databases with object-oriented data modeling and data management facilities; that is, the UniSQL/M MDBS converts the tuples retrieved from relation local databases into objects by augmenting them with OIDs and allowing the users to run methods on them. The

UniSQL/M MDBS also allows the construction of a nested composition structure among relations in local relation databases, making data modeling more natural and providing a basis for improved performance in navigating through tuples of the relation.

Platforms and Driver of External Databases

The UniSQL/M Multidatabase System runs on SUN SPARC and SPARC-compatible workstations under Solaris; UP/Apollo 9000/700 and 800 series workstations under HP-UX; and IBM RS/6000 workstations under AIX. The UniSQL/M Multidatabase System client is available on personal computers running Windows/NT.

The UniSQL/M Multidatabase System currently offers drivers for ORACLE, SYBASE, and INGRES; UniSQL also offers a driver-generator product for generating a driver for any SQL-based relational database system, the UniSQL Driver Development Kit.

7.3   ENTERPRISE AND FEDERATED DATABASES

The terms *enterprise* and *federation* have become very popular within the computer industry and have led some industry observers to conclude that the trendsetters in database technology are aging "Trekkies." Star Trek puns aside, these terms are bantered about with very little regard for their real meanings. The main difference between a federated database and an enterprise database is the ex post facto nature of the federated database. Unlike a true distributed database, a federation attempts to build bridges between existing systems. Consequently, the parts of a federated database tend to be loosely coupled, and the subdatabases continue to maintain their own unique identities. Some consider this loose coupling to be a disadvantage, but the flexibility thus gained can be more practical for systems that change their configurations frequently.

Enterprise	Federation
Planned from inception	Bridges built as an afterthought
Data is uniform	Data is from many database architectures
A single DBMS product	Many DBMSs from many vendors

In a perfect world, it would be very nice to have a system that was well planned and that incorporated a thoroughly designed network of homogeneous databases. The realities of the 1990s show that loose-coupled federations are far more common than are distributed database designs. Federations do have advantages; because the data in a federation may reside in many different database architectures, the designers have the luxury of using the most appropriate database engines for the type of information that they want to store. For example, text information can be stored in Lotus notes, ad hoc marketing databases in Oracle, and online transaction information in Objectivity/DB.

It is also important to recognize that companies are drifting away from the traditional concept of "fielded" data. Today information may take many forms, from bitmaps of photographs to handwritten notes to audio clips, and database architectures are being designed to handle these new data formats.

For example, FoxPro allows for a GENERAL data type in which a bitmap (.BMP) or an audio image (.WAV) may be stored in a table and displayed in the same manner as a traditional field. The widespread use of e-mail has led many companies to treat this information as a data resource. Within the next two years it will be possible to query against an unstructured database full of memos, photographs, and audio material. Several vendors, most notably ConQuest and SandPoint, are creating "concept-based query" engines that access this information. SandPoint markets an information vacuum "Hoover" (pun intended) that allows information to be disseminated and routed to people who need the information (Figure 7.6). With hundreds of terabytes of data on the Internet, new data retrieval methods are emerging to allow users to target the specific data that is of

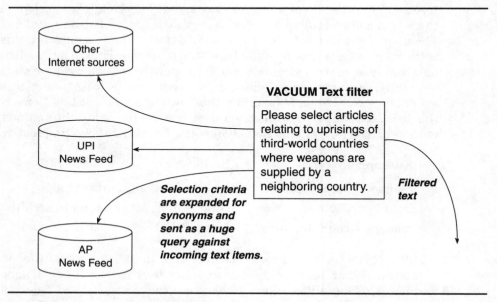

Figure 7.6   The information Hoover vacuum.

interest to them. Gophers can be programmers to visit nodes searching for information, and "bots" can be used to filter through text, searching for on-point material.

There are many ways that companies are exploiting the idea of nonfielded, unstructured databases. Many companies are using word-indexing systems such as ConQuest and Fulcrum to add value to their massive repositories of memos, and these "concept-based" query engines are beginning to replace SQL as a means of extracting information.

Offerings such as SandPoint's Hoover now allow end-users to specify selection criteria for retrieving information, and incoming text streams such as Dow Jones and UPI news feeds are used as giant queries against the query filter. These types of routing/query systems have demonstrated a high degree of precision and recall for routing relevant information to individuals with very specific data requirements.

7.4   OBJECT TECHNOLOGY SOLUTIONS

In an object-oriented scheme, "distributed object messaging" can be used, whereby new applications can be constructed from a menu of pretested objects. Object technology also promises to allow hardware-independent distributed processing. A Sun workstation can be used to solve one component of a complex problem while an HP-9000 simultaneously works on another component of the problem. The object technology principle of "late binding" allows these code snippets to be combined and executed without having to compile or link a program on a specific hardware platform. For example, an application programmer can assemble a system from objects on Sparc workstations, DEC VAXs, and HP UNIX platforms. Because these objects are precompiled and tested on their specific hardware platforms, the new application can dynamically access these objects via distributed messaging, and a seamless application can be created from these distributed components. In other words, with a distributed object approach you do not need to worry about the format of the data or the physical location of the process. Programs (through object "methods") can now be distributed just as data is distributed.

The problem with this approach is that the programming staff will need to become proficient in object technology concepts and object-oriented programming languages such as Smalltalk or C++. The distributed object approach also requires an object request broker or ORB. The ORB is the central component of the CORBA standard, and is used to manage the interfaces to the different hardware platforms and handle the differences in the network protocols. Tools such as IBM's DSOM have shown that distributed object systems can be made to function very elegantly, but that there may be a very significant start-up cost in training the programming staff and building the ORB. Today, CORBA skills are in very high demand, but it will be several years before CORBA talent will be readily available in the marketplace.

The CORBA Architecture

Many organizations are recognizing the importance of standards in the emerging area of object-oriented systems development. In the spring of 1992 the Object Management Group (OMG), a nonprofit corporation dedicated to developing object standards, published the CORBA standard for object-oriented development. CORBA, the Common Object Request Broker Architecture, was developed jointly by Sun, Hewlett-Packard, Digital Equipment Corp., NCR, and Hyperdesk Corporation. CORBA creates a standard protocol for an object to place requests and to receive responses from other objects. These competing vendors, who have a vested interest in proprietary software, have agreed to adhere to the CORBA standard in the development of new object-oriented systems. Selections from the CORBA text are reproduced in Chapter 9 of this book.

Chris Stone, the president and CEO of the Object Management Group, states, "The OMG's goal is to get everybody to agree on a messaging format and how objects talk to each other; get them to agree to the language and a model of how to structure the data; get them to agree to some common interfaces; get them to agree on how to do security and containment. . . . The real significance of the CORBA specification is for application developers who want to build new client/server applications that will work across disparate platforms."

The object request broker (ORB) is the main component of CORBA and provides the mechanisms by which objects transparently make and receive requests and responses. In so doing, the ORB provides interoperability between applications on different machines in heterogeneous distributed environments and seamlessly interconnects multiple object systems.

The OMG object model defines an object request and its associated result (response) as the fundamental interaction mechanism. A request names an operation and includes zero or more parameter values, any of which may be object names identifying specific objects. The ORB arranges for the request to be processed. This entails identifying and causing some method to be invoked that performs the operation using the parameters. After the operation terminates, the ORB conveys the results to the requester.

The ORB itself might not maintain all of the information needed to carry out its functions. In the process of conveying a request, the ORB may generate requests of its own to object services, or otherwise use them. For example, in order to find the specific method to be executed for a given request, the ORB might use a class dictionary service or might search run-time method libraries.

The CORBA architecture has been adhered to by IBM in its Distributed

Systems Object Model (DSOM), by Sunsoft in Distributed Objects Everywhere (DOE), and by Hewlett-Packard in its Distributed Object Management Facility (DOMF) product. Notably missing is Microsoft. Microsoft has recognized the CORBA standard and has stated that its new operating system, Cairo, will "closely" follow the CORBA standard.

7.5   THE DISTRIBUTED DATA ISSUE

The same arguments for and against distributed processing can apply to the distribution of data. The centralized database advocates argue that the only reasonable approach is to have all of the data in a large, centralized data repository on the server, while opponents claim that distributing the data across many processors and platforms is the most beneficial approach.

The centralized data advocates tout the mature and time-tested control mechanisms that are built into the centralized databases. Data access and security can be controlled, and the systems managers can be assured that all of the information is being distributed according to their predefined rules. Physical control of the data is also an issue. In a centralized environment, the data can be backed up and restored as a single unit, and there is never a synchronization problem when a distributed portion of the data is lost or corrupted.

There is also the serious issue of confidential information. When information resides in a remote node, there is far more possibility that it can be accessed or copied. If a system allows information to be transferred to a PC for processing, there is absolutely no assurance that the information will not be copied onto a diskette.

On the other hand, the distributed data advocates argue that the end-users want complete control over their data, and that they do not want their data to be centrally managed. In a distributed data environment, the data resides in nodes that physically reside at the end-users' working location.

It may never become clear which approach is the most beneficial for large companies, but it is clear that the complexion of databases is changing rapidly and that databases are far more than the centralized "pack-farms" that characterized the mainframe databases of the 1980s.

7.6   SUMMARY

While the future of DDS looks very promising, most managers are still faced with today's reality of coupling widely distributed database systems. Even more challenging are the problems of large corporations within which newly acquired companies are constantly changing the configuration of the distribution problem. There seems to be a common thread among companies that are successful in their commitment to distributed databases. Successful MIS departments have the commitment of their top management and invest up to 15 percent of their companies' gross revenue on information management. These companies are also very proactive, and the MIS departments are always planning for the unseen possibilities of new problems. It is only with this high level of support that MIS managers can hope to fulfill the promise of complete and seamless information sharing.

REFERENCES

Abiteoul, S., P. Kanellkis, and E. Waller. 1990. *Method schemas*. Communications of the ACM.

Ahad, R. and D. Dedo. 1992. OpenODB from Hewlett-Packard: a commercial object-oriented database system. *Journal of Object-Oriented Programming* 4:9 (February).

Ahmed, S., A. Wong, D. Sriram, and R. Logcher. 1990. *A comparison of object-oriented database management systems for engineering applications*. MIT Technical Report IESL-90-03.

Atkinson, et al. 1990. *The object-oriented database systems manifesto*. Deductive and object-oriented databases. Elsevier Science Publishers.

Bloor, R. 1993. The patterns of change: Are you ready for the third major computer technology wave? *DBMS Magazine* 6:1 (January).

Brathwaite, K. 1993. *Object-oriented database design: concepts and applications*. Academic.

Brown, A. W. 1991. *Object-oriented databases and their applications to software engineering*. McGraw-Hill.

Burleson, D. 1993. *Practical application of object-oriented techniques to relational databases*. Wiley\QED.

———. 1994. Managing distributed databases—an enterprise view. *Database Programming & Design*, June.

———. 1993. SQL generators. *Database Programming & Design*, July.

———. 1993. Distributed object technology. *First Class Magazine*, October.

———. 1994. An update on object-oriented databases. *Software Magazine*, November.

Burleson, D., S. Kassicieh, and R. Lievano. 1986. Design and implementation of a decision support system for academic scheduling. *Information and Management* 2:2 (September).

Cattell, R. G. G. 1991. *Object data management: object-oriented and extended relational database systems*. Addison-Wesley.

Cattell, R. G. G. and T. Rogers. 1986. *Combining object-oriented and relational models of data.* Proceedings of the International Workshop on Object-Oriented Database Systems. IEEE Computer Society Press.

Chung, Y. and G. Fischer. 1992. Illustration of object-oriented databases for the structure of a bill of materials. *Computers in Industry* 19 (June).

Codd, E. F. 1990. *The relational model for database management*, version 2. Addison-Wesley.

Comaford, C. 1993. At long last, a true query tool for end users. *PC Week*, March.

Date, C. J. 1990. *An introduction to database systems.* Addison-Wesley.

De Troyer, O., J. Keustermans, and R. Meersman. 1986. *How helpful is object-oriented language for an object-oriented database model?* Proceedings of the International Workshop on Object-Oriented Database Systems. IEEE Computer Society Press.

Dittrich, Dayal, Buchmann. 1991. *On object-oriented database systems.* Springer Verlag.

Dittrich, K. 1986. *Object-oriented database systems: the notions and the issues.* Proceedings of the International Workshop on Object-Oriented Database Systems. IEEE Computer Society Press.

Gidman, J. 1994. Practical applications of distributed object technology. *Object Magazine*, March–April.

Gorman, K. and J. Choobineh. *An overview of the object-oriented entity relationship model (OOERM).* Proceedings of the Twenty-Third Annual Hawaii International Conference on Information Systems, vol. 3, 336–345.

Kim, W. 1988. *Issues of object-oriented database schemas.* Doctoral thesis, University of Texas at Austin.

———. 1990. *Introduction to object-oriented databases.* MIT Press.

———. 1990. *Research directions in object-oriented database systems.* Communications of the ACM.

———. 1993. *Object-oriented database systems: promises, reality, and future.* Proceedings of the Very Large Database Conference, Dublin, Ireland.

Loomis, M. 1991. Integrating objects with relational technology. *Object Magazine*, July/August.

———. 1991. Object and relational technology—can they cooperate? *Object Magazine*, July/August.

Loomis, M., T. Atwood, R. Cattel, J. Duhi, G. Ferran, and D. Wade. 1993. The ODMG object model. *Journal of Object-Oriented Programming*, June.

Lyngbaek, P. and W. Kent. 1986. *A data modeling methodology for the design and implementation of information systems.* Proceedings of the International Workshop on Object-Oriented Database Systems. IEEE Computer Society Press.

Martin, J. and J. Odell. 1992. *Object-oriented analysis and design.* Prentice-Hall.

McFadden, F. 1991. Conceptual design of object-oriented databases. *Journal of Object-Oriented Programming* 4 (September).

Meyer. 1988. *Object-oriented software construction*. Prentice-Hall.

Roy, M. and A. Ewald. 1994. Locating and managing ORB objects. *Object Magazine*, March–April.

Ruben, K. and A. Goldberg. 1992. *Object behavior analysis*. Communications of the ACM, September.

8

Distributed Object Technology and Distributed Databases

8.1 INTRODUCTION

There has been an increasing need within the computer industry to effectively manage distributed computing systems. Thousands of companies, from small engineering firms to multibillion-dollar conglomerates, now have their mission-critical information on more than one computer. Distributed computing is inherently complex, and methods must be devised to control the interfacing between the hardware platforms. Distributed object-oriented systems offer a solution. Independent "objects," or representations of physical constructs, can be created to manage all of the complexities of client/server and distributed processing, allowing the user to freely connect and exchange information across widely diverse hardware and software systems.

The general trend of the 1990s has been to move away from the cumbersome mainframe computers into a distributed network of smaller processors, often with client/server technology. The term *client/server* is used to describe the interaction between the data repositories and the applications. The data may be a centralized database on an IBM mainframe, a distributed database on a set of minicomputers, a PC network, or any combination of platforms. The server resides on the same platform as the data, and interacts, via a network, to retrieve and update data. The distributed nature of these systems has a tremendous impact on the future of object technology. In order for an object-oriented application to function in a distributed environment, a standardized set of interfaces must be established. These interfaces will insure that all requests for objects adhere to a standard protocol.

8.2   HISTORICAL BACKGROUND

In the early 1960s, corporations began to change their attitudes about information. Prior to this time, corporate information was considered a burden, a thing to be managed and controlled. However, the widespread availability of commercial databases caused corporations to rethink their attitude about information. Corporations began to consider their information to be an asset, an asset that could be exploited to make better and faster decisions. As most companies adopted database systems, reaction time to changes in the marketplace dropped significantly, and companies had to be able to consult their databases quickly to stay ahead of their competition. By the 1970s, corporate databases were firmly entrenched, and companies struggled to collect and disseminate their information (Figure 8.1).

One of the main goals of database management systems was the concept of the central repository to store all of the corporation's information and allow information to be accessed and distributed to all areas of the corporation. Many companies underwent expensive conversion efforts, and established mega-databases that contained many gigabytes of corporate information. The centralized repository promised to allow complete control and sharing of information for all areas within the organization.

As the idea of the corporate repository matured, companies discovered that many of the promises of database technology were not being fulfilled. Even

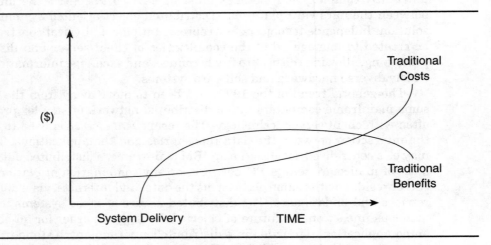

Figure 8.1   Traditional systems—Systems eventually become too cumbersome to maintain.

though the data was stored in a central repository, the managers complained that some information was not being provided to them, or the information was not in a form that the managers could use. Many areas within the company also felt that they were hostages to their information systems department. In order to make changes to their systems, they were forced to work with a team of programmers who they felt were unresponsive to their needs. Often simple changes could take many months and cost thousands of dollars.

The promise of perpetual systems also proved to be a fallacy. As a result of ongoing maintenance, systems that were designed to have a useful life of several decades and that were delivered with complete documentation and well-structured code became unmanageable conglomerations of "spaghetti" that were very hard to maintain. An excellent example was the Social Security system. When its programs were first delivered, they were well structured and completely documented, and processed hundreds of thousands of social security checks each month. This very same system received Senator Proxmire's "Golden Fleece" award several years later, when it was paying Social Security benefits to many people who were not entitled to them. The system, once pristine and well structured, now had become so unmanageable that even the programming staff had trouble describing the functions of each program. The system had to be scrapped and redesigned.

Even with centralized databases, users were still faced with the problem of diverse data platforms. Many companies embarked on downsizing or "rightsizing" to take advantage of the cheaper processing of minicomputers and PC platforms. In the process, many users abandoned the idea of a central repository of data and attempted to build bridges between the applications. Unfortunately, these bridges were often quite complex and difficult to manage. For example, establishing communications between a PC relational database and a CODASYL mainframe database is very cumbersome.

Companies found that frequent reorganization and corporate acquisitions led to many diverse platforms for their information. Most large companies have many different database management systems, and perhaps dozens of hardware platforms. These market conditions have led many information systems administrators to develop systems in a reactive mode, focusing on the immediate need for these systems to communicate, rather than on a common, centralized access method.

In the 1980s, IBM introduced the concept of enterprise modeling, whereby the entire organization's information was modeled, and the overall system was composed of a large client/server environment. This model was based on the idea that data should become independent of its source and that information can be accessed regardless of the type of database manager and hardware platform.

Today, many companies adopt the posture that their systems should exploit the "right" database systems, and it is acceptable to have many different database systems on many different platforms. A marketing system, for example, is ideal for a relational database, while a CAD system is well suited for an object-oriented database.

Friendly application interfaces also have helped to foster downsizing. As end-users are exposed to windowing systems on PC networks, they begin to view the block-mode systems on the mainframe as unacceptable, and to be more demanding on the information system staff to produce systems that are friendlier and more intuitive.

8.3   THE DATA DUALITY

The evolution of database systems has led to two major dualities. (A duality is defined as two concepts that can be thought of as separate, but can also be conceptualized as a single entity.) The first duality was between data and data relationships. Prior to the availability of the first commercial databases, data was stored in VSAM-type files without any direct way to store relationships between the data entities. Even though an entity may have strong relationships with other entities (e.g., each customer places many orders; an order may be for many items, and an item may participate in many orders), there was no direct way to incorporate these relationships into the data.

With the introduction of the IMS database, computer shops began to realize that the data relationships *were* data in the sense that they add value to the data. IMS allowed these relationships to be embedded within each record, and the data and data relationships became a single entity.

The second duality is being addressed with object technology. Prior to object technology systems, data and the behaviors of the data was separated. Traditional systems had a centralized database to store the data and the data relationships, but the programs that manipulated the data were external to the database residing in program load libraries. Object technology insures that the data, the data relationships, and the behavior of the data all be considered a single entity. The feature has a tremendous impact on the development of systems. Reports indicate that most computer shops spend more than 50 percent of their effort maintaining existing programs, and the tight coupling of data with behavior allows object systems to dramatically reduce maintenance costs and time. The code snippets that comprise the behaviors are easy to locate, and the ability to encapsulate behaviors allows these systems to be very quickly modified, without concern for unintended side effects.

8.4   THE PROBLEM OF STANDARDS

Creating distributed systems that communicate effectively has always been one of the foremost problems of distributed data processing. Vendors have an incentive to provide software that is proprietary, that is, software that adheres to a unique protocol that another vendor does not share.

Recall that there are two types of standards. "De jure" standards are established by a standards committee such as ANSI, while "de facto" standards evolve from usage—in this case, by vendor organizations. As an example of a de facto standard, the Object Database Modeling Group (ODMG), a consortium of object database vendors, has adopted a common protocol for object database products. Similarly, the Object Management Group (OMG) is a consortium of vendors that are working to provide a common interface for distributed object systems. Their standard, the Common Object Request Broker Architecture (CORBA), has been adopted as an industry protocol by many but not all of the vendors.

8.5 DISTRIBUTED OBJECT-ORIENTED TECHNOLOGY

There are many problems with client/server and distributed database systems that have influenced many corporations to postpone entry into this technology. The foremost reason for not using client/server technology is a fear of the complexity of the interfaces between the systems. "This [object-oriented] technology will provide an evolutionary approach to the development of this much-needed solution," says Chris Stone, president of the Object Management Group. Corporations that have invested millions of dollars in their information systems tend to be very conservative, and while many have acknowledged that object technology is a great idea, they continue to wait until the technology is fully tested and widely accepted.

While object technology and distributed systems technology may seem to be very different in scope and purpose, they complement each other very nicely for the development of distributed systems. Object technology has been used successfully by numerous vendors to hide the complexity of client/server systems. Connection to a remote database has now become as simple as selecting and dragging an icon. All of the complex interactions between presentation managers and data managers are now hidden from the users and developers, and object-oriented application programming interfaces (APIs) are revolutionizing the way that people think about distributed systems.

Even though millions of people now have personal computers at their desks, most personal computers are vastly underutilized. For most nontechnical users, a PC is nothing more than a tool for simple word processing or spreadsheet tasks. The users have neither the time nor the inclination to learn all of the technical details of a product, and seldom take advantage of all of the advanced features. The introduction of object-oriented operating systems will tap into a huge market of users who want their software to do anything they want without requiring knowledge of the complex details. When functionality is encapsulated into objects, users will be able to assemble and

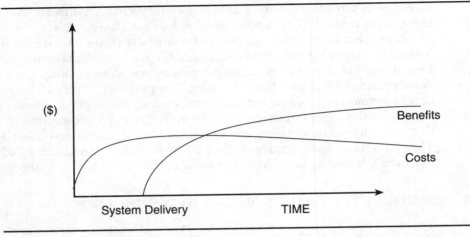

Figure 8.2   Object-oriented systems—Systems continue to be cost-effective for an indefinite period.

combine objects, and many more users will enjoy more functionality in their everyday tasks.

Companies are also frustrated with their "mature" legacy systems that require expensive programming staffs to support. The user community has been clamoring for a technology to create systems that do not decay over time, and systems that do not become unmanageable as a result of constant maintenance. Object-oriented methods promise to deliver systems with a long life span, because maintenance of encapsulated code is easier, and all side effects of a program change can be isolated and identified. Since object-oriented technology has gained market acceptance, vendors have begun to sell object libraries containing all of the building blocks to create a myriad of new distributed networks. This nascent technology will see a wild surge in popularity as more and more companies discover the benefits of coupling object technology with distributed systems.

Vendors are developing distributed object technology tools that will revolutionize the software market in the 1990s. IBM, Hewlett-Packard, DEC, and many others have recognized the huge market potential for object-oriented distributed systems. The GUI front-end market is exploding with object-oriented tools such as Powersoft's PowerBuilder, which is easy to master because it features an object-oriented graphical environment.

Many LAN packages are now offering object-oriented interfaces. The new IBM product for OS/2 and Windows clients is called Thunderbird Networking software. Thunderbird serves as a "transport layer," allowing the user to select from a series of objects to create a LAN-to-WAN gateway. Users of Thunderbird can select an object, dial in to a remote LAN, and behave just as if they were on site. The popular Raima database server also offers an object-oriented GUI for establishing connections to SQL servers.

There are numerous vendor projects to create distributed object-oriented systems. These new offerings will herald the beginning of the distributed object technology (DOT) paradigm. Some of the major efforts include:

- The "Pink" system by Taligent Inc.
- NeXTSTEP by NeXT Inc.
- OS/2 by IBM
- Windows/NT (Cairo) by Microsoft
- DOMF by Hewlett-Packard and Sunsoft
- DOE by Sunsoft

Each of the players in this market will continue to jockey for position and align its products to capture market share. Some vendors may be able to "force" their products on the market with massive marketing campaigns or by bundling their software with other system components. The good news for the user community is that each of the products will comply with the CORBA standard, and a new type of interoperability will become widely available.

REFERENCES

Babcock, C. 1993. Object Lessons. *Computerworld*, May 3.

Bloor, R. 1993. The patterns of change: Are you ready for the third major computer technology wave? *DBMS Magazine* 6:1 (January).

Burleson, D. 1993. *Practical application of object-oriented techniques to relational databases*. Wiley/QED.

———. 1993. Distributed object technology. *First Class Magazine*, October.

———. 1994. Mapping object-oriented applications to relational databases. *Object Magazine*, January.

———. 1994. Objects, objects, everywhere: the role of object administrator. *COMPUTERWORLD*, March 14.

Dittrich, Dayal, Buchmann. 1991. *On object-oriented database systems*. Springer Verlag.

Gidman, J. 1994. Practical applications of distributed object technology. *Object Magazine*, March–April.

Kim, W. 1990. *Research directions in object-oriented database systems*. Communications of the ACM.

———. 1993. Object-oriented database systems: promises, reality, and future. Proceedings of the Very Large Database Conference, Dublin, Ireland.

Loomis, M., T. Atwood, R. Cattel, J. Duhi, G. Ferran, and D. Wade. 1993. The ODMG object model. *Journal of Object-Oriented Programming*, June.

Magedson. 1991. Building OT from the bottom up. *Object Magazine*, July/August.

Rowe, L. 1986. *A shared object hierarchy*. Proceedings of the International Workshop on Object-Oriented Database Systems. IEEE Computer Society Press.

Soloviev, V. 1992. *An overview of three commercial object-oriented database management systems: ONTOS, ObjectStore, and O/sub 2/. SIGMOD Record* 21 (March).

Stileleather, J. 1994. Why distributed object computing is inevitable. *Object Magazine*, March–April.

Stonebraker, M. and E. Neuhold. 1977. A distributed data base version of Ingres. Berkeley Workshop on Distributed Data Management and Computer Networks.

CORBA—A Common Architecture for Distributed Systems

The following text is selected from the Object Management Architecture Guide (1993) and is reproduced with the permission of the Object Management Group.

9.1 INTRODUCTION

As the twin business pressures of decentralization and globalization became apparent, technology again came to the rescue in the form of personal computer and desktop computing. All of the information about the running of a business, however, was distributed throughout the many computing resources of the business.

To make use of information effectively, the information must be accurate and accessible across many departments, even across the world. This means that the CPUs must be intimately linked to the networks of the world and be capable of freely passing and receiving information, not hidden behind glass and cooling ducts or the complexities of the software that drives the technology.

The major hurdles in entering this new world are provided by software: the time to develop it, the ability to maintain and enhance it, the limits on how complex a given program can be in order to be profitably sold, and the time it takes to learn and use it. This leads to the major issue facing corporate information systems today: the quality, cost, and lack of interoperability of software. While the hardware costs are plummeting, software costs are rising.

The Object Management Group (OMG) was formed to help reduce complexity, lower costs, and hasten the introduction of new software applications. OMG plans to accomplish this through the introduction of an architectural framework with supporting detailed interface specifications. These specifications will drive the industry towards interoperable, reusable, portable software components based on standard object-oriented interfaces.

OMG is an international trade association incorporated as nonprofit in the United States. OMG receives funding on a yearly basis from its diverse membership of two hundred and fifty + information systems corporations. The mission of OMG is as follows:

- OMG is dedicated to maximizing the portability, reusability, and interoperability of software. OMG is the leading worldwide organization dedicated to producing the framework and specifications for commercially available object-oriented environments.
- The Object Management Group provides a Reference Architecture with terms and definitions upon which all specifications are based. OMG will create industry standards for commercially available object-oriented systems by focusing on Distributed Applications, Distributed Services, and Common Facilities.
- OMG provides an open forum for industry discussion, education, and promotion of OMG-endorsed object technology. OMG coordinates its activities with related organizations and acts as a technology/marketing center for object-oriented software.

OMG defines the object management paradigm as the ability to encapsulate data and methods for software development. This models the "real world" through representation of program components called "objects." This representation results in faster application development, easier maintenance, reduced program complexity, and reusable components. A central benefit of an object-oriented system is its ability to grow in functionality through the extension of existing components and the addition of new objects to the system.

The software concept of "objects," as incorporated into the technology of OMG, will provide solutions to the software complexities of the 1990s. Object-oriented architectures will allow applications acquired from different sources and installed on different systems to freely exchange information. Software "objects" will mirror the real-world business objects they support, in the sense that the architect's blueprint mirrors a building. OMG envisions a day where users of software start up applications as they start up their cars, with no more concern about the underlying structure of the objects they manipulate than the driver has about the molecular construction of gasoline.

9.2 GOALS OF THE OBJECT MANAGEMENT GROUP

The members of the Object Management Group, Inc. (OMG) have a shared goal of developing and using integrated software systems. These systems should be built using a methodology that supports modular production of software; encourages reuse of code; allows useful integration across lines of developers, operating systems, and hardware; and enhances long-range maintenance of that code. Members of OMG believe that the object-oriented approach to software construction best supports their goals.

Object orientation, at both the programming language and applications environment levels, provides a terrific boost in programmer productivity, and greatly lends itself to the production of integrated software systems. While not necessarily promoting faster programming, object technology allows you to construct more with less code. This is partly due to the naturalness of the approach, and also to its rigorous requirement for interface specification. What is missing is only a set of standard interfaces for interoperable software components. This is the mission of the OMG.

9.3 BENEFITS OF OBJECT MANAGEMENT

As mentioned above, the technological approach of object technology (or object orientation) was chosen by OMG member companies not for its own sake, but in order to attain a set of end-user goals. End-users benefit in four ways from the object-oriented approach to application construction:

- An object-oriented user interface has many advantages over more traditional user interfaces. In an object-oriented use interface, applications objects (computer-simulated representations of real-world objects) are presented to end-users as objects that can be manipulated in a way that is similar to the manipulation of the real-world objects. Examples of such object-oriented user interfaces are realized in systems such as Xerox Star, Apple Macintosh, NeXTSTEP from NeXT Computer, OsF Motif and HP NewWave and to a limited degree, Microsoft Windows. CAD systems are also a good example in which components of a design can be manipulated in a way similar to the manipulation of real components.

This results in a reduced learning curve and common "look and feel" to multiple applications. It is easier to see and point that to remember and type.

- A more indirect end-user benefit of object-oriented applications, provided that they cooperate according to some standard, is that independently developed general-purpose applications can be combined in a user-specific way. It is OMG's central purpose to create a standard that realizes interoperability between independently developed applications across heterogeneous networks of computers.

This means that multiple software programs appear as "one" to the user of information no matter where they reside.

- Common functionality in different applications (such as storage and retrieval of objects, mailing of objects, printing of objects, creation and deletion of objects, or help and computer-based training) is realized by common shared objects leading to a uniform and consistent user interface.

Sharing of information drastically reduces documentation redundancy. Consistent access across multiple applications allows for increased focus on application creation rather than application education.

- Transition to object-oriented application technology does not make existing applications obsolete. Existing applications can be embedded (with different levels of integration) in an object-oriented environment.

Pragmatic migration of existing applications gives users control over their computing resources, and how quickly these resources change.

Likewise, application developers benefit from object technology and object-oriented standards. These benefits fall into two categories:

- Through encapsulation of object data (making data accessible only in a way controlled by the software that implements the object), applications are built in a truly modular fashion, preventing unintended interference. In addition, it is possible to build applications in an incremental way, preserving correctness during the development process.
- By reusing existing components, specifically, when the OMG standard is in effect, thereby standardizing interaction between independently developed applications (and application components), cost and lead time can be saved by making use of existing implementations of object classes.

In developing standards, OMG keeps these benefits of object orientation in mind, together with a set of overall goals:

- Heterogeneity. Integration of applications and facilities must be available across heterogeneous networks of systems independent of networking transports and operating systems.

- Customization options. Common Facilities must be customizable in order to meet specific end-user or organizational requirements and preferences.
- Scope. The scope of OMG adopted technology is characterized by both workgroup support and mission-critical applications.
- Management and control. Issues such as security, recovery, interruptability, auditing, and performance are examined.
- Internationalization. As OMG is itself an international group, the standard reflects built-in support for internationalization of software.
- Technical standards. Standards to meet these user goals are the central goal of the OMG, as well as the content of this manual.

9.4 OBJECT MANAGEMENT ARCHITECTURE

The Object Request Broker component of the Object Management Architecture is the communications heart of the standard. This is referred to commercially as CORBA (Common Object Request Broker Architecture). It provides an infrastructure allowing objects to communicate, independent of the specific platforms and techniques used to implement the addressed objects. The Object Request Broker component will guarantee portability and interoperability of objects over a network of heterogeneous systems.

The Object Services component standardizes the life cycle management of objects. Functions are provided to create objects (the Object Factory), to control access to objects, to keep track of relocated objects, and to control the relationship between species of objects (class management). The Object Services component provides the generic environment in which single objects can perform their tasks. Standardization of Object Services leads to consistency over different applications and improved productivity for the developer.

The Common Facilities component provides a set of generic applications functions that can be configured to the specific requirements of a specific configuration. Examples are printing facilities, database facilities, and electronic mail facilities. Standardization leads to uniformity in generic operations and to options for end-users to configure their configurations (as opposed to configuring individual applications).

The Application Objects part of the architecture represents those application objects performing specific tasks for users. One application is typically built from a large number of basic object classes, partly specific for the application, partly from the set of Common Facilities. New classes of application objects can be built by modification of existing classes through generalization or specialization of existing classes (inheritance) as provided by Object Service. The multi-object class approach to application development leads to improved productivity for the developer and to options for end-users to combine and configure their applications.

9.5 THE OMG OBJECT MODEL—OVERVIEW

This model defines a common object semantics for specifying the externally visible characteristics of objects in a standard and implementation-independent way. The common semantics characterize objects that exist in an OMG-compliant system. These systems perform operations and maintain state for objects.

The externally visible characteristics of objects are described by an interface which consists of operation signatures. The external view of both object behavior and object state (information needed to alter the outcome of a subsequent operation) are modeled in terms of operation signatures.

Objects are grouped into types, and individual objects are instances of their respective types. A type determines what operations can be applied to its instances. Types participate in subtype/supertype relationships which affect the set of operations that are applicable to their instances.

Types also have implementations. An implementation of an object type is typically a set of data structures that constitutes a stored representation, and a set of methods or procedures that provide the code to implement each of the operations whose signature is defined by the type.

Implementation details are encapsulated by operations, and never directly exposed in the external interface. For example, the stored representation is only observable or changeable through an operation request. The OMG Object Model formally says nothing about implementations of a type other than that they exist and that there can be multiple implementations for a given type (although it is not a requirement that systems support multiple implementations).

The OMG Object Model defines a core set of requirements that must be supported in any system that complies with the Object Model standard. This set of required capabilities is called the Core Object Model. The core serves as the basis for portability and interoperability of object systems across all technologies and across implementations within technology domains.

While the Core Object Model serves as the common ground, the OMG Object Model also allows for extensions to the Core to enable even greater commonality within different technology domains. The Object Model defines the concept of components which are compatible extensions to the Core Object Model but are not required to be supported by all systems. For example, relationships are defined as components. The OMG OM Components guide contains descriptions of components that have been accepted as a standard.

The Object Model also defines a mechanism, called profiles, for technology domains to group pertinent components. Profiles are groups of components that combine to serve as a useful set of extensions for particular domains. For example, a subset of components could be combined to form an Object Database profile of a PCTE profile.

Object Management Architecture

An application that is "OMA-compliant" consists of a set of interworking classes and instances that interact via the ORB (as defined below). Compliance therefore means conformance to the OMA and the protocol definitions and ORB enables objects to make and receive requests and responses.

- Object Services (Os) is a collection of services with object interfaces that provide basic functions for realizing and maintaining objects.
- Common Facilities (CF) is a collections of classes and object interfaces that provide general-purpose capabilities, useful in many applications.
- Application Objects (AO) are specific to particular end-user applications.

In general terms, the Application Objects and Common Facilities have an application orientation, while the Object Request Broker (ORB) and Object Services are concerned more with the "system" or infrastructure aspects of distributed object management. Common Facilities may, however, provide higher-level services, such as transactions and versioning, that make use of primitives provided within Object Services.

The three categories (Object Services, Common Facilities, and Application Objects) reflect a partitioning in terms of functions, from those basic to most applications or common enough to broad classes of applications to standardize, to those too application-specific or special-purpose to standardize at this time, thus, the Object Request Broker, Object Services, and Common Facilities will be the focus of OMG standardization efforts.

In general, Object Services, Common Facilities, and Application Objects all intercommunicate using the Object Request Broker. Objects may also use non-object interfaces to external services, but these are outside the scope of the OMA. Although not explicit in the Reference Model, objects may (or may not) communicate with the Object Services via object interfaces. For example, the addition of a new class may be cast as a request to an object that provides this service, but equivalently, it could be performed by editing a class definition script of a C++ include file.

The Application Objects and Common Facilities use and provide functions and services via object interfaces. In general, objects can issue as well as process requests. Thus, objects categorized as Application Objects can provide services for other applications or facilities. For example, an application-specific service, such as printer rendering, could be cast as an Application Object that is invoked by a Common Facility, such as a print queue. Equally, objects categorized as Common Facilities may use services provided elsewhere.

It is important to note that applications need only provide or use OMA-compliant interfaces to participate in the Object Management Architecture. They need not themselves be constructed using the object-oriented paradigm. This also applies to the provision of Object Services. For example, existing relational or object-oriented database management systems could be used to provide some or all of the Object Services. Figure 9.1 shows how existing applications, external tools and system support software can be embedded as objects that participate in the Object Management Architecture, using class interface front ends (otherwise called "adapters" or "wrappers").

The Reference Model does not impose any restrictions on how applications and common facilities are structured and implemented. Objects of a given application class may deal with the presentation of information, interaction with the user, "semantics," functionality, the persistent storage of data, or a combination of the above.

The OMA assumes that underlying services provided by a platform's operating system and lower-level basic services such as network computing facilities are available and usable by OMA implementations. Specifically, the Object Management Architecture does not address user interface support. The interfaces between applications and windowing systems or other display support are the subjects of standardization efforts outside the OMG. Eventually, however, Common Facilities may provide standard user interface classes. In addition, the Reference Model does not deal explicitly with the choice of possible binding mechanisms (e.g., compile time, load time, and run time).

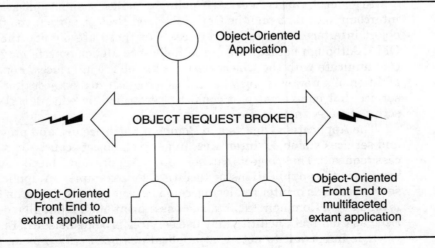

Figure 9.1   Wrapping existing applications.

Object Request Broker (ORB)

The Object Request Broker (ORB) provides the mechanisms by which objects transparently make and receive requests and responses. In so doing, the ORB provides interoperability between applications on different machines in heterogeneous distributed environments and seamlessly interconnects multiple object systems.

The OMG Object Model defines an object request and its associated result (response) as the fundamental interaction mechanism. A request names an operation and includes zero or more parameter values, any of which may be object names identifying specific objects. The ORB arranges for the request to be processed. This entails identifying and causing some method to be invoked that performs the operation using the parameters. After the operation terminates, the ORB conveys the results to the requester.

The ORB itself might not maintain all of the information needed to carry out its functions. In the process of conveying a request, the ORB may generate requests of its own to Object Services, or otherwise use them. For example, in order to find the specific method to be executed for a given request, the ORB might use a class dictionary service or might search run-time method libraries.

In order to satisfy the OMG Technical Objectives, the ORB is expected to address all of the following areas, at least to some degree:

- Name services. Object name mapping services map object names in the naming domain of the requester into equivalent names in the domain of the method to be executed, and vice versa. The OMG Object Model does not require object names to be unique or universal. Object location services use the object names in the request to locate the method to perform the requested operation. Object location services may involve simple attribute lookups on objects. In practice, different object systems or domains will have locally preferred object naming schemes.
- Request dispatch. This function determines which method to invoke. The OMG Object Model does not require a request to be delivered to any particular object. As far as the requester is concerned, it does not matter whether the request first goes to a method that then operates on the state variables of objects passed as parameters, or whether it goes to any particular object in the parameter list.
- Parameter encoding. These facilities convey the local representation of parameter values in the requester's environment to equivalent representations in the recipient's environment. To accomplish this, parameter encodings may employ standards or de facto standards (e.g., OSF/DCE, ONC/NFS/XDR, NCA/SCS/NDR, ASN.1).
- Delivery. Requests and results must be delivered to the proper location as

characterized by a particular node, address, space, thread, or entry point. These facilities may use standard transport protocol (e.g., TcP/UDP/IP, ISO/TPn).

- Synchronization. Synchronization primarily deals with handling the parallelism of the objects making and processing a request and the rendezvousing of the requester with the response to the request. Possible synchronization models include: asynchronous (request with no response), synchronous (request; await reply), and deferred synchronous (proceed after sending request; claim reply later).

- Activation. Activation is the housekeeping processing necessary before a method can be invoked. Activation and deactivation ("passivation") of persistent objects is needed to obtain the object state for use when the object is accessed, and save the state when it no longer needs to be accessed. For objects that hold persistent information in non-object storage facilities (e.g., files and databases), explicit requests can be made to objects to activate and deactivate themselves.

- Exception handling. Various failures in the process of object location and attempted request delivery must be reported to requester and/or recipient in ways that distinguish them from other errors. Actions are needed to recover session resources and resynchronize requester and recipient. The ORB coordinates recovery housekeeping activities.

- Security mechanisms. The ORB provides security enforcement mechanisms that support higher-level security control and policies. These mechanisms insure the secure conveyance of requests among objects. Authentication mechanisms insure the identities of requesting and receiving objects, threads, address spaces, nodes, and communication routes. Protection mechanisms assure the integrity of data being conveyed and assure that the data being communicated and the fact of communication are accessible only to authorized parties. Access enforcement mechanisms enforce access and licensing policies.

The Object Management Group has been very active in the establishment of standard interfaces for object-oriented distributed systems; their common object request broker architecture (CORBA) has been widely accepted, and vendors are developing distributed object technology tools which will revolutionize the software market in the 1990s. IBM, Hewlett-Packard, DEC, and many others have recognized the huge market potential for object-oriented distributed systems.

Powersoft's PowerBuilder is easier to learn, primarily because it features an object-oriented graphical environment.

Many LAN packages are now offering object-oriented interfaces. The new

IBM product for OS/2 and Windows clients is called Thunderbird Networking Software. Thunderbird serves as a "transport layer," allowing the user to select from a series of objects to create a LAN-to-WAN gateway. Users of Thunderbird can select an object and dial in to a remote LAN, and behave just as if they were on site. The popular Raima database server also offers an object-oriented GUI for establishing connections to SQL servers.

9.6   CONCLUSION

The commitment of the major vendors to develop object-oriented distributed environments indicates that distributed object technology (DOT) is not a "flash in the pan." DOT will become an integral part of all new operating systems, and with the growing desire for client/server architectures, it seems clear that object-oriented technology will become ingrained in mainstream systems development in the late 1990s.

With all of the simultaneous development, it is apparent that all of the offerings will attempt to carve out the largest market share. Being "first to market" is a very important part of market share, and many vendors will be tempted to release their DOT systems become they are fully debugged. It remains to be seen how the market will react to this new technology, but it is clear that all distributed operating systems will employ an object-oriented engine, and that systems developers must learn to employ the new technology.

The greatest threat to the vendors is the large promises of DOT as a panacea for all of the troubles of client/server computing. While object-oriented technology will clearly improve the usefulness and maintenance of client/server implementations, the initial development time may not live up to the users' expectations. The next two years will be critical for the DOT vendors, and the fierce competition that is sure to result among the vendors will bode well for the users. Competition always helps the users, and the vendors will continue to scramble to improve their offerings.

When each of these is eventually introduced and evaluated, the marketplace will decide which environments will become dominant. Regardless of which operating system achieves market dominance, it is clear that object-oriented operating systems will become a major force in the next decade.

REFERENCES

Loomis, M., T. Atwood, R. Cattel, J. Duhi, G. Ferran, and D. Wade. 1993. The ODMG object model. *Journal of Object-Oriented Programming*, June.

Stone, C. 1992. The rise of object databases: can the Object Management Group get database vendors to agree on object standards? *DBMS*, July.

10

Distributed Database Connectivity

10.1 INTRODUCTION

Database connectivity involves much more than establishing communications with another database; it is the glue that holds the entire federation together. Connectivity is achieved with many mechanisms, including application programming interfaces (APIs), remote procedure calls (RPCs), and a variety of vendor solutions. Each mechanism imposes strict rules for establishing database connections. This chapter will review the most popular ways of making connectivity a reality.

There is a great deal of confusion about the functions of APIs and how they communicate with connectivity tools and databases. In fact, some client/server architectures impose so many layers of interfaces that it is often very difficult to track the flow of information.

Ignoring the physical details, we can look at the logical methods for establishing connectivity. The most common type of logical connectivity is between remote databases of the same type. Oracle provides this type of mechanism with its SQL*Net software, which allows Oracle databases to connect with each other in a seamless fashion. Connectivity is established in Oracle by creating "database links" to the remote databases. Once defined by the DBA, these remote databases can participate in queries and updates from within any Oracle application. For example, a database in London and Paris can be defined to the Denver system with the following SQL extension:

```
CREATE PUBLIC DATABASE LINK london
    CONNECT TO london_unix;

CREATE PUBLIC DATABASE LINK paris
    CONNECT TO paris_vms;
```

We can now include any tables from these remote sites by qualifying their remote site name in the SQL query. This example joins three tables—a local ORDER table in Denver, a CUSTOMER table in Paris, and an ORDERLINE table in London:

```
SELECT customer.customer_name, order.order_date,
orderline.quantity_ordered
    FROM customer@london, order, orderline@paris
    WHERE
    customer.cust_number = order.customer_number
    AND
    order.order_number = orderline. order_number;
```

But what about remote databases that reside in other relational systems such as Sybase or FoxPro? And what about legacy data from a hierarchical database like IMS or a network database such as IDMS? Here we enter a more complicated scenario. Fortunately there are a variety of tools to accomplish this type of cross-architecture connectivity. The most popular connectivity gateway is Microsoft's Open Database Connectivity (ODBC) product, but many users have successfully implemented cross-architecture systems using custom-written remote procedure calls (RPCs) and APIs.

10.2 DATABASE APIs

An API is an interface that is generally embedded into an application program to interface with an external database. Databases APIs come in two flavors, embedded and call-level. Embedded APIs are placed within an application program to interface with the database management system:

```
WORKING-STORAGE SECTION.

01 CUST-RECORD.

    05 CUSTOMER-NAME              PIC X(80).
    05 CUSTOMER ADDRESS       PIC X(100).
    05 CUSTOMER-PHONE         PIC 9(7).
```

```
EXEC-SQL  INCLUDE SQLCA  END-EXEC.

PROCEDURE DIVISION.

OPEN INPUT INPUT-FILE.
READ INPUT-FILE AT END MOVE 'Y' TO EOF-SWITCH.

EXEC-SQL

    CONNECT TO :REMOTE_SITE;

END-EXEC

EXEC-SQL

    SELECT*FROM CUSTOMER
    WHERE
    DB-CUST-NAME = INPUT-CUSTOMER-NAME

END-EXEC

IF SQLCODE <> O THEN PERFORM NOT-FOUND-ROUTINE.

NOT-FOUND-ROUTINE.

    DISPLAY "ERROR IN READING DATABASE"

CLOSE INPUT-FILE.
END RUN.
```

Here we see SQL that has been embedded in a COBOL program for access to a relational database. However, these special sections are foreign to the COBOL compiler. In this sample, the SQL commands are started with EXEC-SQL and ended with END-EXEC. An SQL pre-compiler is invoked to preprocess these statements, commenting them out and replacing them with native calls statements that the COBOL compiler will recognize:

```
WORKING-STORAGE SECTION.

01 CUST-RECORD.

    05 CUSTOMER-NAME              PIC X(80).
    05 CUSTOMER ADDRESS      PIC X(100).
```

```
          05 CUSTOMER-PHONE              PIC 9(7).

   * EXEC-SQL INCLUDE SQLCA  END-EXEC.

   01 SQLCA.
          05 SQL-FIELD1     PIC 99.
          05 SQL-FIELD2     PIC X(20).

   PROCEDURE DIVISION.

   OPEN INPUT INPUT-FILE.
   READ INPUT-FILE AT END MOVE 'Y' TO EOF-SWITCH.

   * EXEC-SQL

   *    CONNECT TO :REMOTE_SITE;

   * END-EXEC

   CALL RDBINTC USING (SQLCA,45,:REMOTE_SITE);

   * EXEC-SQL

   *    SELECT*FROM CUSTOMER
   *    WHERE
   *    DB-CUST-NAME = INPUT-CUSTOMER-NAME

   *END-EXEC


   CALL RDBINTC USING (SQLCA,23,"CUSTOMER", DB-CUST-NAME,
        INPUT-CUSTOMER-NAME);

   IF SQLCODE <> 0 THEN PERFORM NOT-FOUND-ROUTINE.

   NOT-FOUND-ROUTINE.

        DISPLAY "ERROR IN READING DATABASE"

   CLOSE INPUT-FILE.
   END RUN.
```

At execution time, the COBOL program will interface with the database by making native calls to the database interface, called RDBINTC in this example.

The interface will manage all of the I/O against the database on behalf of the COBOL program, and will pass the result set (or a cursor) back to the application program using the SQLCA, the SQL communications area.

Note how the COBOL program checks the value of the SQLCODE field. When the database is accessed from a remote program, the calling program must explicitly check the value of the SQLCODE to insure that the intended statement executed successfully.

10.3 ODBC—AN OVERVIEW

The Open Database Connectivity (ODBC) product was initially developed by Microsoft as a generic database driver. Its architecture has now been generalized, and many different vendors are offering open database connectivity products that are based on ODBC. ODBC is the predominant common-interface approach to database connectivity and is a part of Microsoft's Windows Open Service Architecture (WOSA). ODBC and WOSA define a standard set of data access services that can be used by a variety of other products when interfacing with an MS-Windows application.

ODBC consists of more than 50 functions that are invoked from an application using a call-level API. The ODBC API does not communicate with a database directly. Instead, it serves as a link between the application and a generic interface routine. The interface routine, in turn, communicates with the database drivers via a service provider interface (SPI) (Figure 10.1).

Each custom application within Windows will have call-level API calls to the ODBC database driver, which in turn directs the request to the appropriate database driver for execution. The database driver manages the communication between the database and handles all returning data and messages, passing them back to the ODBC driver, which, in turn, passes them back to the invoking application.

As ODBC becomes more popular, database vendors are creating new ODBC drivers that will allow ODBC to be used as a gateway into their database products. Note that while most programmers can be successful with ODBC in a simple application, effective use of ODBC in multi-database environments is a very difficult task. The programmers must be aware of all of the different dialects of SQL, and they must also be aware of the native API to the database engines. However, despite the steep learning curve, there are some tips that can reduce the effort needed to use ODBC.

Essentially, ODBC serves as the "traffic cop" for all data within the client/server system. When a client requests a service from a database, ODBC receives the request and manages the connection to the target database. ODBC

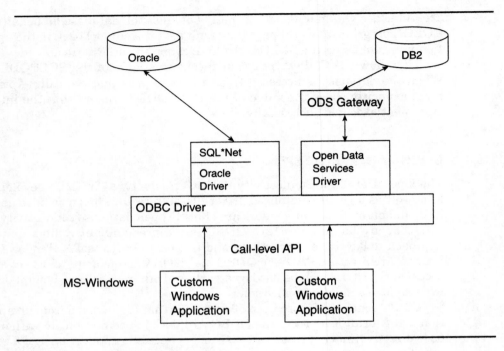

Figure 10.1   ODBC architecture.

manages all of the database drivers, checking all of the status information as it arrives from the database drivers.

The database drivers should be able to handle more than just SQL. Many databases have a native API that requires ODBC to map the request into a library of functions. An example would be an SQL-server driver that maps ODBC functions to database library function calls. Databases without a native API (e.g., non-SQL databases) can also be used with ODBC, but their calls go through a much greater transformation than the native API calls.

When accessing multiple databases with ODBC, it is up to the API programmer to manage the multiple database connections and the multiple SQL requests that are being directed to the connections. In ODBC, "handles" are used to point to each database connection. A handle is usually a pointer into the database, and the value of the handle is a record key, a row ID, or an object ID.

Most people associate ODBC with SQL. While SQL is now the single most common access method for databases, there are many important non-SQL databases that are widely used. Popular non-SQL databases include IMS, IDMS,

Basis Plus, and almost all of the new object-oriented databases. It is a misconception that a database that does not support SQL cannot use ODBC.

10.4 PROGRAMMING FOR PORTABILITY

The key to success with ODBC in a distributed relational database environment is to create the illusion of location transparency. This transparency is best maintained by requiring that all cross-database applications handle their queries with "vanilla" SQL. The term "vanilla" refers to the common features of SQL that are shared by all of the vendors. Determining what features are vanilla can often be a difficult task, because each major database vendor has implemented SQL with its own "enhancements" that are not shared by other vendors. Fortunately, most of these differences are found in the CREATE TABLE and referential integrity syntax and are not germane to SQL queries. For queries, the most common extensions relate to syntax tricks that are used to force the SQL to use a specific index. For example, in Oracle SQL a null string can be concatenated into the query to force the transaction to use a specific index.

Note that ODBC can also be used to interrogate the system tables of the target database. With additional programming effort, an ODBC routine can be written to interrogate the metadata in the target database and determine the SQL features that are supported by the database product.

For example, a database such as Oracle can be interrogated to see if it has stored procedures associated with a database event, and these procedures can be accessed by ODBC and displayed as a list. Users of the system can then choose from the list if they want ODBC to utilize the stored procedure.

This approach can be very cumbersome, and most users of ODBC recommend the "generic SQL" approach.

There are two ways that non-vanilla SQL can cause trouble:

- The SQL is rejected as a syntax error.

This is the simplest problem to correct and can be fixed in the testing phase, long before delivery of the completed system. The introduction of a new database into the federation may also cause problems if the existing SQL relies on nonstandard extensions that the new SQL dialect will not support.

- The SQL performance is different on each target database.

This happens when the SQL optimizer uses different access paths for different implementations of SQL. An identical SQL request that is valid for both Oracle and DB2 will return identical results sets, but may use different access methods to retrieve the data. For example, DB2 SQL uses the concept of "sargeable predicates" to determine the optimization of an SQL query. Depending upon how the SQL request is phrased, the SQL optimizer may choose to invoke sequential prefetch, use a merge scan, or employ other access techniques that can affect performance. Whenever possible, it is recommended that the programmer ignore this issue initially, because rewriting an SQL query for performance reasons can be very time consuming. Of course, performance remains an issue, but the SQL tuning can be left to the final stages of the project.

Anyone who is considering ODBC should also be aware that ODBC does not support all of the SQL extensions that a database server may offer. In order to accommodate these nonstandard features, ODBC offers a back door that the programmer can use to send native API commands directly to the target database. Again, this procedure is not recommended unless the feature is absolutely necessary to the application. Mixing ODBC calls with native API calls creates a confusing combination of access methods and makes the application much more difficult to support. Another problem with this approach to ODBC is maintaining the portability of the application. As new releases of the database add new extensions to the SQL, the ODBC component must be changed to accommodate these enhancements.

Some people argue that the "least common denominator" approach to ODBC SQL is too limiting. They state that learning the common syntax and facilities of SQL is too time consuming, and that a generalization of SQL would remove the most powerful features, making the system far less functional.

10.5 INTERSYSTEM CONNECTIVITY

In systems that allow cross-database access, a very common method of distribution uses the idea of *horizontal partitioning*. For example, customer service organizations commonly allow their remote sites to maintain customer information while still maintaining a location-transparent access mode to every customer, regardless of the customer's physical location. The horizontal partitioning is achieved by taking a subset of each remote site's customer table, and populating a master lookup table that is accessible from any node in the distributed system (Figure 10.2).

In a UNIX-based distributed system, the CRON utility can be used to schedule a periodic refresh of the master table. CRON is a time-dependent task activation utility that starts tasks at predetermined dates and times. An SQL script would automatically extract customer_name from the remote site and repopulate the master customer table, leaving the customer details at the remote site. The Oracle SQL might look like this:

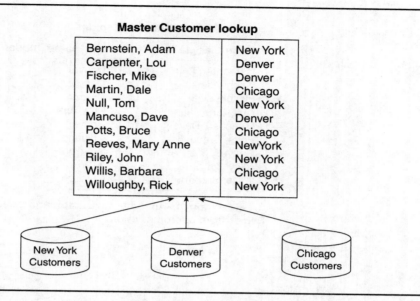

Figure 10.2   Horizontal partitioning for master lookup. Customer detail remains at remote databases.

```
/* Delete remote rows in the master table... */

DELETE FROM customer@master
WHERE
LOCATION = :OUR_SITE;

/* Re-populate the master table... */

SELECT customer_name, ":our_site"
FROM customer@:OUR_SITE
AS
INSERT INTO customer@master
VALUES customer_name, site_name;
```

Once populated, the master lookup can be accessed by any node and used to redirect the database query to the appropriate remote database for customer detail (Figure 10.3).

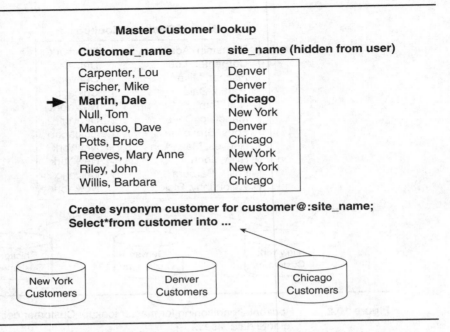

Master Customer lookup

Customer_name	site_name (hidden from user)
Carpenter, Lou	Denver
Fischer, Mike	Denver
Martin, Dale	**Chicago**
Null, Tom	New York
Mancuso, Dave	Denver
Potts, Bruce	Chicago
Reeves, Mary Anne	NewYork
Riley, John	New York
Willis, Barbara	Chicago

Create synonym customer for customer@:site_name;
Select*from customer into ...

New York Customers   Denver Customers   Chicago Customers

Figure 10.3   Location transparency with dynamic location—user of system is unaware of the location of the customer.

Because of the dynamic substitution in the SQL, a common application can be made to access any customer in the federation regardless of the location, and without any coding changes.

10.6   A CLOSER LOOK: POWERBUILDER

Courtesy of Powersoft Incorporated

Powersoft Enterprise Series

PowerBuilder is now a member of the Powersoft Enterprise Series, a family of scalable client/server application development tools encompassing all users within the organization—IS developers, departmental developers, and end-users. Built upon the unifying client/server platform and Powersoft's Common Object Technology, the Enterprise Series represents the first Enterprise Development Architecture. Using objects as the medium, the Powersoft Enterprise Series defines a new collaborative development relationship among all users. This results in an Object Empowered Enterprise enabled to rapidly develop and deliver strategic business solutions in a dynamic, fast-paced environment.

PowerBuilder Desktop is designed to eliminate barriers to entry for desktop developers by allowing organizations to implement scalable client/server solutions in phases. Used in conjunction with PowerBuilder Desktop, the PowerBuilder Team/ODBC Kit enables organizations to scale client/server application development and deployment from the individual to departmental level. The organization can access the native drivers of server databases including Oracle, Sybase, Informix, and DB2 throughout the PowerBuilder Enhanced Database Kit.

The Powersoft Enterprise Series gives IS the power to distribute the benefits of client/server in a controlled environment. Since the underlying object technology is the same for all products, end-users can build applications that can at any time be turned over to IS for continued development, maintenance, and support. At the same time, IS can supply end-users with application components that can help them get a quick start on their own development. This gives IS and the end-user community the tools to fully exploit the power of client/server throughout the organization.

Introduction to PowerBuilder

PowerBuilder is becoming the standard for client/server application development. It allows professional developers to build applications faster, at a lower cost, and with greater quality and more functionality, than any other client/server development environment. PowerBuilder provides comprehensive support for application development that is SQL Smart, Object Easy, Enterprise Enabled, and Developer Designed.

SQL Smart

PowerBuilder's SQL Smart capabilities provide tight integration to underlying database systems. PowerBuilder supports a variety of relational database management systems and fully exploits the specific features of each database. Information from multiple databases can be accessed and then displayed in a single window. Developers can utilize a built-in, high-performance relational database engine, WATCOM SQL, for creating standalone applications or for working on server-based applications away from the server.

Only PowerBuilder possesses the DataWindow object. A DataWindow in an intelligent object that manipulates data from a relation database without any need to code SQL. With a DataWindow, data can be retrieved, updated, inserted, deleted, scrolled, printed, and saved in any of 10 file formats. The DataWindow manages the interaction and manipulation of a database directly.

The DataWindow also simplifies the creation of reports. In PowerBuilder, a broad spectrum of business reports can be created in a point-and-click fashion. These include complex band-oriented tabular, free-form, crosstab, label, and multicolumn reports with multilevel grouping and sorting and user-defined calculated fields, columns, and totals. In addition, PowerBuilder includes a fully featured, built-in business graphics capability for combined text and graphics reporting.

PowerBuilder provides interactive facilities for creating and maintaining SQL databases, eliminating the need to learn and code SQL. Developers can create tables and views, assign primary and foreign keys, run database script files, maintain security, and edit data in the database, all in a single integrated environment.

Object Easy

PowerBuilder utilizes a practical approach to object orientation that allows IS developers to quickly make the transition to object-oriented development without knowledge or use of specialized, learning-intensive languages. It provides full support for inheritance, polymorphism, and encapsulation.

A PowerBuilder application is composed of a series of objects, including windows, menus, functions, structures, and DataWindows. Objects that perform common functions, such as a Print button, can be reused across many applications, substantially reducing development time while increasing programmer productivity as well as software quality.

PowerBuilder includes a graphical painting environment for creating user-defined objects, events, and functions that greatly facilitate code reusability and maintainability. Multilevel inheritance is supported, allowing for easy development and maintenance of object class libraries. Access to third-party controls such as VBX and C++ objects is supported seamlessly through PowerBuilder's User Object painter.

Enterprise Enabled

PowerBuilder's unique graphical approach to development supports large-team IS projects through a common object library manager and a central design repository. The library manager contains a check-in/check-out facility to prevent multiple developers from updating a single object at the same time and facilities to browse through the libraries, do impact analysis, and produce detailed developer reports on the libraries and their components. The library manager can be extended to integrate with industry-leading CASE tools and popular third-party version control systems such as PVCS from Intersolv Corporation, allowing the developer to leverage existing investments in such products.

In addition, PowerBuilder includes a central application design repository that is available to the entire development team and allows developers to define extended table and column attributes (e.g., headings, labels). The central design repository serves to enforce application development standards and speeds up the development process. Powersoft is the first in the industry to provide graphic behavior as part of a high-level development tools repository.

PowerBuilder is an open development environment with interfaces to best-of-breed client/server software technologies. CASE tools, version control systems, host connectivity tools, multimedia, imaging, pen-based computing, DCF, and many other technologies are fully integrated through Powersoft's open library API.

Developer Designed

PowerBuilder provides a completely integrated environment for the developer. All of the various components of an application including windows, menus, business logic, database access, database creation graphics, and reports can be developed entirely with PowerBuilder without having to bounce in and out of the environment to get the job done. This greatly enhances and speeds up the development process.

PowerBuilder is a rapid iterative development environment. Because PowerBuilder includes an incremental compile capability as well as integrated debugging and testing facilities, an application can be built and tested wholly from within the development environment. The prototypes developed are fully functional and can be tightly or loosely coupled with the database. PowerBuilder's incremental compile capability greatly facilitates the design, development, and deployment process.

PowerBuilder provides complete support for Microsoft Windows 3.1, including all Windows messages and controls as well as Multiple Document Interface (MDI), Object Linking and Embedding (OLE), Dynamic Link Library (DLL), and calls to integrate with existing PC applications. Robust graphical user interface (GUI) applications can be created by developers without all of the low-level coding necessary in C or in the Windows Software Developer's Kit (SDK).

PowerBuilder contains a powerful BASIC-like 4GL, PowerScript, which enables the developer to easily incorporate simple or complex business logic into an application. It consists hundreds of functions for: manipulating objects, numerics, and text, date/time processing, full support for DDE both as a client and server, and full text I/O. PowerBuilder's Function painter allows the developer to easily extend the scripting language by adding his or her own user-defined functions. External functions can be declared and easily accessed, as with built-in PowerBuilder functions, from within a PowerBuilder application, enabling communication with external 3GL routines operating on the client or the server.

PowerBuilder has an extensive context-sensitive online Help facility that supplements the information in PowerBuilder reference manuals, providing a comprehensive reference within the development environment. Online Help supports searches for key words, step-back capability, browsing, adding notes, and cutting, copying, and pasting help information.

Database views, which join multiple tables, can be created in the Database View painter using a point-and-click style. Column names indicate the contents of the view. Other view requirements, such as row selection and grouping, can also be specified.

While performing database operations graphically, the Database painter keeps a log of the SQL statements that it generates and then submits these to the database management system. In addition, database table syntax can be exported to a log file and saved for future use. Database log files provide for easy migration from one DBMS to another.

The Database painter provides access to the Data Administration painter, an interactive notepad for typing or graphically painting SQL statements for immediate execution by the DBMS. SQL scripts can be painted, typed, or read in from a DOS (SQL) file, optimized, and immediately executed or saved for later use. The Database Administration painter also allows the creation, deletion, and modification of users to the database management system, including the assignments of access privileges and restrictions that are tailored to the access control features supported in the target DBMS.

The Data Manipulation painter provides a facility to preview existing data, populate a new table, or test display formats, validation rules, and edit styles on real data. Database information can be retrieved, manipulated, and saved in a variety of PC formats (such as Excel, dBASE, or Lotus 1-2-3). Developers can also add, modify, or delete rows and update the database with any changes.

PowerBuilder's Database Development and Deployment Kits are available for a variety of database management systems. These kits provide the link between PowerBuilder and the back-end database, during both development and deployment of the application. They enable PowerBuilder to take advantage of the advanced features of each database, including stored procedures, triggers, scrolling cursors, referential integrity rules, and so on for those databases that provide this functionality.

Objects, Controls, and Events

PowerBuilder development is based on the creation of objects, controls, and events. PowerBuilder applications are comprised of objects (such as windows,

DataWindows, menus, and user objects) and controls (such as command buttons and radio buttons).

Each PowerBuilder object and control has a set of attributes that describe its size, position, tab sequence, and current status (visible, enabled). Other attributes, such as text or list contents, presence of scroll bars, foreground and background colors, text fonts and sizes, and others are available where appropriate.

Changing object attributes is as easy as clicking the right mouse button. Context-sensitive pop-up menus list the appropriate items and provide a shortcut for modifying attributes. Pop-up menus are available throughout PowerBuilder.

PowerBuilder is an event-driven system that uses scripts to process events associated with a given object or control. Developers specify the attributes and behavior of objects and controls as the application is constructed.

Object Management

The objects created during the course of developing an application are stored in PowerBuilder libraries. Developers can use objects from one library or multiple libraries in an application. Each library used by the application is specified in the library search path, which PowerBuilder uses to find referenced objects during application execution.

Object Technology

PowerBuilder's unique object technology permits developers to quickly create industrial-strength object-oriented applications without knowledge or use of specialized, learning-intensive languages. PowerBuilder utilizes a practical approach to object orientation that allows IS developers to quickly make the transition to object-oriented development. PowerBuilder fully supports true inheritance, class libraries, encapsulation, and polymorphism.

For IS, the single greatest advantage of object orientation is the dramatic improvement in productivity through reuse. Inheritance permits developers to easily enhance an ancestor object and automatically pass its new characteristic along to all of its descendants. Inheritance also makes it easier to maintain applications and insure consistency. If a developer adds or removes an object, or fixes a bug, PowerBuilder makes the change automatically—without recompilation—in all the objects that inherit from that object.

PowerBuilder supports encapsulation by storing both an object and its associate functionality, or script, together as an encapsulate object. Encapsulation is provided automatically for all objects created in PowerBuilder, including objects placed within others (such as a Common Button placed on a window).

Polymorphism is supported in PowerBuilder by allowing objects to send the same message to objects of similar but unknown type. As long as the receiving object is part of a polymorphic family for which the message being sent is meaningful, the sender can trust that the receiving object will interpret the message in a manner that makes sense for it. In addition, PowerBuilder supports function overloading. Function overloading allows the developer to define multiple functions with the same name, but potentially different arguments, scripts, and return values. Based on the argument(s) passed to the function, the appropriate version of the function is executed.

Adding Data to the Application Using the DataWindow Painter

PowerBuilder's DataWindow is an intelligent object that retrieves, displays, and manipulates data from databases without requiring the developer to know specific SQL syntax. The DataWindow drastically reduces the developer's coding time and effort by managing the interaction and the manipulation of the database. DataWindow can retrieve, update, insert, delete, sort, filter, scroll, print, and save data. The sophisticated design of the DataWindow offers the flexibility to represent data in a variety of formats including radio buttons, check boxes, edit fields, drop-down list boxes, OLE objects, crosstabs, and graphs.

Creating a DataWindow

The DataWindow painter is a visual editor for specifying the data source, presentation style, and data attributes such as display formats, validation rules, and sort and filter criteria.

Each DataWindow is populated by data from one of five generic sources: Quick Select, SQL Select, Query, External, and Stored Procedures. An SQL SELECT statement is generated by choosing Quick Select, SQL, Select, or Query as the data source. Quick Select, geared toward the novice user, creates a SELECT statement based on a single table and having no retrieval arguments. SQL Select, geared toward the experienced user, creates a SELECT statement based on multiple tables and retrieval arguments. When desired, the Query data source accesses a list of predefined queries created in the Query painter.

External is chosen as the data source if the DataWindow object will not be associated with a database table. The DataWindow can process data from standard PC files using scripts or exchange data with other desktop applications (through Dynamic Data Exchange).

The option for selecting Stored Procedures as the data source for the DataWindow is available for those DBMSs that support it. Stored procedures are a database-specific set of features that allow for pre-optimized/pre-compiled result plans, centralized storage, security enforcement, and other robust capabilities.

The DataWindow painter provides eight options for initial presentation layout:

Tabular	Standard report for optimal list display
Freeform	Facilitates data entry
Grid	Similar to a spreadsheet with dotted lines separating rows and columns
Group	Presents a tabular style with one level of grouping and automatic subtotals
Labels	Allows for the selection of a predefined label format
N-Up	Displays multiple rows of data side by side
Crosstab	Displays data in a spreadsheet-like grid for summary and analysis
Graph	Displays data as a graph (Bar, Column, Pie, Line, Area, Scatter, and more)

The Generation Options feature allows for the definition of DataWindow background colors and text and column borders and colors for each DataWindow style. Developers can quickly define a standard for creating a consistent DataWindow appearance by using the Generation Options feature. Once these options are set for a particular style, each new DataWindow created in that style will have identical color and border characteristics.

If the SQL Select data source was specified, PowerBuilder displays the Select painter, which lets developers graphically paint an SQL SELECT statement. The Select painter presents developers with no previous SQL experience with a mechanism for learning SQL. Experienced SQL developers can view the SQL, verify it, and later modify and save it in order to retain control over database processing.

PowerBuilder developers can seamlessly return to the Select painter to SQL. PowerBuilder displays a graphic representation of the database table(s) so that data can be re-specified by selecting the columns from the table. This feature is useful for adding additional columns to the data selection or for defining retrieval arguments.

Once the developer specifies the selection criteria that determine what data will be manipulated by the DataWindow, PowerBuilder generates a DataWindow object and displays the DataWindow banded workspace for form or reporting editing. The DataWindow painter enables easy customization of the layout and contents of the DataWindow. Developers can:

- Preview the DataWindow with the actual data
- Reposition the data
- Change font type, style, size, and color
- Modify and insert headers, labels, and text
- Add drawing objects and bitmaps
- Insert computed columns and business graphs
- Insert OLE client objects
- Magnify the DataWindow display using the Zoom feature
- Specify initial values, validation expressions, and error messages
- Create groups
- Modify the result set (add, delete columns)

Using a DataWindow

After the DataWindow is built, it can be used in a window to display and process information from the database. For example, the DataWindow can retrieve data from the database, format and validate data, analyze data through graphs and crosstabs, create reports, and update the database.

DataWindows respond to PowerScript functions that process data. The following lists a few of the PowerScript functions that can be used to manipulate data in a DataWindow:

Retrieve	Retrieves data from the database
Update	Applies all inserted, modified, or deleted data from the DataWindow to the database Update; also allows for updating multiple tables
SetItem	Sets the value of a specific row and column in the DataWindow
Sort	Sorts the rows in the DataWindow using the sort criteria specified
Filter	Allows for limiting or changing the data that displays in the Data Window Object when the application executes
GetItem	Obtains data from specific row and column in the DataWindow

For added flexibility, developers can program the DataWindow to change at run time based upon input from end-users. Dynamic DataWindows allow end-users to create ad hoc queries or tailor the DataWindow text font, colors, and other properties.

PowerBuilder provides an object-oriented, professional client/server development environment that supports centralized management and broad connectivity to front-end design tools and enterprise-wide back-end data servers. The Powersoft Enterprise Series of family of tools gives large and small corporations the technology to support collaborative IS and end-user developments of enterprise-wide applications.

PowerBuilder gives IS the tools and technology that they need to steer their organizations into a successful future. Powersoft's CODE strategy enables users to mix-and-match products within their client/server solutions based on specific economic and performance needs for each of the three client/server components—client, network, and server.

Powersoft is focused on supplying the best application development tools and building the interfaces to other application life cycle products that enable the development of large-scale mission-critical applications.

10.7   A CLOSER LOOK: ORACLE'S SQL*NET

Client/Server and Server/Server Communications

When a connection is made to SQL*Net, it passes the request to its underlying layer, the TNS, where the request is transmitted to the appropriate server. At the server, SQL*Net receives the request from TNS and passes the SQL to the database. TNS is the "transparent network substrate": a single, common interface to all protocols. TNS has the ability to connect to databases in physically separate networks. At the lowest level, TNS communicates to other databases with message-level send-receive commands.

> Client side—The User Programmatic Interface (UPI) is the central client component. The UPI converts SQL to associated parse, execute, and fetch statements. The UPI parses the SQL, opens the SQL cursor, binds the client application, describes the contents of returned data fields, executes the SQL, fetches the rows, and closes the cursor. Oracle attempts to minimize messages to the server by combining UPI calls whenever possible.

> Server side—The Oracle Programmatic Interface (OPI) is the central server component. The OPI is the obverse of the UPI; it responds to all possible messages from the UPI and returning requests.

For server-to-server communication there is no UPI; instead there is a Network Programmatic Interface (NPI) at the initiating server. SQL*Net supports network transparency such that the network structure may be changed without affecting the SQL*Net application. Location transparency is achieved with database links and synonyms.

Recent enhancements to SQL*Net version 2 include multiple "community" access (e.g., TCP/IP to LU6.2), where databases can connect across diverse protocols, and the multithreaded server that allows all communications to a database to be handled through a single dispatcher, rather than with separate processes on each database (Figure 10.4).

A *community* is a group of computers that share a common protocol (TCP/IP, LU6.2). SQL*Net version 2 is able to cross between different communities, such that the remote request is specified by database name, and all protocol conversion is automatically managed by the SQL*Net software.

System Components of SQL*Net

TSNAMES.ORA—This file defines *incoming* database requests. It contains all database names (sid's) running on the processor. When a new database is added to a box, /etc/tnsnames.ora must be updated. This file also describes each domain name, with protocol, host, and port information.

LISTNER.ORA—A list of destinations for *outgoing* database connections. When a new destination database is added to a box, it must be added to /etc/listener.ora, and the listener must be bounced.

/usr/etc/HOSTS—UNIX level—lists all network addresses.

/usr/etc/SERVICES—lists the SQL*Net services.

Application Connection with SQL*Net

Connections to remote databases can be made by specifying either "service names" or "connect strings." Connect strings use the full connection, and in the example below, "t:" means a TCP/IP connection, "host:" is the name of the remote processor, and "database:" is the name of the databases on that processor.

To connect with a service name, use:

```
sqlplus /@database
```

To connect with a server connect string, use:

```
sqlplus /@t:host:database
```

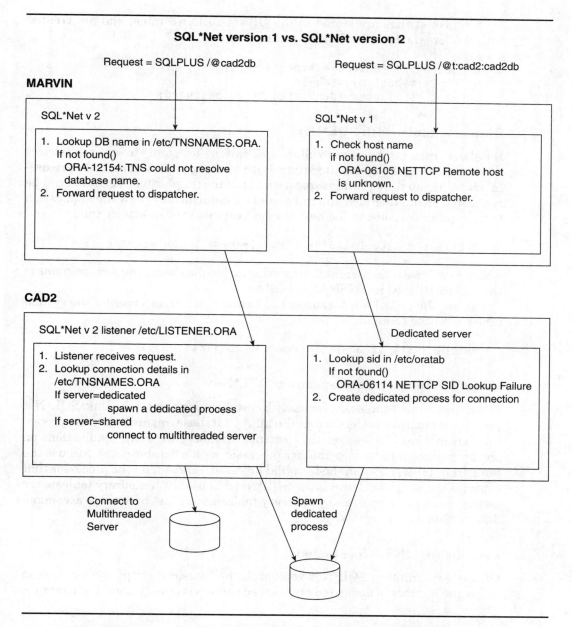

Figure 10.4   SQL*Net version 2: multithread server enhancement.

Connect strings are stored in the DBA_DBLINKS table, and are created with the "create database link" command:

```
create public database link ny_emp for
ny_emp@t:myhost:mydatabase
connect to my_user identified by my_password;
```

Database Links with SQL*Net

Database links can be used to allow applications to "point" to other databases without altering the application code. With banking applications, links are useful when a system requests restoration of a "quarterly" table. The table can be replicated on another box, and links can be established to allow the application to transparently point to the new box that contains the quarterly table:

```
CREATE (PUBLIC) DATABASE LINK linkname USING service_name:
```

where *linkname* is the name of an existing global database, and *service_name* is the service defined in TNSNAMES.ORA.

To see the links for a database, the Oracle user can interrogate the system tables with the command:

```
Select distinct db_link from dba_db_links;
```

Use of Temporary Tablespaces in SQL*Net

When a database is accessed remotely by establishing a database link, SQL*Net uses the temporary tablespace on the target database, regardless of the processor that invokes the task, or the "original" database location. Applications on one processor that accesses another processor with a database link will use the temporary tablespaces on the terminal processor, and not on the processor that contains the link. The moral is the SQL*Net will use the temporary tablespaces on the remote database, and temporary tablespaces must be sized to accommodate remote data requests.

Establishing SQL*Net sessions

On systems running SQL*Net version 2, the "session" script can be used to query the number of dedicated and shared servers on the system. For example:

```
[oracle]cad2: sqlx session
Wed Sep 14
```

```
Page 1
cad2db Database
Sessions for SQL*Net

SERVER      Oracle user   O/S        User    Machine Program
---------   -----------   --------   ------  ------------------------------
DEDICATED   SYS           oracle     cad2    sqldba@cad2 (Pipe Two-Task)

DEDICATED   OPS$REDDY     reddy      cad2    runform30@cad2 (Pipe Two-Task)

DEDICATED   GLINT         lkornake   cad2    sqlplus@cad2 (Pipe Two-Task)

DEDICATED   OPS$ORACLE    oracle     clt2    sqlplus@clt2 (TNS interface)

DEDICATED   SECTION125    dburleso   syspro  sqlplus@syspro (TCP Two-Task)

DEDICATED   OPS$JCONNORS  jconnors   cad2    ? @cad2 (TCP Two-Task)

DEDICATED   OPS$WWRIGHT   wwright    cad2    runmenu50@cad2 (Pipe Two-Task)

DEDICATED   OPS$ORACLE    oracle     ensc    sqlplus@ensc (TCP Two-Task)

DEDICATED   SECTION125    OraUser            C:\PB3\PBSYS030.DLL

DEDICATED   OPS$ORACLE    oracle     cad2    sqlplus@cad2 (Pipe Two-Task)

DEDICATED   OPS$JSTARR    jstarr     cad2    sqlforms30@cad2 (Pipe Two-Task)

DEDICATED   OPS$WWRIGHT   wwright    cad2    RUN_USEX@cad2 (Pipe Two-Task)


12 rows selected.
```

Here we see four types of connections:

- Pipe Two-Task—used for internal tasks (e.g., SQLPLUS /)
- TNS Interface—used when connection is made with a v2 service name. (e.g., SQLPLUS /@cad2)
- TCP Two-Task—used when connection is made with a v1 "connect string." (e.g., SQLPLUS /@t:cad2:cad2db)
- PC connection task—denoted by the PC DLL name (e.g., C:\PB3\PBSYS030.DLL = initiated via PowerBuilder DLL)

The Listener

The listener is a software program that runs on each remote node and "listens" for any incoming database requests. When a request is detected, the listener may direct the request to:

- A dedicated server
- A multithreaded server
- An existing process—prespawned shadow

Basic Listener Commands To see what the Oracle listener is doing, Oracle provides a series of listener commands. They include:

lsnrctl reload	refreshes the listener
lsnrctl start	starts the listener
lsnrctl stop	stops the listener
lsnrctl status	shows the status of the listener

```
[oracle]cad2: lsnrctl stat

LSNRCTL for HPUX: Version 2.0.15.0.0 - Production on 16-SEP-94 15:38:00

Copyright (c) Oracle Corporation 1993. All rights reserved.

Connecting to (ADDRESS=(PROTOCOL=TCP)(HOST=cad2)(PORT=1521))
STATUS of the LISTENER
----------------
Alias                     LISTENER
Version                   TNSLSNR for HPUX: Version 2.0.15.0.0 -
                             Production
Start Date                29-AUG-94 13:50:16
Uptime                    18 days 1 hr. 47 min. 45 sec
Trace Level               off
Security                  OFF
Listener Parameter File   /etc/listener.ora
Listener Log File         /usr/oracle/network/log/listener.log
Services Summary...
 dev7db                   has 1 service handlers
 cad2db                   has 1 service handlers
The command completed successfully
```

The lsnrctl services command lists all servers and dispatchers:

```
[oracle]marvin: lsnrctl services

LSNRCTL for HPUX: Version 2.0.15.0.0 - Production on 16-SEP-94 15:36:47

Copyright (c) Oracle Corporation 1993. All rights reserved.

Connecting to (ADDRESS=(PROTOCOL=TCP)(HOST=marvin)(PORT=1521))
Services Summary...
  tdb000          has 4 service handlers
  DISPATCHER established:1 refused:0 current:2 max:55 state:ready
   D001 (machine: marvin, pid: 4146)
   (ADDRESS=(PROTOCOL=tcp)(DEV=5)(HOST=141.123.224.38)(PORT=1323))
  DISPATCHER established:1 refused:0 current:2 max:55 state:ready
   D000 (machine: marvin, pid: 4145)
   (ADDRESS=(PROTOCOL=tcp)(DEV=5)(HOST=141.123.224.38)(PORT=1321))
  DISPATCHER established:0 refused:0 current:1 max:55 state:ready
   D002 (machine: marvin, pid: 4147)
   (ADDRESS=(PROTOCOL=tcp)(DEV=5)(HOST=141.123.224.38)(PORT=1325))
  DEDICATED SERVER established:0 refused:0
The command completed successfully
```

Note that the configuration of an Oracle listener is a direct result of the parameters that are specified in the start-up deck for the Oracle database. This parameter file, called init.ora, will contain the following parameters to define the multithreaded server and listener.

```
# ----------------
# Multi-threaded Server
# ----------------

MTS_DISPATCHERS = "tcp,3"

MTS_LISTENER_ADDRESS = "(ADDRESS=(PROTOCOL=tcp) (HOST=marvin) (PORT=1521))"

MTS_MAX_DISPATCHERS = 5

MTS_MAX_SERVERS = 20

# ----------------
# Distributed systems options
# ----------------

DISTRIBUTED_LOCK_TIMEOUT = 60

DISTRIBUTED_RECOVERY_CONNECTION_HOLD_TIME = 200

DISTRIBUTED_TRANSACTIONS = 6
```

Two-Phase Commit Processing (2PC)

When a distributed update (or delete) has finished processing, SQL*Net will coordinate commit processing such that if any portion of the transaction fails, then the entire transaction is rolled back. The first phase is a "prepare" phase to each node, followed by the commits, and terminated by a "forget" phase.

If a distributed update is in the process of issuing the 2PC, and a network connection breaks, Oracle will place an entry in the dba_2pc_pending table, and the recoverer background process, RECO, will rollback or commit the good node to match the state of the disconnected node, thereby insuring consistency. RECO can be turned on by using the ALTER SYSTEM ENABLE DISTRIBUTED RECOVERY command.

The dba_2pc_pending table contains an advise column that directs the database to either commit or roll back the pending item. The "alter session advise" syntax can be used to direct the 2PC mechanism.

For example, to force the completion of an insert we could enter:

```
alter session advise commit;
insert into payroll@PX010 ....;
```

When a 2PC transaction fails, say due to a network disconnection, the dba_2pc_pending table can be queried to check the STATE column. You can enter the SQLDBA utility and use the recover in-doubt transaction dialog box to force either a rollback or a commit of the pending transaction. If you do this, the row will disappear from the dba_p2c_pending table after the transaction has been resolved. If you force the transaction the wrong way (roll back when other nodes are committed), the RECO process will detect the problem and set the MIXED column to "yes" and the row will remain in dba_2pc_pending.

10.8   CROSS-DATABASE CONNECTIVITY ON IBM MAINFRAMES

There is a great deal of interest in database connectivity as more and more companies are choosing diverse database platforms. Database designers are working actively to develop bridges between the divergent database systems, and many tools are becoming available to assist with multi-database connectivity.

There are currently three classes of products for database connectivity:

Transparency products—products that allow applications written for a database to run on another product.

Fourth-generation languages that access multiple databases.

"Hook" products that allow exits to other databases.

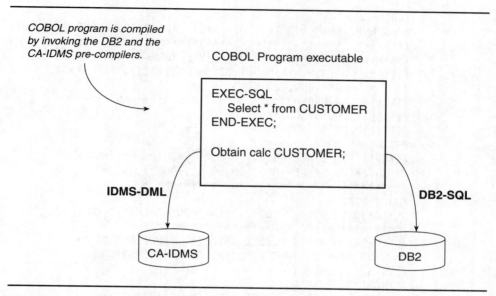

COBOL program is compiled by invoking the DB2 and the CA-IDMS pre-compilers.

COBOL Program executable

```
EXEC-SQL
    Select * from CUSTOMER
END-EXEC;

Obtain calc CUSTOMER;
```

IDMS-DML

DB2-SQL

CA-IDMS

DB2

Figure 10.5   Cross-database communication for IBM mainframes.

This is a very exciting area of technology. There is a very simple way to begin working with multiple databases, in the batch environment. By embedding database commands from two databases in a single COBOL program, compile procedures can be developed to separately pre-compile each set of database statements, and create a single program that concurrently accesses two different databases (Figure 10.5). In this example, a COBOL program was created to read DB2 tables and dynamically store them into an IDMS database. The statements for DB2 and IDMS remain as they would in a single database program, but a special compile procedure is set up to pre-compile each set of statements separately. The trick is to invoke the DB2 pre-compiler before the IDMS pre-compiler. Because all DB2 commands are bracketed with EXEC-SQL.....END-EXEC, all DB2 commands will be processed before the IDMS pre-compiler begins its job. Here is some JCL that works for compiling a COBOL program to simultaneously access DB2 and IDMS:

```
//DB2IDMSC PROC PROGRAM=,SYSTEM=PROD,DICT=LCPDICT
//************************************
//* THIS IS THE IDMS/DB2 COBOL COMPILER (BATCH IDMS/DB2 COBOL)
//************************************
```

```
//DB2 EXEC
PGM=DSNHPC,PARM='HOST(COBOL),APOST,APOSTSQL,NOSOURCE,NOXREF'
//***********************************
//DBRMLIB DD DSN=DB2.LCP.DBRMLIB(&PROGRAM),DISP=SHR
//SYSCIN  DD DSN=&&DSNHOUT,DISP=(MOD,PASS),UNIT=SYSDA,
//        SPACE=(800,(50,50))
//SYSLIB  DD DSN=DB2.LCP.DCLGNLIB,SUBSYS=LAM
//SYSPRINT DD SYSOUT=*
//SYSTERM DD SYSOUT=*
//SYSUDUMP DD SYSOUT=*
//SYSUT1  DD SPACE=(800,(50,50),,,ROUND),UNIT=SYSDA
//SYSUT2  DD SPACE=(800,(50,50),,,ROUND),UNIT=SYSDA
//***************************************
//DMLC EXEC
PGM=IDMSDMLC,REGION=1024K,PARM='DBNAME=&DICT',COND=(4,LT)
//***************************************
//STEPLIB DD DSN=LCP.IDMS.&SYSTEM..PRODLIB,DISP=SHR
//       DD DSN=LCP.IDMS.&SYSTEM..CDMSLIB,DISP=SHR
//SYSLST  DD DUMMY
//SYSPRINT DD SYSOUT=*
//SYSCTL  DD DSN=LCP.IDMS.&SYSTEM..SYSCTL,DISP=SHR
//SYSJRNL DD DUMMY
//SYSPCH DD DSN=&&WRK1WORK,UNIT=SYSDA,DISP=(NEW,PASS),
//       DCB=BLKSIZE=800,SPACE=(CYL,(5,1))
/SYSIPT  DD DSN=&&DSNHOUT,DISP=(OLD,DELETE,DELETE)
//***********************************
//COMP  EXEC PGM=IKFCBL00,COND=(4,LT),
//PARM='&CPARM,&PAYPR,STA,LIB,DMAP,CLIST,APOST,NOSXREF,BUF=28672'
//***********************************
//STEPLIB DD DSN=SYS1.VSCOLIB,DISP=SHR
//SYSPRINT DD SYSOUT=*
//SYSUDUMP DD SYSOUT=*
//SYSLIN  DD DSN=&&LOADSET,DISP=(MOD,PASS),UNIT=SYSDA,
//        SPACE=(800,(50,50),RLSE)
//SYSLIB  DD DSN=ISD.COBOL.TEST.COPYLIB,DISP=SHR
//      DD DSN=ISD.COBOL.COPYLIB,DISP=SHR
//SYSUT1 DD SPACE=(800,(50,50),RLSE),UNIT=SYSDA
//SYSUT2 DD SPACE=(800,(50,50),RLSE),UNIT=SYSDA
//SYSUT3 DD SPACE=(800,(50,50),RLSE),UNIT=SYSDA
//SYSUT4 DD SPACE=(800,(50,50),RLSE),UNIT=SYSDA
//SYSIN DD DSN=&&WRK1WORK,DISP=(OLD,DELETE,DELETE)
//***********************************
//LKED  EXEC PGM=IEWL,PARM='XREF,LIST,&LPARM',
//       COND=((12,LE,COMP),(4,LT,DB2))
```

```
//************************************
//SYSPRINT DD SYSOUT=*
//SYSUDUMP DD SYSOUT=*
//SYSLIN DD DSN=&&LOADSET,DISP=(OLD,DELETE)
//       DD DSN=LCP.IDMS.TEST.PROCLIB(IDMSCOB),DISP=SHR
//SYSUT1 DD SPACE=(1024,(50,50)),UNIT=SYSDA
//SYSLIB DD DSN=SYS1.DB2.DSNLINK,DISP=SHR
//       DD DSN=SYS1.VSCOLIB,DISP=SHR
//       DD DSN=SYS1.VSCLLIB,DISP=SHR
//       DD DSN=LCP.IDMS.&SYSTEM..CDMSLIB,DISP=SHR
//SYSLMOD DD DSN=LCP.IDMS.&SYSTEM..LINKLIB(&PROGRAM),DISP=SHR
//LIB    DD DSN=LCP.IDMS.&SYSTEM..OBJLIB,DISP=SHR
//************************************
//BIND EXEC PGM=IKJEFT01,DYNAMNBR=20,COND=((8,LT),(4,LT,DB2))
//************************************
//SYSTSIN DD DSN=ISD.TEST.PARMCARD(PCRDB21),DISP=SHR
//DSNTRACE DD SYSOUT=*
//SYSUDUMP DD SYSOUT=*
//SYSPRINT DD SYSOUT=*
//SYSTSPRT DD SYSOUT=*
//SYSIN  DD DSN=LCP.IDMS.&SYSTEM..LINKLIB(&PROGRAM),DISP=SHR
```

The execution of the COBOL program is normally achieved by running it under the domain of the DB2 foreground processor. Here is what the execution JCL for a DB2/IDMS COBOL program would look like:

```
//GOFORIT JOB (CARD)
//GOFORIT EXEC PGM=IKJEFT01,DYNAMNBR=20
//************************************
//SYSTSIN DD *
  DSN SYSTEM  (DB2P)
  RUN PROG   (MYCOBOL) -
  LIB        ('MY.LINK.LIB') -
  PLAN       (MYCOBOL)
//DSNTRACE DD SYSOUT=*
//SYSUDUMP DD SYSOUT=*
//SYSPRINT DD SYSOUT=*
//SYSTSPRT DD SYSOUT=*
//STEPLIB  DD DSN=MY.IDMS.LIBRARIES,DISP=SHR
```

With this technique, batch programs on IBM mainframes can be created to share information between architectures.

REFERENCES

Batelle, J. et al. 1992. Planning for 1995: the future is now. *Corporate Computing*, December.

Baum, D. 1993. Middleware: Unearthing the software treasure trove. *InfoWorld*, March.

Beech, D. 1993. *Collections of Object in SQL3*. Proceedings of the ninteenth VLDB Conference, Dublin, Ireland.

Bloomer, J. 1991. *Power programming with RPC*. O'Reilly & Associates.

Burleson, D. 1992. Performance and tuning for the very large database. *Database Programming & Design*.

———. 1993. *Practical application of object-oriented techniques to relational databases*. Wiley\QED.

———. 1993. Distributed object technology. *First Class Magazine*, October.

———. 1994. Managing distributed databases—an enterprise view. *Database Programming & Design*, June.

Cellary, W., E. Gelenbe, and T. Morzy. 1988. *Concurrency control in distributed database systems*. Elsevier Science Publishing.

Demers, R. et al. 1992. Inside IBM's distributed data management architecture. *IBM Systems Journal*, September.

Franklin, M. 1993. Local disk caching for client/server database systems. Proceedings of the ninteenth VLDB conference, Dublin, Ireland.

Gray, B. 1993. Database/file servers. *Computing Canada*, March.

Lawton, G. 1993. Protecting integrity of distributed data. *Software Magazine*, January.

Ricciuti, M. 1992. Terabytes of data—how to get at them? *Datamation*, August.

Stodder, D. 1992. Return of the process: client/server computing forces us to reexamine the data-centric approach. *Database Programming & Design*, March.

Watt, P. and J. Celko. 1993. Hewlett-Packard's relational/object paradigm. *DBMS*, February.

11

Database Access Control and Concurrency

11.1 INTRODUCTION

While most commercial database products provide for locking and concurrency control, there are new issues when using a distributed heterogeneous database architecture. This problem is especially prevalent when a run-unit updates several databases. When these databases are of differing architectures, say relational and network, the concurrency control must be provided for inside the application program, since neither database can be expected to manage the internals of the other database.

The popularity of client/server interfaces has also changed the ways in which concurrency is handled. Many client/server systems disable their database locking and rely upon procedural tricks to maintain data integrity.

This chapter explains the basic features of database access control and describes the issues involved when concurrency and database integrity must be maintained in a distributed database environment.

11.2 THE PROBLEM OF COHESIVE UPDATING

In order to insure that a database transaction properly retrieves and updates information, it is important to understand the differences between two processing modes, conversational and pseudo-conversational. In a conversational scenario, the unit of work is extended to include the entire wall-clock time that the user spends in the transaction. In pseudo-conversational mode, the unit of work is partitioned. The task begins when the user requests a database service, and ends when the database delivers the response to the user. The system then stands idle, releasing any locks that may have been held by the previous transaction (Figure 11.1).

To illustrate, consider an example in which a user displays a customer's information, waits five minutes, and then issues an update of the customer information. If processing takes place in fully conversational mode there is never a problem of database corruption because "exclusive" record locks are held for the entire duration of the terminal session. However, the resources required to hold the locks may cause a burden on the database, and the locks will impede other transactions that desire to retrieve (and possibly update) the information that is being held by the session.

The solution to the locking problem is to process in pseudo-conversational mode, and release the record locks after the screen has mapped out to the user. However, this processing mode can lead to a variety of problems.

- Dirty reads

In a dirty read, a record has been retrieved while it is held by another transaction with intent to update. Assume that a transaction starts and grabs

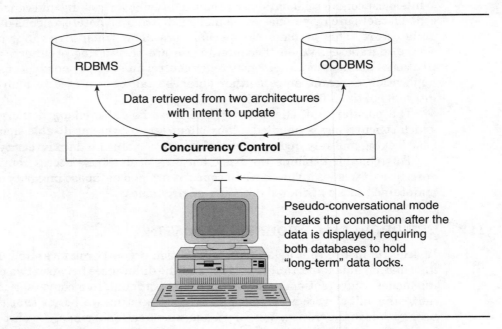

Figure 11.1   Pseudo-conversational processing and data locking.

customer ABC with an intent to update. The information for ABC is displayed on the screen and the user changes the value of the CUSTOMER-STATUS field. At this time, the change has been written to the database, but the information is not made permanent until either a commit or abort statement is issued. During the original transaction the change may be nullified with an abort statement. Unfortunately, a transaction may have read the value of CUSTOMER-STATUS for ABC before the transaction was aborted, thereby reading incorrect information.

• Nonreproducible results

This most commonly occurs when a report is being run against a database that is actively being updated. The report may be run in "local mode," a processing mode that bypasses the services of the database manager and ignores all database locks, reading the database files directly from the disk. The local mode report sweeps the database pages, obtaining the requested information, but it also reports on information while it is in the process of being changed. This can also result in "phantom rows," rows that are read by other database tasks while they are being deleted or added.

• Database corruption (bad pointers)

This can occur when local mode reports are run against a system that is being updated. The report attempts to retrieve a record (usually via an index) while the index nodes are readjusting after an insert or delete. The result is that the report terminates with a message indicating a bad pointer. Many DBAs have gone into a panic over this scenario until they realize that the "bad" pointer was not really corrupt and their database is intact.

Conversational processing is usually associated with a pessimistic locking scheme—that is, the transaction manager assumes that the transaction is going to be "interfered with" during the session, and the locks are held for the entire time that the record is being viewed. Pseudo-conversational processing mode is associated with an optimistic locking scheme whereby the system "hopes" that the transaction will remain isolated.

11.3   DATABASE LOCKING AND GRANULARITY

Database locking can take place at many levels. For relational databases, the locks can be set for the entire database, a tablespace within the database, a table within the tablespace, or a row within the table (Figure 11.2). Some relational databases also offer page-level locking. A database page is a unit of storage, usually associated with a physical block, upon which rows are stored.

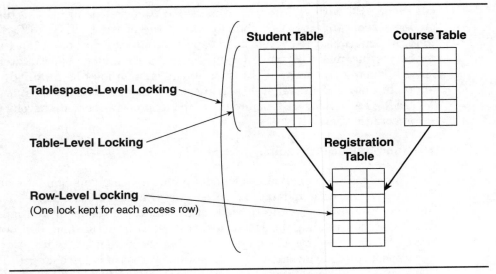

Figure 11.2   Relational database granularity and data locking.

For example, a page in the Oracle database is usually 2 KB, and the IDMS database allows page sizes to range from 2 KB up to 32 KB, depending on the size of the records.

In object-oriented databases, locking can take place at the level of the database, the *container* within the database, or the object within the container. The concept of a container is an innovation of the object-oriented databases. A container is defined as a partition of disk memory of arbitrary size that is used to hold objects. Containers can be thought of as analogous to the pages that are used within IDMS and DB2. In commercial object-oriented databases, most vendors only support locking at the container level, although most of the vendors recognize the necessity of providing object-level locking mechanisms. As a general rule, the finer the locking level, the higher the demands on lock manager resources, but the potential for database deadlocks is reduced.

In some databases the programmer has some control over whether a database lock is issued. In CODASYL databases such as IDMS, the programmer may issue a GET EXCLUSIVE command to expressly hold a record lock for the duration of the transaction, and some relational databases allow for locks to be controlled with the SQL. Most relational databases offer commands that can allow an application to hold shared or exclusive locks on database rows.

Most commercial databases offer two types of locks, shared and exclusive.

The most common types of locks are shared locks that are issued with SQL SELECT statements, and exclusive locks that are issued with DELETE and UPDATE statements. In shared locking, whenever a unit of data is retrieved from the database, an entry is placed in the database storage pool. This entry records the unit ID (usually a row or database page number). The usual size of a lock ranges from 4 to 16 bytes, depending on the database. This lock will be held by the database until a COMMIT, END, or ABORT message releases it. Most locking schemes use a "coexistence" method. For example, many clients have shared locks against the same resource, but shared locks cannot coexist with exclusive locks. Whenever an update event occurs, the database attempts to post an exclusive lock against the target row. The exclusive lock will wait if any other tasks hold a shared lock against the target row (Figure 11.3).

This locking scenario insures that all database integrity is maintained and that updates do not inadvertently overlay prior updates to the database. However, there is a penalty to be paid for maintaining shared locks. In most databases, a lock requires 4 bytes of RAM storage within the storage pool, and large

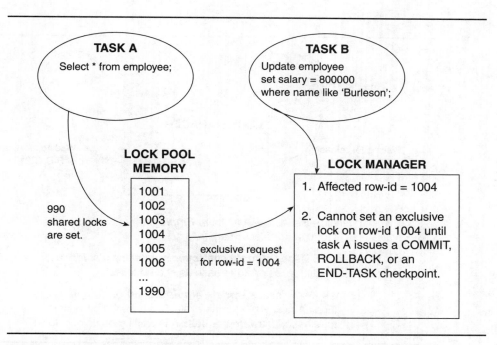

Figure 11.3   Exclusive and shared locks.

SQL SELECT statements can create S.O.S. (short-on-storage) conditions that can cripple the database. A SELECT statement that retrieves 1,000 rows into the buffer will require 4,000 bytes of lock space. This condition can also cause the "deadly embrace," or DB-KEY deadlocks. A deadlock condition exists when a task is waiting on resources that another task has locked (Figure 11.4).

Most programmers do not realize that database deadlocks occur most commonly within the database indexes. It is important to note that a SELECT of a single row from the database may cause more than one lock entry to be placed in the storage pool. The individual row receives a lock, but each index node that contains the value for that row will also have locks assigned (Figure 11.5). If the "last" entry in a sorted index is retrieved, the database will lock all index nodes that reference the indexed value, in case the user changes that value. Since many indexing schemes always carry the high-order key in multiple index nodes, an entire branch of the index tree can be locked, all the way up to the root node of the index. While each database's indexing scheme is different, many developers recommend that tables with ascending keys be loaded in descending order, such that the rows are loaded from Z to A on an alphabetic key field. Others

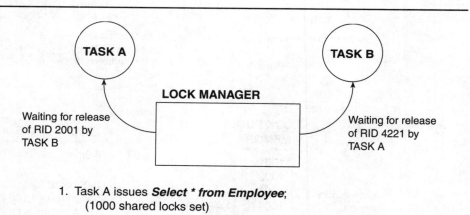

1. Task A issues *Select * from Employee*;
   (1000 shared locks set)

2. Task B issues *Update employee set salary = salary*1.1*;
   (waits for Task A to release its shared locks)

3. Task A now issues *Update employee set bonus_flag = 1*;
   (Task A now waits for the exclusive locks set by Task B
   to release, unaware that Task A is waiting on its own locks)

Figure 11.4   Database deadlocks (the perpetual embrace).

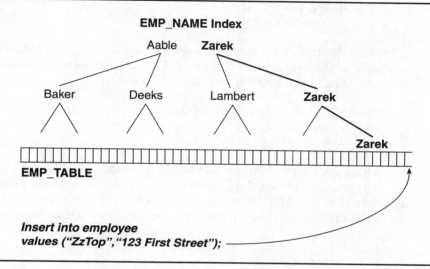

EMP_NAME Index

Figure 11.5   Locking of a single table row and many index rows.

such as Oracle recommend that the indexes be dropped and re-created after the rows have been loaded into an empty table.

When an update or delete is issued against a row that participates in the index, the database will attempt to get an exclusive lock on the row, which requires the task to check if any shared locks are held against the row, as well as any index nodes that will be affected. Many indexing algorithms allow for the index tree to dynamically change shape, spawning new levels as items are added, and condensing levels as items are deleted.

Because most commercial databases only issue locks against a row when they need to, programmatic solutions can be used to minimize the amount of locking that is used for very large update tasks. For example, in Oracle SQL, a programmer can use the SELECT...FOR UPDATE clause to explicitly lock a row or a set of rows prior to issuing the UPDATE operation. This will cause the database to issue exclusive locks (sometimes called "preemptive" locks) at the time of retrieval, and hold these exclusive locks until the task has committed or ended. In the following SQL, an exclusive lock is placed upon the target row, and no other task will be able to retrieve that row until the update operation has completed:

```
Select*
     from employee
```

```
      where emp_name = "Findlay"
      for update of salary;
```

For large updates, statements can be issued to lock an entire table for the duration of the operation. This is useful when all rows in the table are going to be affected, as in this salary adjustment routine:

```
lock table emp_table in exclusive mode nowait;
update emp_table
      set salary = salary * 1.1;
```

There are times when the user wants to update all of the rows in a table, but it is not practical to lock the entire table. An alternative to the exclusive update is to use the SQL FETCH statement to lock a small segment of the table, perform the update, and then release the lock with a COMMIT statement:

```
declare      cursor total_cursor is
      select emp_name from emp_table;

declare cursor update_cursor is
      select rowid
      from emp_table
      where emp_name = :my_emp_name
      for update of salary;

begin
      count = 0;
      open total_cursor;
      begin_loop;

            open update_cursor;

            fetch total_cursor into :my_emp_name;

            fetch update_cursor into :my_rowid;

            if (update_cursor%found) then
            {
                  update emp_table
                        set salary = salary * 1.1
                  where
                        rowid = :my_rowid;

                  count++;
```

```
                           if (count = 20) then
                           {
                                   commit;
                                   count = 0;
                           }
                   }
           }
   close update_cursor;
   close total_cursor;
   end;
```

As we see from this code, the locks are set as the rows are fetched, 20 at a time, and then released with a COMMIT. This technique consumes less memory in the lock pool and also allows other SQL statements to access other rows in the table while the update is in progress. Of course, if this code should fail, it would have to be restarted from the point of the last COMMIT statement. This would require additional logic to be inserted into the update program to record the row ID of the last COMMITted row, and to restart the program from that row.

Lock Escalation

Some databases attempt to alleviate locking problems by performing "lock escalation." Lock escalation increases the granularity of the lock in an attempt to minimize the impact on the database lock manager. In a relational database, the level of locking is directly proportional to the type of update that is being executed. Remember, for row-level locking, a lock must be placed in the lock storage pool for every row that the SQL statement addresses. This can lead to very heavy resource consumption, especially for SQL statements that update numerous records in many tables. For example, an SQL query that selects many but not all of the records in the registration table might state:

```
SELECT *
FROM REGISTRATION
    WHERE
    registration.grade = 'A'
    FOR UPDATE OF REGISTRATION;
```

Depending on the number of students affected, this type of query will begin to hold row locks until the task has successfully completed or until the SQL statement terminates because of a lack of space in the lock pool. However, if the database supports lock escalation, the database will set a single lock for the entire table even if only a portion of the rows in registration are affected.

If the statement SELECT * FROM REGISTRATION FOR UPDATE OF REGISTRATION is used to return all rows in the registration table, the database will escalate from row-level locking to page-level locking. If the REGISTRATION table resides in a single tablespace, some database engines will escalate to tablespace-level locking. This strategy can greatly reduce strain on the lock pool, but some lock mechanisms will escalate locks even if it means that some rows are locked whether or not they are used by the large task. For example, SELECT * FROM EMPLOYEE WHERE DEPARTMENT = 'MARKETING' FOR UPDATE OF EMPLOYEE may cause the entire EMPLOYEE table to lock, preventing updates against employees in other departments.

Whenever possible, large SQL updates could be run using table-level locks, thereby reducing resource consumption and improving the overall speed of the query. Some implementations of SQL provide extensions that allow for the explicit specification of the locking level and granularity. This mechanism could allow exclusive locks to be placed on a result set if the user intends to update the rows, or to turn off shared locks if the rows will never be updated.

In all relational databases the engine must be sure that a row is "free" before altering any values within the row. The database accomplishes this by issuing an exclusive lock on the target row. The exclusive lock mechanism then sweeps the internal "lock chain" to see if shared locks are held by any other tasks for any rows in the database. If shared locks are detected, the update task will wait for the release of the shared locks until they are freed or until the maximum wait time has been exceeded. While the task is waiting for the other tasks to release their locks, it is possible that one of these tasks may issue an update. If this update affects the original update task's resources, a database deadlock will occur, and the database will abort the task that is holding the least amount of resources.

Unlike object, network, or hierarchical databases that update a single entity at a time, relational databases may update hundreds of rows in a single statement. For example:

```
Update Registration
set registration.grade = 'A'
where
course_id = 'CS101'
    AND
    course.instructor_id = 'BURLESON';
```

This single statement may update many rows, and the concurrency manager must check for contention (e.g., shared locks). If any other tasks are viewing any other rows in the database, the engine will set as many exclusive locks as it can, and put the statement into a wait state until the shared locks from other tasks have been released. Only after all the desired rows are free will the transaction be completed.

11.4   ALTERNATIVE INTEGRITY MECHANISMS

The problems of lock pool resources and database deadlocks have led to some creative alternatives to shared and exclusive locks. Locking can be turned off in any database by issuing a COMMIT statement immediately after the SELECT. Without long-term shared locks, lock pool utilization is reduced and the potential for database deadlocks is eliminated. But we still must deal with the problem of insuring that updates are not overlaid.

Consider the example of updates without locking shown in Figure 11.6. Both tasks have selected Kevin Nally's employee record and issued COMMIT statements to release the locks. Task B now changes Nally's performance rating to a 12 and issues an UPDATE that writes the column back to the database. Task B, which is now looking at an obsolete copy of Nally's performance_flag, changes the salary to $21,000, improperly assigning Nally's raise. This is a type

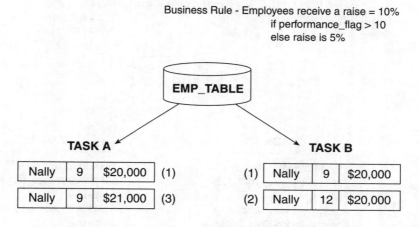

Business Rule - Employees receive a raise = 10%
if performance_flag > 10
else raise is 5%

EMP_TABLE

TASK A

| Nally | 9 | $20,000 | (1) |

| Nally | 9 | $21,000 | (3) |

TASK B

| (1) | Nally | 9 | $20,000 |

| (2) | Nally | 12 | $20,000 |

1. Task A and Task B retrieve Nally (issuing COMMITs).
2. Task B sets performance_flag to 12 for Nally (COMMITs).
3. Task A, not knowing about the change to performance_flag, improperly sets salary = salary*1.05.

Figure 11.6   Example of update anomalies.

of "logical" corruption whereby a user may rely on outdated values in other rows, updating the target column based upon the obsolete information.

Some databases such as SQL/DS and Oracle allow SELECT FOR UPDATE commands. With SELECT FOR UPDATE, the update is not allowed until the before image of the row is compared with the current image of the row. If your database does not support SELECT FOR UPDATE, there are several clever techniques to release locks and still maintain database integrity.

- Issue all updates with a WHERE clause on all updatable columns in the row.

For example, if Kevin Nally's row contains the fields shown in Figure 11.7, each of the fields will be specified in the update command, even if the user has not changed the item. If any of the values has changed since the row was initially retrieved, the database will reject the transaction with a "not found" SQL code. The application could interpret this code, re-retrieving the updated record and presenting it to the user with its new value.

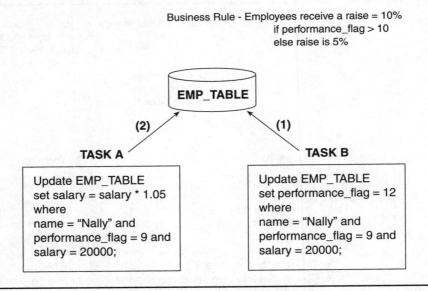

Figure 11.7　Update anomaly solution: TASK A's update fails with "not found" due to the change to performance_flag.

It is very important to run the EXPLAIN utility with this type of update statement to be sure that the SQL optimizer uses the employee index to locate the row. With so many items in the WHERE clause, some optimizers may become confused and service the request by using a full table scan, causing significant performance delays. Some implementations of SQL allow the programmer to specify the index that will be used to service the query, while other implementations of SQL require that the indexed field be specified first in the WHERE clause. Regardless, it is important to run an EXPLAIN PLAN on the SQL to be sure that the additions to the WHERE clause do not impede performance.

Some databases have SQL extensions that can explicitly "turn off" unwanted indexes. Oracle, for example, allows indexes to be turned off by altering the key field that is used in the WHERE clause. Assume that EMP-TABLE has the following definition:

```
create table emp-table (
    emp-name            char(20),
    sex                 char(1),
    performance-flag    number,
    salary              decimal(8,2) );
```

Also assume that EMP-NAME has a unique index and the fields SEX, PER-FORMANCE-FLAG, and SALARY have nonunique indexes. To insure that the index on EMP-NAME is used, the index key fields will be "altered" by concatenating a null string to the end of the char columns and adding a 0 to the end of each numeric column. Hence, the SQL update would read:

```
Update emp-table
    set salary          = salary*1.05
where
    emp-name            = "Nally"   and
    performance_flag+0  = 9         and
    sex !! ''''         = 'M'       and
    salary+0            = 20000;
```

There is another method to insure that the EMP_NAME index will be used. It is possible to alter the EMP_NAME index to include the nonunique fields of PERFORMANCE_FLAG, SEX, and SALARY, creating a large concatenated index on every column in the table. There will be a slight index overhead, but you can be assured that all index updates perform efficiently without relying on the SQL programmers to alter their SQL.

- Add a date-time stamp to each row.

This solution requires that a date-time stamp column be added to each table that may be updated. All applications are required to select this column and include it in the WHERE clause when issuing any UPDATE SQL. Of course, if the row has changed, the date-time stamps will not match, and the transaction will fail with a "not found" SQL code.

11.5 DISTRIBUTED DATABASE CONCURRENCY

Whether the database administrator chooses to purchase an API or to create a custom API, it is very important to realize that the nature of the data access can tremendously impact the complexity of the processing. For read-only databases, API processing is relatively simple, but for systems that require cohesive updating, the processing problems increase exponentially. In fact, it is impossible to implement any cohesive updating scheme with 100 percent reliability.

There is an inherent updating problem with distributed databases that is common to all systems. This exposure occurs when a federated database attempts to simultaneously update two distributed databases. Commonly known as the "two-phase commit" (2PC), the procedure is illustrated in the following example:

```
Apply update A
Apply update B
If A-OK and B-OK
      Commit A
                        < ==== "Here is the deadly exposure"
      Commit B
else
      Rollback A
      Rollback B
```

As you can see, updates A and B get posted to the database. If the SQL code indicates that the transactions have completed successfully, then the system will issue COMMIT statements to A and B. The point of exposure occurs when a failure happens after the commit of A and before the commit of B. Of course, the exposure can only happen when the failure occurs *exactly* between the commit of A and the commit of B, but it is an exposure that has a potential to cause a major loss of integrity within the federation, and an exposure for which there is no automated recovery. The only remedy is to notify the DBA that the transaction has terminated, and manually roll back the updates to A and B. This type of corruption has a *very small* probability, and most databases do not worry about it.

Stages of Two-Phase Commits

Following the receipt of a message from each remote database that the transaction was successful, the initiating processor begins the two-phase commit. To demonstrate, here is an SQL query that simultaneously updates all rows in a horizontally partitioned table residing in London and Paris. Assume that the SQL originates from a remote database in Denver, and that the Denver database will manage the two-phase commit.

```
UPDATE    employee@london,
          employee@paris
   set salary = salary * 1.1;
```

The initiating database in Denver is elected to manage the transaction, and will direct all stages of the two-phase commit. Most two-phase commit mechanisms have three phases.

Prepare Phase The prepare phase insures that all of the remote databases will not inadvertently issue a COMMIT or a ROLLBACK unless the initiating transaction directs the remote database to do so. In Oracle, the remote databases "promise" to allow the initiating request to govern the transaction. The initiating request then converts its own locks to "in-doubt" locks that prevent both read and write operations against the data in question.

Commit Phase The initiating database commits and then instructs each remote database to commit. Each remote database then informs the initiating database that its commit transaction has been executed.

Forget Phase After all remote databases have committed, the initiating database "forgets" about the transaction, releasing all in-doubt locks. Each remote database then releases its transaction locks.

Some of the more sophisticated databases allow the database administrator to manually recover any in-doubt transactions that remain after a failure in a distributed database network. For example, a common reason that distributed database transactions fail is from problems with the communications lines. These failures may cause an update against several remote databases to fail during any point of the prepare, commit, or forget phases. The database will detect the lost connection, and depending upon the state of the transaction, it will direct the online component to either commit or roll back its part of the update. The remaining transaction piece, since it cannot be accessed due to the line failure, will be posted to an in-doubt system table. When the remote database returns online, the database will direct the failed node to either commit or roll back.

In the meantime, the DBA may wish to manually direct the operation of the in-doubt transactions.

REFERENCES

Bacon, J. 1993. *Concurrent systems, an integration approach to operating systems, database and distributed systems.* Addison-Wesley.

Beech, D. 1993. *Collections of objects in SQL3.* Proceedings of the ninteenth VLDB Conference, Dublin, Ireland.

Bloomer, J. 1991. *Power programming with RPC.* O'Reilly & Associates.

Burleson, D., *Practical application of object-oriented techniques to relational databases.* Wiley\QED.

————. 1994. Building your own SQL generator. *Database Programming & Design*, January.

————. 1994. Managing distributed databases—an enterprise view. *Database Programming & Design*, June.

Cellary, W., E. Gelenbe, and T. Morzy. 1988. *Concurrency control in distributed database systems.* Elsevier Science Publishing.

Franklin, M. 1993. *Local disk caching for client/server database systems.* Proceedings of the ninteenth VLDB Conference, Dublin, Ireland.

Lawton, G. 1993. Protecting integrity of distributed data. *Software Magazine*, January.

Distributed Database Backup and Recovery

12.1   INTRODUCTION

While many of the basic principles of backup and recovery continue to apply to distributed databases, advances in technology such as redundant arrays in inexpensive disk (RAID) have changed the approach to managing distributed database integrity. This trend is seen in many of the new object databases that do not contain roll-forward or roll-back facilities. Recording all of the before images takes resources, and it has become largely unnecessary.

12.2   PROCESSING MODES

There are several processing modes that have an impact on recovery of very large processes. Unlike online transactions that may change the values of several rows, large processes are usually run in background mode (or "batch" mode) and often touch every row in the databases. An example of this type of process would be an account update for a set of banking tables that interrogates each account, computes the interest, and writes the new balance back to the database. Traditionally there have been three approaches to running this type of task.

• Full database processing

In this scenario, all database services are in effect, and all database recovery and locking mechanisms are available. This processing mode is the safest because it insures concurrent access and data recovery. Tasks may run slowly in this mode, especially if they are update-intensive and require the locking of many database rows. Without the prudent and frequent use of COMMIT SQL statements to release row locks, database storage pools are at risk of becoming full and locking up the entire database. The logging of before and after images also consumes resources. In case of program failure, the task must be restarted at the point of the last SQL commit. This requires additional logic to be placed within the application program.

- Local mode processing

In local mode processing, the large update process is run directly against the database tables without the intervention of the database. A subset of the database software is invoked to manage I/O against the database tables, and the standard database functions such as automatic recovery and record locking are bypassed. The task will thus run as much as 70 percent faster than it would if it ran under the full supervision of the database. Of course, the online database must be offline or the database tables must be offline when the local mode processing is executing.

The down side to this type of processing is that there can be no other activity against the database while the task is running, and there will not be automatic recovery if the program crashes. In the case of a failure, the database tables must be restored and the task rerun from the beginning.

- Local mode with logging (journaling)

In this processing mode, the task runs in local mode, bypassing the database lock manager, but the database software continues to write the before and after images to a log. If the task abnormally terminates, these logs may be used to recover the database to its prior state. Unlike regular processing, in which a terminated update automatically rolls back, local mode would require the DBA to manually apply the logs to roll back the update job.

Another common method for backup and local mode processing is to move or "vary" a database or a set of tables offline to the online database (Figure 12.1). When a table is offline, all database activity stops, and a "quiesce" point is reached. From this point, the database can be backed up, or local mode tasks may be run against these tables. Once the backup or local tasks have successfully completed, the tables may be "varied" online to the online database.

The concept of a database "instance" comes into play here. When a database is started, a set of control parameters direct the database software to allocate spaces in memory for buffer pools, record locking pools, and other system resources. Many sites configure their database instances to conform to the pro-

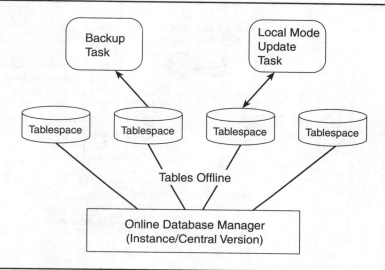

Figure 12.1   Tables may be moved offline for local mode processing.

cessing requirements of their immediate tasks. For example, a shop that performs short online updates during working hours, followed by full database scans and updates of all of their tables in the evenings, may benefit from the dual-instance approach.

The solution is to custom-tailor the instance to the type of task that will be processed. A special instance is configured for online processing, one with smaller locking pools and a large buffer allocation. After the online time session, the database is "bounced" and another version of the database is started with a different internal configuration of buffers and storage pools.

12.3   CONCURRENT PROCESSING

In order for a database to manage simultaneous updates by many users, a method must be devised to insure that each object is updated without interference from other concurrent users. Most commercial databases use the concept of locking. As a row of data is retrieved from a table, the row ID is locked, so that the row is unavailable for update by any other transactions until the unit of work has been completed. These locking mechanisms are used only for managing update and insert operations, and read-only transactions can be made to bypass locking.

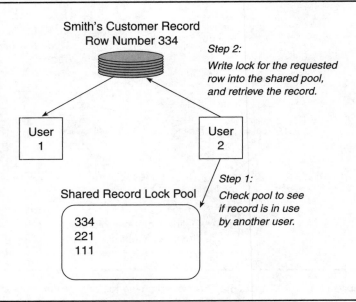

Figure 12.2   Database concurrency control.

Consider the situation where two users are simultaneously viewing the record for customer 334 (Figure 12.2). User 1 updates the customer information. User 2 is unaware that this change has taken place because his unit of work has already ended and the record appears on his online screen before user 1 made the change. Under this scenario, if user 2 then updates the information for customer 334, the changes made by user 1 would be overlaid with user 2's information, resulting in update anomalies, whereby information can be lost. This pseudo-conversational mode thus requires the database manager to issue locks upon the retrieval of any database record.

The problem with indiscriminate record locking in pseudo-conversational mode is in the resources required to hold the lock. Once a record is displayed on the screen, the record lock must be maintained for the duration of that user's session. For example, a user could call up the information for customer 334, at which time a shared lock would be placed on this customer record, prohibiting anyone else from updating the row until it has been released. User 1 could then hold this lock for minutes or even hours before releasing the record back to the database. Unfortunately, the only way to alleviate this problem is to run the online sessions with exclusive locks.

For object-oriented databases, a customer screen may consist of objects from different areas of the database. Because there is no one-to-one correspondence between an object and its data components, a record-locking mechanism for a single object might need to lock numerous objects from numerous containers in the database.

For most commercial database systems, record locks are held in RAM memory and consist of the row ID for relational databases, or a DB-key for CODASYL records. A DB-key is used for some databases to uniquely identify a record, and consists of a database page (physical block) and an *offset* or displacement into the database page.

Before any database retrieval occurs, the storage pool is scanned to be sure that no other active programs have requested the record with intent to update. If a program has set a lock on the desired record, the database will return a message code that can be trapped by the application. The application can then decide to wait for the record or to abort the transaction and provide the appropriate message to the user. Because most transactions are relatively short, this type of contention seldom occurs. However, background tasks or large updates can often create thousands of record locks. In traditional database systems, this problem is overcome by issuing commit statements, which release all pending locks issued since the beginning of the job, or since a previous commit checkpoint. Please refer to Chapter 11 for a complete description of concurrency management.

12.4   TRANSACTION LOGGING MECHANISMS

In order to maintain data integrity within a distributed database, a scheme must be devised that will allow the system to recover from hardware or software failure. Software failure occurs when a unit of work abnormally terminates prior to its normal end of processing. Under this circumstance, the program is rolled back, and the database is returned to the state it existed in prior to the start of the task.

Hardware failure can occur when disk media become unusable. When this happens, the database must allow for the recovery of the bad media and a roll forward of all objects up to the time at which the disk failure occurred. Hardware failure can also occur if the system crashes in the middle of online processing. When the database is restarted, a warmstart utility will be automatically invoked to detect all unfinished transactions and to roll them back to their state at the beginning of the task.

This roll-forward and roll-back capability is accomplished by taking "before" and "after" images of all objects. In order to insure that data integrity is maintained, these before and after images are written to a file prior to physically updating the object in the database. Just about every commercial database has a different name for these recovery files. In Oracle they are called Redo logs, in IDMS they are called journals, and in DB2 they are called logs, but they all serve the same basic function.

In cases where a software problem occurs, a user-exit will detect the abnormal termination of the task and will go to the system logs to apply all of the before images, restoring all of the objects to their initial state. In the case of media failure, the database administrator will restore the database using the most current backup copies, and then apply the after images from the database log to this newly restored database, rolling it forward to the time of the disk crash (Figure 12.3).

Database logs contain five types of records:

- Begin job
- Before image
- After image
- Commit checkpoint
- Abort checkpoint

A *begin-job* checkpoint is issued at the start of each program within the system. This record contains a unique system identifier for the program and the precise time that the task was invoked. Following the begin-job checkpoint, a series of *before* and *after* images are written to the log. These contain the run

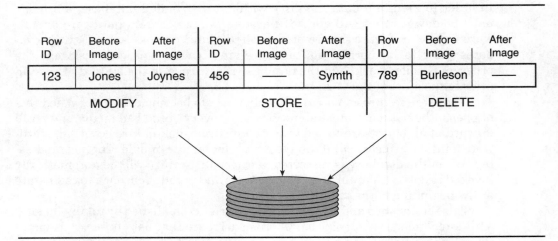

Row ID	Before Image	After Image	Row ID	Before Image	After Image	Row ID	Before Image	After Image
123	Jones	Joynes	456	——	Symth	789	Burleson	——
	MODIFY			STORE			DELETE	

Figure 12.3   Database logging mechanism.

unit ID number, the object ID number (OID), and the complete contents of the data that has changed. In the case of a deletion, only the before image is written to the log. Conversely, in the case of an add operation, only the after image is written to the log.

A run unit may terminate in one of two ways. If the program successfully completes, an *end-job* checkpoint is written to the log containing the run unit ID and the precise time of task termination. If the program aborts, an *abort checkpoint* is written to the log. For high-volume update transactions, the program may issue *commit* checkpoints. A commit checkpoint consists of the run unit ID and the time at which the checkpoint was issued. A commit checkpoint serves two functions within the database. First, it will release any record locks that are being held within the database storage pool. Second, it serves as the termination point for any roll-back activity. For example, the database will detect an abnormally terminated task, and will go to the logs and apply all *before* object images until either a *commit* checkpoint or a *begin* checkpoint is encountered (Figure 12.4).

In the event of a system crash, the database start-up routine must be directed to interrogate the system logs to see if there are any abnormally terminated tasks from the last database session. If the database administrator detects an abnormal condition, he or she will go to the logs and apply the before images for all of these tasks, thereby insuring that each object in the database maintains its integrity.

After commercial databases entered mainstream business systems, a method was devised to allow these databases to remain running for indefinite

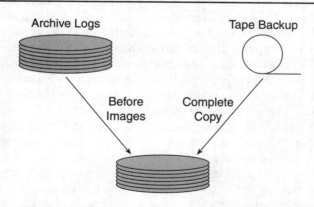

Figure 12.4   Database recovery: rolling forward.

periods of time. These 24-hour-a-day, seven-day-a-week system present a diffi-cult problem for the maintenance of backup tapes. In a normal environment, the database is shut down and a full-image copy of the files is taken before the database is restarted. However, a 24 × 7 database cannot be stopped while backups are taken. In other words, the database may be updated *during* the backup session. In order to restore a database from this type of backup, the backup utility must be carefully synchronized with the system logs. This method is sometimes called a "flying dump." When the backup begins, the database system is *quiesced*—the database does not allow any new transactions to begin until all in-process transactions have completed. This creates one brief moment when the database has no active work (the quiesce point). At this precise mo-ment a synchronization point is written to the system logs and the backup begins. Because the backup and the system logs are in exact harmony, recovery is possible to any point in time.

12.5 CENTRALIZED BACKUP METHODS: ENTERPRISE DATA MANAGERS

As distributed databases continue to add remote nodes, the maintenance of control over backup and recovery has become an important issue. With central-ized hardware, logically distributed databases can be backed up and recovered in a synchronized fashion. All tape archives are managed by a tape manage-ment system that prevents accidental loss of archive data. With open systems, dozens of remote databases may exist in widely distributed geographic loca-tions, and backup and recovery is generally handled by each remote node as an independent process. There is no guarantee that backups are being taken at specified intervals, and synchronized recovery, where two nodes share updates and must be recovered together, are very difficult. Tape management systems are almost unheard of in distributed midrange processors, and lost backup tapes can cripple a distributed system. Also, hundreds of individual PC work-stations may contain subsets of production data, and it has been the responsi-bility of the PC users to back up and restore their own hard drives.

One solution has been to centralize all of the backup and recovery for all of the distributed databases. The logical place for this type of operation is on mainframes. Mainframe computers have well-tested tape management sys-tems, logging mechanisms, and communications channels that make them ideal for centralized backup and recovery.

This type of strategy, called an "enterprise backup system," can greatly reduce the manual labor involved when backing up each of the nodes sepa-rately. Some commercial enterprise backup systems take the initial backups at the server level and then transfer them to the mainframe for permanent stor-age (Figure 12.5). Some even offer the ability to automatically backup data from

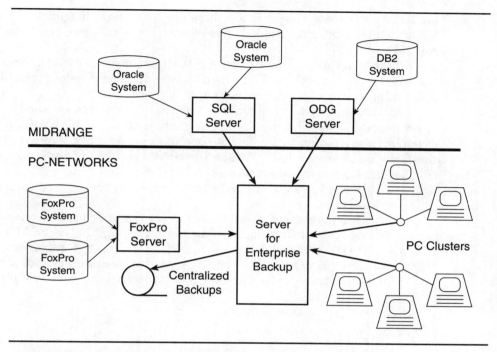

Figure 12.5   Enterprise data backup architecture.

hard drives of individual PC workstations. However, these systems can cost as much as $100,000. Many IS managers are willing to incur these costs because of the reduction in human resources and because they can be assured of a secure recovery environment.

Some enterprise data administrators do not back up all of the remote databases each night. Rather, they understand where data is replicated, and back up only a master copy without any redundancy. Recoveries are also coordinated to replicate data where it has been defined to the data manager. Not all enterprise data managers require the use of a mainframe. Some vendors are now offering centralized backup tools that run on UNIX servers. Vendors for tools of this type include Legato systems and Epoch systems.

12.6 RAID BACKUP TECHNOLOGY

Advances in disk technology are making some of the traditional database recovery mechanisms obsolete. Disk memory schemes such as RAID (redundant arrays of inexpensive disk) now offer a very high degree of reliability and availability. As a consequence of RAID there are many new distributed object-oriented database offerings that do not contain the traditional roll-forward and roll-back utilities.

Unlike traditional database recovery mechanisms where a disk crash causes the application to go offline while the disk is restored and rolled forward, RAID offers almost instantaneous recovery from disk failure.

RAID technology was the brainchild of three researchers at the University of California, who found that by creating an array of small disks, they could create software to duplicate all write operations, and quickly recover if one of the disks in the array fails. Essentially, RAID consists of three components (Figure 12.6): an array of small disk devices, a controller to manager the I/O against the disks, and software to distribute the data across the disk array and manager recovery.

The most complex part of RAID is the array management software. The algorithms for RAID differ widely, and as of 1994 there are eight RAID "levels" or types of RAID software that can be used with the array management software, numbered from zero to seven. New vendors continue to add new RAID level numbers as they develop new algorithms to improve data availability.

| RAID 0 | Disk striping |
| RAID 1 | Disk mirroring |

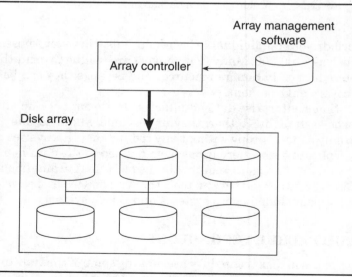

Figure 12.6   RAID architecture.

RAID 2	Block interleaf with check disk
RAID 3	Byte interleaf
RAID 4	Byte interleaf with error correcting code
RAID 5	Byte interleaf with parity checking
RAID 6	Byte interleaf with double parity checking

It must be understood that RAID is a software technique; the array controller and the disks are purchased from standard industry hardware vendors. One need only purchase the RAID level software of one's choice, and purchase the disk and controllers separately.

When evaluating disk recovery methods there are two acronyms worth noting. The MTBF (mean time between failures) is a statistic that can be provided by the disk vendor, and the MTTR (mean time to recovery) is a function of the recovery software. With RAID it would be necessary for several disks to fail within the same hour to get a failure. For a four-disk array, this can mean astounding improvements in the MTBF. If each disk in a five-disk array has an MTBF of 150,000 hours, RAID 5's redundancy will increase the MTBF of the disk array to 46,000,000 hours! (Assuming, of course, that individual failed disks are promptly replaced with new disks.)

When a disk failure occurs, the RAID software redirects any new write operations to temporary storage. Once the bad disk is replaced, the RAID software resynchronizes the new disk automatically. This is a huge improvement over the traditional recovery from disk failure, when the application users sat idle while a new disk was initialized, restored to the last backup, and rolled forward from archive log tapes.

REFERENCES

Bell, D. 1992. *Distributed database systems*. Addison-Wesley.

Bobak, A. 1993. *Distributed and multidatabase systems*. Bantam Books.

Burleson, D. 1992. Performance and tuning for the very large database. *Database Programming & Design*.

Chorafas, D. 1989. *Handbook of database management and distributed relational databases*. TAB Books.

Chu, W., ed. 1986. *Distributed database systems*. Books on Demand.

Fiorio, T. 1992. Managing distributed applications. *DEC Professional*, December.

Lawton, G. 1993. Protecting integrity of distributed data. *Software Magazine*, January.

13

Distributed Database Security

13.1 INTRODUCTION

For many system administrators, the terms *open system* and *security* can seem impossibly opposed. Maintaining security for a centralized system is difficult enough, and when faced with a network of networked databases, maintaining a level of access and update security is a formidable challenge. Often, security is an afterthought—there has been no up-front planning of system-wide security, especially for distributed databases that are created as a result of external factors such a corporate acquisitions.

Security tools have been lagging behind the development of client/server and distributed databases, leaving security exposures. A few tools such as CA-Unicenter by Computer Associates and OmniGuard by Axent Technologies attempt to address these issues, but there remains no single product on the market that can easily address the security needs for a broad multiarchitecture distributed database.

Many companies are developing security systems that tie security to the data that feeds the distributed applications rather than the applications themselves. This data-level approach insures that the database controls access to the data and eliminates the possibility that someone may bypass the application and the security.

13.2 DATA-LEVEL SECURITY

Data-level security is generally implemented by associating a user with a "role" or a "subschema." There are profiles of acceptable data items and operations, and the profiles are checked by the database engine at data request time, regardless of the application that the end-user is using to query or update the information (Figure 13.1).

While data-level security insures that all access is controlled by the database, some relational database products allow GRANTs only to entire tables, and do not have facilities that control access to specific rows or columns. Many database administrators must thus choose between using application-level security or denormalizing their tables so that the database software will be able to control data access. Neither of these choices is ideal.

13.3 APPLICATION-LEVEL SECURITY

The other common method for controlling security is to program the database security into the application logic, and have the application govern the access to the data (Figure 13.2). This method is sometimes used in situations where the default database security is inadequate. An application of the method might be controlling access to specific rows within a table, or specific columns within a row. This method of security can be a problem with distributed databases, especially since it is possible to bypass the application and access the secured information directly by using an online query tool such as IBM's SPUFI or Oracle's SQL*Plus.

Subschema Data Access Control

Many databases, especially those written for the CODASYL DBTG standard, use subschemas to control data access. The subschema is a subdivision of the overall database description or *schema*. The subschema defines the areas, records, and sets that the user may access, and further describes the actions that the user may take on each data item. Following is a sample subschema for a customer database. Note that the user has the ability to retrieve the customer, order, and item records, but may only add orders and update the order and customer records. Because subschemas are associated with individual users, they provide very tight control over the access to the data.

```
SUBSCHEMA custrecs of SCHEMA custschema

    AREA cust-area default usage is shared retrieval
         exclusive retrieval is not allowed
```

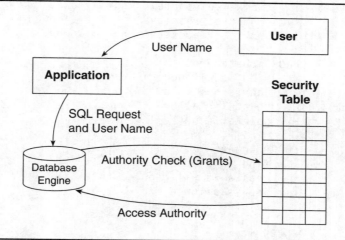

Figure 13.1   Data-level security.

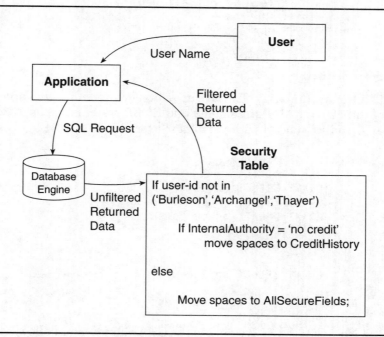

Figure 13.2   Application-level security.

```
                        exclusive update is not allowed
                        protected retrieval is not allowed
                        protected update is not allowed

                RECORD customer
                        find is allowed
                        add is not allowed
                        update is allowed
                        delete is not allowed

                RECORD order
                        find is allowed
                        update is allowed
                        add is allowed
                        delete is allowed

                RECORD item
                        find is allowed
                        add is not allowed
                        update is not allowed
                        delete is not allowed

        MODIFY USER Burleson add SUBSCHEMA custrecs.
```

SQL Security

Relational databases also have a facility for governing data access. Through use of the SQL GRANT statements and ROLE statements, user "roles" can be created and associated with particular users.

```
    CREATE ROLE custrecs

        GRANT SELECT on customer
        GRANT INSERT on customer
        GRANT UPDATE on customer

        GRANT ALL on order

        GRANT SELECT on item;

    ALTER USER xxxx ROLE custrecs;
```

Note that the ALL clause of the GRANT statement allows the user to do any valid SQL operation (with the exception of DROP) on the specified table.

13.4   SECURITY FOR DISTRIBUTED DATABASES

While there is no single standard definition of security, at a basic level security can be defined as a mechanism to insure that the corporation's information is protected from accidental or willful corruption. Security can extend beyond the databases and might include e-mail as well as hardware. In a distributed database system there are special considerations due to the increased complexity of the environment.

- Multiple entry points

    Unlike a traditional centralized database, distributed systems have many entry points. These entry points might include a file server on a PC LAN, an individual workstation, or any one of the multitude of databases that participate in the federation. When dealing with literally hundreds of entry points, special care must be taken to insure that harmful viruses are not introduced into the system. For example, many viruses attach themselves to common system software components such as COMMAND.COM, and can be propagated at a very rapid rate to all of the nodes of the enterprise. UNIX systems can be penetrated by viruses that infect the telnet, remsh, and rlogin programs.

- Weakest link problem

    When dealing with such a wide variety of entry points and platforms, the overall system is only as secure as the weakest link in the network. No matter how much care is taken to insure security at the database level, problems can still be introduced from a variety of other sources.

- Workstation issues

    The widespread use of PC workstations presents another significant problem in a distributed database environment. With workstations, users "check out" a unit of data from one of the databases, process it on a standalone basis, and then check the edited material back into the database. It is very difficult to insure that the incoming data from the workstation is entirely free of viruses. There are also some advantages to distributed database security:

- Varying levels of security

    Unlike a centralized environment, a distributed database offers the ability to custom-tailor the security for each database in the enterprise. Because each database can operate independently of the other databases in the federation, highly confidential information can easily be isolated and maintained independently from the rest of the system.

- Isolated risk

In the case of a breach in security, in a distributed system the breach can be contained to one single node and not affect the entire federation of databases. For example, a malicious programmer who obtains "super-user" access to a single processor can only wreak havoc on that one machine; the breach will not affect the operation of the entire system.

The system administrator, who can control security for each remote database component, must choose the level of security that the system will have at each node. In general, the following levels of security can exist simultaneously within a distributed system:

1. *Unprotected free access to information.* This is most commonly used in situations of read-only access to nonconfidential information.
2. *Access control.* This level of security gives users access only to information for which they have been explicitly granted privileges.
3. *Update control.* This level of security allows users only to update information that they have been specifically granted authority to change.
4. *Row-, column-level security.* This level of security allows users to manipulate only that information directly associated with their departmental job functions. For example, a user in the finance department may be granted the ability to update only those rows in a personnel table that indicate the employees are affiliated with the finance department. Of course, there are very few security packages capable of this level of access control, and consequently this level of security is very expensive in terms of both programming effort and resource consumption.

13.5   DEVELOPING A DISTRIBUTED DATABASE SECURITY PLAN

When initially planning system-wide security for a network of distributed databases, many companies follow an evolutionary approach. In most cases each node within the enterprise already has security features, and integration for a new enterprise consists primarily of allowing a unified access method to each node.

For distributed applications that access numerous remote databases, database links can be used to manage the assignment of user IDs to databases. It can be a tremendous chore to assign hundreds of user IDs to dozens of remote databases, and manage access to each separate database.

Common Problems of Distributed Database Security Plans

In a centralized environment, user access to the centralized database sources is controlled by a central security method such as ACF2 or RACF. In an open system environment, access is controlled at the network sign-on level, at the individual workstation, at each database within the federation, and in each application. Many shops have discovered that when users are forced to provide passwords for each component in a distributed database, they commonly compromise system security by choosing passwords that are cyclic in nature. For example, a user may rotate between the passwords "north," "south," "east," and "west" in order to make it easier to keep track of the multiple sign-ons to all of the system components. More sophisticated password devices require the end-user to specify passwords of a minimum length (greater than five characters), prohibit the reuse of passwords, and require that the passwords are changed on a periodic basis.

Without a centralized security component, the end-users are forced to write down the passwords to each system component in order to remember all of them. While this strategy is a tremendous headache for the end-users, it does insure that system-wide security is not jeopardized through a single breach. In system-wide security environments, security tables are kept that allow end-users to specify their user ID and sign-on once; the security subsystem automatically manages their access to networks, operating systems, databases, and applications.

There are several basic approaches to distributed database security. The most common approach utilizes a common security system. This security system maintains a single password, and controls access to all of the system components. This idea has been borrowed from mainframe systems such as RACF and ACF2. Another approach is password propagation, where the end-user is prompted for a password change and the password change is then propagated to each of the target subsystems (Figure 13.3).

While this is a great simplification for the end-user of the system, it also increases the risk of a breach to the system-wide security that could have widespread ramifications. In addition, a failure on the processor that contains the propagation routine could conceivably lock up the entire enterprise. Another potential problem of centralized security is that a user might decrypt a password on one component, thereby gaining access to the entire federation.

Another method for controlling security is to make each of the distributed systems components access the security tables directly (Figure 13.4). This eliminates the exposure of redundant passwords stored in each processor, and provides a simple point of control for the entire federation.

This approach requires user-exits to be installed at the level of each sign-on, at the network, operating system, and database level. The security files of

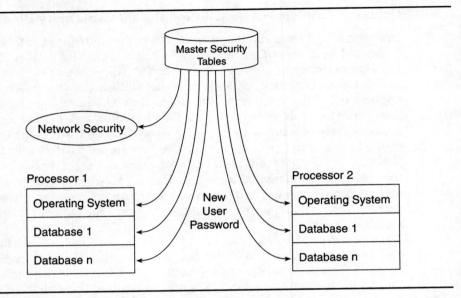

Figure 13.3   Password propagation security.

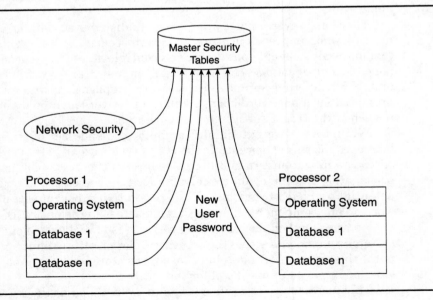

Figure 13.4   Centralized password security.

each component continue to exist, but the password fields contain random, unchanging values. While it is nice to have a single point with which to control security, there is also the possibility that a failure on the security system would block access to the entire federation. To reduce this exposure, security tables are stored redundantly on two processors, and a failure on one processor will trigger the security mechanism to check the other processor. Security at each level of the system is still maintained because each individual security component is still active, with random passwords that are never actually used for signing on to the component.

How Security Is Breached

There are many ways that a malicious programmer can bypass the security of systems. The news media are full of reports of adolescent hackers who have breached top-secret systems. While there are new approaches to breaking into systems being developed constantly, most approaches fall into some general categories.

Decryption Methods A malicious programmer (or even an end-user) can write routines that decrypt a password. In many databases, sign-on security programs are relatively easy to locate—for example, IDMS uses a program called IDMSPSWD. Once located, the password programs can be accessed directly if the file system allows it, or they can be read from leftover RAM memory in the program pool. The sign-on program can then be decompiled, and a trial-and-error program can be built to reverse the encryption process, thereby giving someone the ability to reverse any encrypted password.

In almost all databases, security encryption is done on a one-way basis, that is, the unencrypted password is never stored in any tertiary memory (Figure 13.5). This method insures that the unencrypted password is never stored on disk memory, and provides security from all but the most diligent hacker. However, the encrypted password is left in RAM by some software packages, on the assumption that it is safe to do this because the password is encrypted. As we have seen from the previous discussion, this safety is an illusion.

To decrypt a password, a routine can be written to unscramble the strings that make up the password until they are found in a standard word dictionary or a dictionary of common names. Using this method, a malicious programmer could start a background task to run until the decrypted string matched a dictionary entry. While this process might take hundreds of thousands or even millions of attempts, it is relatively simple to create this type of program and gain access to a system within a week.

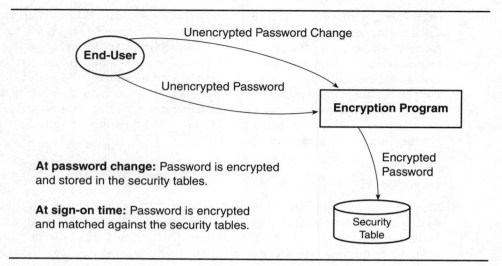

At password change: Password is encrypted and stored in the security tables.

At sign-on time: Password is encrypted and matched against the security tables.

Figure 13.5   One-way password encryption.

Cruising RAM Another common way that password security is breached is by finding and interrogating the leftover RAM that has been used by the database or operating system sign-on process. Some security mechanisms do not bother to physically erase the contents of RAM that they use during the sign-on process, and consequently, user IDs and unencrypted passwords are left in RAM. To get a user ID and password, the malicious programmer simply writes a program that requests core memory, and then sweeps the memory looking for strings that might represent user IDs. In a C program, the malloc command can be used to access memory, and in COBOL a large array can be defined in the working-storage section of the program. This technique is especially effective for sites that use a common letter or series of letters to identify users (e.g., Maureen A. Thayer becomes user UMATHAYE). Once a string is identified, the next 20 bytes of storage can be printed, and the program continues to access RAM and search for passwords.

Shopping and Guessing One of the easiest ways to breach security is to allow the end-user to tell you his or her passwords. While this is not likely to happen deliberately, many end-users are very sloppy in their assignment and keeping of passwords. In distributed databases that do not use centralized security, it is not uncommon to find lists of passwords written down on the end-user's desk, one for the network, one for the application, and one for each database. It is also amazing how many end-users will choose predictable passwords. Names of children and pets are especially popular, and a savvy hacker with access to personal information can sometimes guess the passwords.

Trojan Horses This is a common method for eliciting a password from an unsuspecting user. To build a Trojan horse, the malcontent hacker creates a sign-on screen that is identical to the real sign-on screen. This phony screen solicits the user ID and password, writes it to a file, and then passes the user ID and password to the real sign-on screen (Figure 13.6).

Many sign-on screens, especially those for distributed databases, contain a direct gateway into the system, whereby the sign-on screens for all distributed systems are not displayed if the user ID and password are provided when the initial sign-on program is invoked. These direct gateways are commonly used to get fast, transparent access to information in other databases, but they are also great for the malicious programmer who wants to write a Trojan horse. Some UNIX and MVS databases allow user passwords to be managed by the operating system, and assume that if the user has been able to enter the operating system, he or she may pass freely into the database.

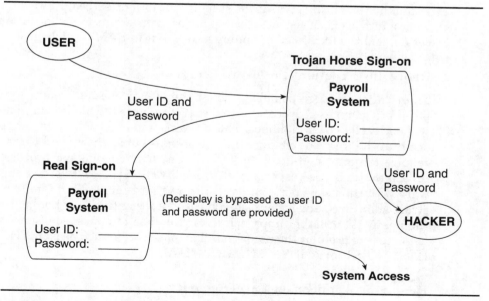

Figure 13.6   The Trojan horse.

13.6   PREVENTING SECURITY BREACHES

While few security systems are perfect (the exception being the retinal eyeball scanners used by the U.S. Department of Defense for top-secret systems), there are some things that can be done to decrease the likelihood of a security breach. Many of these methods are time-consuming and slow down the run-time system, so careful thought must be given to these solutions before implementing them in a production environment.

Enhancing Encryption Processing

One way to insure that a user ID and password are not in RAM is to check each sign-on program for each component and insure that it sets all used RAM memory to binary zeros. If it does not, sign-on exits can be written to reacquire the freed memory and reset the RAM memory.

The memory for the sign-on program itself should also be erased. Even the tightest file-level security can be breached if the entire sign-on program, including the encryption algorithm, continues to reside in RAM, and can be read and stored by a malicious person. Few sign-on programs bother to erase the program memory, because erasing is resource intensive, slowing down the sign-on process, and also because it is assumed that the sign-on program will be overwritten by another executing program as soon as the storage is freed. However, the sign-on program is one of the most commonly used programs in just about any application, and the likelihood of finding a copy of it in RAM is fairly good.

Requiring Frequent Password Changes

There has been a great debate about the effectiveness of requiring frequent password changes. Advocates argue that it reduces the likelihood that the user will use easily guessed names. Those against enforced password changes point out that the frequent changes may be seen as obtrusive by end-users and also require forgetful end-users to write down their current passwords. One approach that has been especially effective is to link the password-changing software with the user's personnel records, so that the names of family members, street addresses, and other easily guessed information may *not* be included in the password. Another approach takes the idea of nonreuse of password, enhancing it to prohibit the use of "similar" passwords, such as NORTH, SOUTH, EAST, WEST, or ANDY1, ANDY2, ANDY3.

Removing Application-Level Security

One way that users in a PC workstation environment can bypass security is through the use of the powerful PC-based access tools. For example, if access authority is governed by an application running on the PC, a savvy end-user could capitalize on PC access, writing an entirely new application with a product such as PowerBuilder or Visual Basic, thereby bypassing the security within the original application on his or her desktop. Some companies that use application-level security attempt to avoid this problem by autotasking the PC user directly into the application, and installing special software to disallow a system boot from anything other than the appropriate initialization routine.

13.7   A CLOSER LOOK: ORACLE SQL SECURITY

Database security for the Oracle relational database is applied with the SQL GRANT statement and removed with the REVOKE statement. While these two basic commands appear simple, there are hundreds of database access privileges that can be granted and revoked. Privileges fall into two categories: system privileges and object privileges.

System privileges give the user the right to perform an action, or perform an action on a particular *type* of object, for example:

```
GRANT select any table TO USER1;
```

There are dozens of system privileges that are used by the database to regulate access to all functions within the database. Systems privileges are expressed in three parts: the action part, the global part (ANY), and the object type. Based on this taxonomy, system privileges are expressed:

```
action:          ANY                      object_type
```

The following are action and object type options:

Action	Object type
alter	cluster
audit (any)	database
backup (table)	database link
become (user)	privilege
create	procedure
drop	profile
force (transaction)	role
grant	sequence

Action	Object type
manage (tablespace)	session
select	snapshot
	synonym
	system
	table
	tablespace
	trigger
	user

Object privileges grant the right to perform an action on a *specific* object type, for instance:

```
GRANT select on cat.food to USER1;
```

Object privileges are in the form *action-object-objectname*, and are delineated in the following table:

object privilege	tables	views	sequences	snapshots
ALL	x	x	x	x
ALTER	x		x	
DELETE	x	x		
INDEX	x			
INSERT	x	x		
REFERENCES		x		
SELECT	x	x	x	x
UPDATE	x	x		

Based on this table, the following object privileges are valid:

```
grant ALL         on my_table to user1;
grant INSERT      on my_view to user1;
```

Functions, Procedures, and Packages

One of the features of Oracle is the ability to enforce access to a table by using procedures. A function is a small code snippet that may contain SQL, accepting input variables and returning a value to the caller of the function. A procedure is a piece of code that has embedded SQL commands within its body. A package is a collection of procedures and/or functions that logically relates the procedures. For example, the following package, human_resources, contains functions and procedures that are required to perform the HR tasks:

```
CREATE PACKAGE BODY human_resources AS;

        PROCEDURE hire_employee
            BEGIN ... END;
        FUNCTION give_raise
            BEGIN ... END;
        PROCEDURE manage_benefits
            BEGIN ... END;
```

The confounding problem with procedures and packages is that their security is managed in an entirely different fashion from other GRANT statements. If a user is given EXECUTE privileges on a package, when the user executes the package he or she will be operating under the security domain of the *owner* of the procedure, and not under his or her own defined security domain. In other words, a user who does not have privileges to update employee rows can get this privilege by being authorized to use a procedure that updates employees. The DBA's database security audits will not reveal this update capability.

Assignment of Privileges to Users

Privileges are GRANTed or REVOKEd to individual users. Since all privileges and users are specified at the most atomic level, a database with 10 tables and 100 users would require 4000 specific GRANTs. Fortunately, SQL provides a method for categorizing privileges and users such that the management of security becomes more practical.

Object privileges can be combined into a single GRANT statement. For example, when a table is created, access to the table is limited to the creator of the table. If user CAT creates a table called FOOD, then access to the table could be granted to all users with the statement:

```
GRANT SELECT, INSERT, UPDATE, DELETE on CAT.FOOD to USER1, USER2;
```

Cascading of Privileges

One problematic feature of SQL is the cascading ability of GRANT privileges after they have been granted with the GRANT or ADMIN OPTION. If USER1 has been given a privilege with the GRANT OPTION, that user gains the ability to grant that privilege to any other users.

For example:

DBA: `GRANT ALL on my_table to USER1 with GRANT OPTION.`

USER1 may now distribute this privilege to USER2:

USER2:   `GRANT ALL on my_table to USER1 with GRANT OPTION.`

USER2 may now, in turn, give this privilege to other users, and so on, ad infinitum.

Fortunately, the GRANT OPTION clause does not work with roles. It is not allowed to:

`GRANT MY__ROLE to USER1 with GRANT OPTION.`

Cascading Revokes

Cascading revokes only apply to non-DDL system privileges and object privileges. For example, consider the following:

DBA: `GRANT create table to USER1 with ADMIN OPTION;`

USER1:   `CREATE TABLE user1.my_table;`

USER1:   `GRANT create table to USER2;`

DBA: `REVOKE create table from USER1;`

In this scenario, USER2 continues to have CREATE TABLE privileges. The moral is not to use the ADMIN OPTION.

In all cases *except* system DDL privileges, the initial REVOKE will cascade to all who have been granted the privilege. The best example is a table owner who GRANTs select privileges to USER1 with the GRANT OPTION, which USER1 then GRANTs to friends. When the table owner revokes the select privilege from USER1, all users who received their grant from USER1 will also lose their privilege. A more extreme example would be when the DBA allows anyone to select from a table (GRANT select any table to PUBLIC), and then revokes the privilege (REVOKE select any table from PUBLIC). Any select references to any tables in the entire database will fail, unless other object privileges have been used to grant access.

Scope of GRANT Statements

When using GRANT statements there is a method to negate all security for a specific object. Security can be explicitly turned off for an object by using PUBLIC as the receiver of the grant. For example, to turn off all security for my_table, we could enter:

```
GRANT ALL on my_table to PUBLIC;
```

Security is now effectively turned off for my_table, and restrictions may not be added with the REVOKE command. For example, if USER1 and USER2 are not allowed to delete rows from my_table, we could not enter REVOKE DELETE on my_table to user1. The PUBLIC parameter cannot be negated with REVOKE statements.

Roles and Security

While it may seem verbose to explicitly specify all of the SQL operators on the table, there are methods for grouping a number of privileges into a "role." In this example, a role called CAT_ALL is created:

```
CREATE role CAT_ALL;

GRANT select, update, insert, delete     on CAT.FOOD to CAT_ALL;
```

We can now apply the role CAT_ALL to the CAT.FOOD table with:

```
GRANT CAT_ALL on CAT.FOOD to public;
```

Session-Level Security

Session-level security can be enforced within the database tools as well as within the database. For example, a user may have update authority when accessing the customer data through an online application, but the authority should be rescinded if the user attempts to update customers within SQL*Plus.

Oracle provides the PRODUCT_USER_PROFILE table to enforce tool-level security, and the user may be disabled from updating in SQL*Plus by making an entry into this table. For example, to disable updates for user KNALLY, the DBA could state:

```
INSERT INTO
PRODUCT_USER_PROFILE (product, userid, attribute, char_value)
```

```
        VALUES ("SQL*Plus", "KNALLY", "UPDATE", "DISABLED");
```

User KNALLY could still perform updates within the application, but would be prohibited from updating while in the SQL*Plus tool. At this time, the following values for the attribute column are being used:

```
BEGIN, COPY, DECLARE, DELETE, EDIT, HOST, INSERT, UPDATE
```

To disable unwanted commands for end-users, a wildcard can be used in the attribute column. To disable the DELETE command for all users of SQL*Plus, the DBA could enter:

```
INSERT INTO
PRODUCT_USER_PROFILE (product, userid, attribute, char_value)
    VALUES ("SQL*Plus", "%", "DELETE", "DISABLED");
```

Unfortunately, while this is great for excluding *all* users, it is not possible to alter the tables to allow the DBA staff to have delete authority. The only acceptable value for the char_value column is DISABLED.

Changing Roles

Roles may be assigned to sessions as well as to individual users. Assume that we want a user to have the role of customer_clerk, but only when the user is within the control of the customer service application. When the user invokes the main menu for the customer service application, the application could disable all previous roles for this user and force the user into the customer_service role:

```
SET ROLE none;
SET ROLE customer_service;
```

Of course, the SET ROLE command cannot authorize a user for a role that he or she has not been granted privileges to use.

Row-Level, Column-Level Security

By using roles with relational views, it is possible to restrict SELECT access to individual rows and columns within a relational table. For example, assume that a person table contains confidential columns such as SALARY. Also assume that this table contains a TYPE column with the values EXEMPT, NON_EXEMPT, and MANAGER. We want our end-users to have access to the person table, but we wish to restrict access to the SALARY columns and the

MANAGER rows. A relational view could be created to isolate the columns and rows that are allowed:

```
CREATE VIEW USER_VIEW as
SELECT name, address, phone, history, comments, type
FROM person
where type <> "MANAGER" ;
```

We may now grant access to this view to anyone:

```
grant select on USER_VIEW to PUBLIC;
```

Oracle also allows GRANT statements to specify individual table columns, but column-level security can only be used with UPDATE, INSERT, or REFERENCES GRANTs. The columns can be specified in the GRANT statement with the columns enclosed in parentheses:

```
GRANT update (salary, date_of_birth) on EMPLOYEE_TABLE to JONES;
```

If we wish to change the GRANT to specify only the SALARY column, Oracle requires that all privileges be revoked, and the individual columns re-added. For example, to revoke update privileges for the SALARY column, we would need to enter:

```
REVOKE update on EMPLOYEE from JONES;
GRANT update (date_of_birth) on EMPLOYEE_TABLE to JONES;
```

GRANTs and Table Synonyms

In a distributed database environment, synonyms are often granted to tables in order to avoid the use of the "location qualifier" in the table name. For example:

```
CREATE public synonym EMPLOYEE for emp.employee@london;
```

Synonyms are also commonly used to "hide" the table owner name, so that the SQL does not always have to specify the table owner. For example:

```
CREATE public synonym CUSTOMER for custowner.customer;
```

A grant to a table automatically allows access to the table by its synonym and also allows grants to be specified for a table according to the synonym. In the following example, the user MYUSER is granted access to the synonym "emp" for access to the table cat.emp. This GRANT will remain in effect even if the synonym "emp" is dropped.

```
create synonym emp for cat.emp;

grant select on emp to MYUSER;

drop synonym emp;
```

GRANTs and Distributed Databases

When a connection is made to a remote database, the security in the remote database is applied to the transaction. In other words, the security is regulated at the destination, and the privileges at the source are irrelevant. Assume that USER1 has:

```
GRANT select any table TO user1; on database1.
```

If USER1 attaches to a remote database, say database2, this grant has no authority on tables that reside in database2.

For distributed queries, the user must have proper privileges on both of the databases involved in the update. For example, a user in London may join two tables from New York and California:

```
CREATE synonym ny_customers for customer@ny;
CREATE synonym ca_customers for customer@ca;
select * from ny_customers, ca_customers;
```

At the time of the select, the user must have SELECT privileges against both of the customer tables or the entire transaction will fail.

Role Strategy

Roles can be organized in a hierarchy, and different users can be assigned roles according to their individual needs. New roles can be created from existing roles, from system privileges, from object privileges, or from any combination thereof (Figure 13.7).

Data-Specific vs. Application-Specific Security

Application-specific security can give much tighter control than data-specific security. The DBA can authorize the application owners with the proper privi-

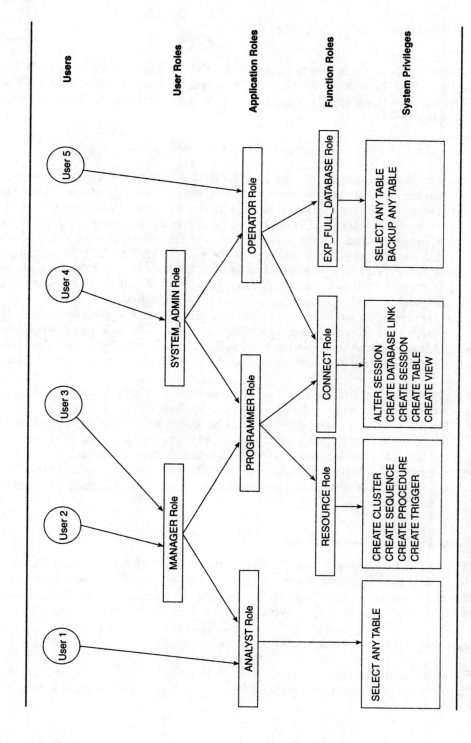

Figure 13.7   Sample role assignment strategy for system privileges.

leges to perform their functions, and all of the end-users will not have any explicit GRANTs against the database. Instead, they are granted EXECUTE on the procedure; the only way that a user will be able to access the data is through the procedure:

```
GRANT EXECUTE on human_resources to JONES;
```

For specific applications, the user ID that serves as the table owner (e.g., custowner.customer) can be used as the creator of the procedures. Since the table owner automatically received *all* authority against the tables the owner creates, no DBA intervention is necessary. Since the procedures govern what the end-user can and cannot perform, the only administration required would be to bundle the procedures into a package and GRANT EXECUTE privileges to the appropriate end-users. There is no need to create huge GRANT scripts for each and every end-user, and there is no possibility of end-users doing an end-run and accessing the tables from within other packages.

Of course, this would require coordination with the application programmers, such that they encapsulate all SQL into functions and procedures. Any SQL that is inserted directly into the application code will fail at run time. The benefits of consciously encapsulating code into functions and procedures is great:

- Reusability—Functions and procedures can be written independently and reused in a variety of places within the application.
- Isolation—Since each procedure can be tested as a finite unit, application changes are simplified, and the programmers can be assured that unintended side effects are not introduced into their environment.
- Security—Security is maintained directly by the procedures and functions, and the data is protected from being altered by anyone outside the domain of the procedures.

Security Recommendations

If the goal of database security is to maintain tight control over willful or accidental corruption of data, then a method must be devised to insure that sensitive operations are controlled without making the security scheme cumbersome or obtrusive to the end-user. While features such as application-specific security have very compelling benefits, the DBA staff must deal with legacy systems that do not use functions, procedures, and packages.

Existing Applications Existing security must be cleaned up and enhanced to simplify the ongoing maintenance of security. A good approach will take the existing applications, one at a time, and perform the following steps. Assume in this example that the existing security is adequate for the protection of confidential information and that any holes in the SQL security are taken care of within the application code.

1. Investigate the current security mechanism. Look at all grants for all application tables, cross-referencing the grants with the users. Check for and remove all GRANT OPTION and WITH ADMIN OPTIONs.
2. Create a role (or roles) to match each category of security. Whenever feasible, role names will begin with the table owner name and end with a function name (e.g., benefits_maintenance, benefits_query).
3. Grant access to the roles for each user based upon the cross-reference table from step 1.
4. Drop all "direct' grants to tables with the exception of the role GRANTs, notify the end-users, and carefully watch for security problems.

New Applications Whenever possible, fine-grained security should be bypassed. If a system does not contain confidential information, then we could GRANT SELECT to table_name to PUBLIC, and only explicitly restrict the INSERT and UPDATE operations. In the same spirit, it is not a good idea to implement column-level GRANTs unless certain columns contain confidential information. For complete control of security, never use the GRANT OPTION or the WITH ADMIN OPTION.

Actively encourage the use of procedures and packages. In addition to making the code easier to maintain, the security benefits are obvious. Also encourage the use of "views," since they can encapsulate SQL into logical pieces, simplifying security administration.

For all new systems, a task should be added to the project called "role-based security." This task will be fulfilled by meeting with the developers and gathering the information required to create roles that will meet their functional requirements. Individual roles will be identified and incorporated into a hierarchical structure. Detailed roles (e.g., benefits_query) will be organized as subsets of general roles (e.g., benefits_manager). Once created, these roles will be attached to the end-users with existing methods.

A Role-Based Security Framework for Distributed Databases

Because SQL security for applications is controlled at the table level, and because an application may consist of hundreds of tables, finding a way to group tables into functional categories can greatly simplify security administration.

Some distributed enterprises have large replicated applications where each application has more than 50 tables. When this is multiplied by 50 horizontal partitions, there are more than 2500 distinct tables. Clearly, maintaining security on 2500 tables is a messy chore.

Functional security can be implemented with either role-based or procedure-based categorization of privileges. For existing systems, role-based security can be implemented without disturbing existing applications.

There are two general types of roles that are used to simplify administration:

- Administrative roles—Roles are created for all administrative personnel including DBA, OPERATOR, DEVELOPER, and SUPPORT.
- Applications roles—Roles are created for each "schema" owner, and special "read-only" roles are created for linking between distributed databases. A schema owner is the same as a table owner, and GRANTs can be created that include only tables that begin with the schema name.

Administrative Roles Administrative roles will address system privileges that are granted to DBAs, operators, and programmers to allow them to perform their functions.

The *database administrator role* will receive all of the standard system privileges; the standard DBA roles as defined by Oracle would be used.

The *operator role* will receive the privileges necessary to perform database compression scripts:

RESOURCE
CONNECT
IMP_FULL_TABLE
EXP_FULL_TABLE
UNLIMITED TABLESPACE

The *developer role* will only exist in test environments and will consist of system privileges that are required to perform application development in a particular area. A developer cannot be granted DROP ANY TABLE, since he or she would then have the ability to drop tables belonging to another application. For example, the table owner BENEFITS would own full privileges on all objects created by BENEFITS, but could not drop tables belonging to SALES. To create a developer role for BENEFITS, the following SQL could be issued to allow full access to any objects WITHIN THE SPECIFIED SCHEMA with:

```
GRANT schema_privilege ON schema TO schema_DEVELOPER:
```

Within their schema, developers would require the following privileges:

operators: create, drop, alter

schema objects: cluster, table, index, sequence, procedure, synonym, tablespace, trigger, view

system privileges: unlimited tablespace, connect, resource

Some developers might require more than one copy of their databases, in which case schemas could be created for BENEFITS1, BENEFITS2, and so on.

The *support role* would grant some system privileges to support personnel. They need the authority to address issues with some DBA authority, but without privileges to tablespace, rollback_segment, or system. Valid privileges might include:

```
CREATE | ALTER | DROP any    table, index, procedure,
profile, sequence, snapshot, synonym, table, trigger, view
(force transaction), (alter user)
```

Application Roles   Each application would get its own role that encompassed all of the valid authorities for the end-users. This role would be similar to the authority of the table owner. Instead of granting benefits to PUBLIC, the tables would be granted to the role associated with the application. Note that roles, just like users, may be assigned passwords.

```
create role BENEFITS_ROLE         identified by xxx;
create role BENEFITS_ROLE_SELECT  identified by xxx;

grant all     on BENEFITS.table1, BENEFITS.table2
      to BENEFITS_ROLE;

grant select on BENEFITS.table1, BENEFITS.table2
      to BENEFITS_ROLE_SELECT;

grant BENEFITS_ROLE to OPS$username;
```

For the purposes of database links, select-only versions of roles could be created. Such read-only versions of the roles would have all of the same tables as the regular roles. If a user required access to an entire system, the roles could be combined:

```
create role BENDB_ROLE         identified by xxx;
create role BENDB_ROLE_SELECT  identified by xxx;
```

```
grant BENEFITS_ROLE_SELECT, S125_ROLE_SELECT to MAIN_ROLE;
```

We are now free to specify bendb_ROLE_SELECT on any target system that requires a database link:

```
create public database link BENDB
       connect to bendb_ROLE_SELECT identified by 't:host:db';
```

Migration of Table-Level Security to Role-Level Security

Once the appropriate roles have been identified and the privileges have been decided, a plan must be devised to replace existing table-level security. This must be done unobtrusively so that the end-users and developers are not aware that a change has occurred. A complete plan for replacing table-based security with role-based security would include the following steps:

1. Make changes to databases, one at a time.
2. Review the existing security for each database, identifying all table GRANTs:

```
select distinct table_name , privilege from dba_tab_privs;
```

3. Also assign all table-level grants to a new role:

```
create role SCHEMA_ROLE   identified by xxx;
create role SCHEMA_ROLE_SELECT identified by xxx;

grant all      on table1, table2 to SCHEMA_ROLE;
grant select  on table1, table2 to SCHEMA_ROLE_SELECT;
```

4. Interrogate all end-users to get their existing grants (if any):

```
select * from dba_tab_privs where grantee like 'OPS$';
```

5. Create and assign the role to all appropriate users:

```
create role schema_ROLE identified by xxx;
grant xxx on table1, table2, to schema_ROLE;
```

6. Revoke the existing grants (except the role) from users:

```
revoke select, update on table1, table2 from ops$username;
```

7. Wait one week; if there are no reported problems, revoke all grants to tables (except the role):

```
revoke select, update on table1, table2 from public;
```

8. Locate all databases that access this database, and alter their database links to specify the read-only role instead of a user ID:

```
alter database link SCHEMA
        connect to SCHEMA_ROLE_SELECT identified by xxx;
```

Once an existing "schema" table owner has been located, the following Oracle SQL script can be used to generate all of the SQL necessary to move from table-based security to role-based security.

ROLE.SQL **To execute, enter from SQL*Plus: start ROLE tableownername**

```
set heading off;
set pause off;
set echo off;
set termout off;
—set termout on;
set linesize 75;
set showmode off;
set feedback off;
set newpage 1;
set verify off;
set pagesize 9999;

spool /tmp/&1.role.sql

select '— Create the two new roles. ' from dual;
select 'create role &1._role_manager  identified by xxx;' from dual;
select 'create role &1._role_ROLE_SELECT  identified by xxx;' from dual;


select '— If there were select privileges, '   from dual;
select '— grant these selects to _role_ROLE_SELECT. ' from dual;

select distinct 'grant SELECT',
        ' on ',
        substr(table_name,1,20),
        ' to ',
        '&1._role_ROLE_SELECT;'
```

```
from dba_tab_privs where
owner = '&1'
and privilege = 'SELECT';

select '- If there were non-select privileges, '    from dual;
select '- grant these privileges to _role_ROLE_SELECT. ' from dual;

select distinct 'grant ',
          substr(privilege,1,12),
          ' on ',
          substr(table_name,1,20),
          ' to ',
          '&1._role_manager;'
from dba_tab_privs where
owner = '&1'
and privilege <> 'SELECT';

select '- If the users were granted to specific privileges, ' from dual;
select '- grant these privileges to the new role. '      from dual;
select distinct 'grant ',
          substr(privilege,1,12),
          ' on ',
          substr(table_name,1,20),
          ' to ',
          '&1._role_manager;'
from dba_tab_privs where
owner = '&1' and grantee <> 'PUBLIC';

select '- If the privilege was granted to PUBLIC, '       from dual;
select '- grant the privilege to all system users.'       from dual;

select distinct 'grant ',
          '&1._role_manager',
          ' to ',
          substr(username,1,12),
          ';'
from dba_ROLEs;

select '- If the privilege was granted to specific users, ' from dual;
select '- grant the role to those users '          from dual;

select distinct 'grant ',
          '&1._role_manager',
          ' to ',
          substr(grantee,1,12),
          ';'
```

```
from dba_tab_privs where
owner = '&1' and grantee <> 'PUBLIC';

select '— Revoke all table-level privileges for the owner. ' from dual;

select distinct 'revoke ',
        substr(privilege,1,12),
        ' on ',
        substr(table_name,1,20),
        ' from ',
        substr(grantee,1,12),
        ';'
from dba_tab_privs where
owner = '&1';
spool off;

set termout on;
prompt Roles for &1 has been written to /tmp/&1.role.sql
```

Auditing SQL Security in a Distributed Environment

The basic tenet of the security function is to create a framework to manage security in a simple fashion. To achieve simplicity, the following guidelines apply:

- Prohibit the use of GRANT .... WITH ADMIN OPTION.
- Prohibit the use of GRANT ... WITH GRANT OPTION.
- Prohibit any object grants to PUBLIC.
- Require the use of role-based security.
- Encourage the use of function-procedure-package security.

To audit a distributed database, each database must be checked for "unusual" grants and situations in which a user has received privileges (either system or object privileges) from an unauthorized source. As each database is visited, an audit file will be produced for the DBA to review. The database dictionary can be interrogated to show the following security breaches:

- Any system privileges that are granted WITH ADMIN OPTION (DBA_SYS_PRIVS table)—Anyone who receives a system privilege WITH ADMIN OPTION can grant his or her privileges to others.
- Any non-DBA roles granted WITH ADMIN OPTION (ROLE_SYS_PRIVS table)—Any system privileges and roles can be granted WITH ADMIN OPTION, and it is important to insure that there are not any roles floating around that could be granted to others.

- End-users with table privileges that are grantable to others (DBA_TAB_PRIVS table)—Just as system privileges and roles can be granted WITH ADMIN OPTION, object privileges can be granted WITH GRANT OPTION. It is important that nobody (except the table's owner, who gets it by default) may grant table privileges to others.
- End-users who have received a grantable privilege (ALL_TAB_PRIVS_RECD table)—Anyone who receives a system or object privilege from anyone except SYS will be reported in this list. The person who granted the privilege will appear in the GRANTOR column, and it should correspond to a GRANTEE name in DBA_TAB_PRIVS and/or DBA_SYS_PRIVS. If the offending GRANTEE has his or her ADMIN or GRANT option revoked (e.g., REVOKE privilege from GRANTEE CASCADE CONSTRAINTS), the revoke should cascade into ALL_TAB_PRIVS_RECD, and these entries will disappear.
- End-users with roles (other than resource/connect) (DBA_ROLE_PRIVS table)—This will list any roles other than resource, and connect for all users except OPS$ORACLE, SYS, SYSTEM, and DBA. This will show anyone who has wrongly acquired DBA privileges.
- End-users with system privileges (DBA_SYS_PRIVS table)—This shows all users who have system privileges. In some cases it is okay for a user to have UNLIMITED TABLESPACE, but other privileges such as DROP TABLE should be carefully reviewed.

The script to check an Oracle database for unusual security might look like this:

```
*************************************************************************
prompt Searching &1 for system privileges granted WITH ADMIN OPTION...
select * from
dba_sys_privs
where
admin_option = 'YES'
and
grantee not in ('DBA','SYSTEM','SYS','OPS$ORACLE');
*************************************************************************
prompt Searching &1 for non-dba roles granted WITH ADMIN OPTION...
select * from
role_sys_privs
where
role <> 'DBA'
and
admin_option = 'YES';
*************************************************************************
```

```
prompt Searching &1 for table privileges that are grantable to others...
select substr(grantee,1,12), substr(table_name,1,20),
    substr(privilege,1,10), substr(grantable,1,3)
from
dba_tab_privs
where
grantable = 'YES'
and
owner not in ('SYS','SYSTEM','GL','APPLSYS','BOM','ENG',
'PO','AP','PER','WIP','LOGGER');
*********************************************************************
prompt Searching &1 for users who have received a grantable privilege...
select * from
all_tab_privs_recd
Where grantable = 'YES'
and
owner not in ('SYS','SYSTEM');
*********************************************************************
prompt Searching &1 for folks with roles (other than resource/connect)...
select * from
dba_role_privs
where
granted_role not in ('RESOURCE','CONNECT')
and
grantee not in ('OPS$ORACLE','OPS$ADMOPR','DBA','SYS','SYSTEM');
*********************************************************************
prompt Searching &1 for folks with system privileges...
select * from
dba_sys_privs
where
privilege <> 'UNLIMITED TABLESPACE' and
grantee not in
('COMMON','OPS$ORACLE','RESOURCE','CONNECT','OPS$TPSOPR',
'IMP_FULL_DATABASE','DBA','SYS','SYSTEM','OPS$ADMOPR',
'EXP_FULL_DATABASE');
*********************************************************************
```

Propagating Security to Many Distributed Databases

When an enterprise consists of more than 50 databases, the propagation of
database code and audits can become a major headache. The following script
can be used in a UNIX environment to read a list of remote processors and
access each one, finding all databases on the processor, and performing the
same function on each database. The script has been used to run SQL security

audits on more than 70 distributed databases, all from a single task on the master processor.

An audit of SQL security must sweep each processor, interrogating the system to get a list of all databases on the processor. Once found, the audit script will be run against the database and the results will be piped into an audit file.

```
for HOST1 in 'cat hostlist| cut -d":" -f1'
do
    echo " "
    echo "════════════════"
    echo "HOST= $HOST1"
    echo "════════════════"
    # Now, get all of the database names on each box...
    for DB in 'remsh $HOST1 -n "cat /etc/oratab | grep /usr/oracle:Y|cut
-d":" -f1"'
        do
            echo " "
            echo " --------------"
            echo " DB= $DB"
            echo " --------------"

            #Now, we log into the database
            TWO_TASK=t:$HOST1:$DB
            export TWO_TASK DB
            su oracle -c "sqlplus /<<!
            spool $DB.audit
            start audit $DB
            exit;
            !"

        done

done
```

REFERENCES

Baum, D. 1993. Middleware: unearthing the software treasure trove. *InfoWorld*, March.

Bobak, A. 1993. *Distributed and multidatabase systems*. Bantam Books.

Goulde, M. 1992. Open systems: analysis, issues and opinions. *Open Information Systems*, December.

Performance and Tuning for Distributed Databases

14.1 INTRODUCTION

Performance and tuning of database systems is not trivial, especially in distributed database environments, because of the many components within the database software that can contribute to the overall performance. The number of concurrent users, the availability of space within the buffer and lock pools, and the balancing of application access all can have an effect on the performance of a database. In the case of distributed databases, the database administrator (DBA) must now look at more than the individual databases. Performance problems can be introduced by PC hardware, LAN and network bottlenecks, router overloads, and a plethora of other sources. Only by examining each component individually can a DBA reach an understanding of the overall performance of a distributed database.

There is a methodology that most DBAs use when tuning distributed database systems:

1. *Tune SQL statements and applications*—By starting at the application level, the DBA can insure that all access requests follow proper protocols and conventions. Since any query in SQL can be written in many forms, the DBA reviews all SQL statements within applications (with the EXPLAIN and the PLAN table), and insures that distributed requests properly connect to the remote databases.

2. *Tune memory allocation*—Efficient memory utilization within each remote database depends upon the characteristics of the application, which must be understood in order to allocate the buffer storage and lock pool storage for maximum performance.

3. *Tune system I/O*—This step involves table placement on the disk devices, table "striping" (spanning a table over several physical files), and the proper creation and maintenance of indexes to insure maximum performance.

14.2   MULTITASKING AND MULTITHREADING

The widespread acceptance of distributed processing and multitasking operating systems has heralded a new mode of designing and implementing business systems. Instead of the traditional "linear" design of systems, tomorrow's system will incorporate massively parallel computers simultaneously processing information. Indeed, the entire definition of data processing is changing. The corporate data resource has been expanded to include all sources of information, not just databases. Corporate information lies within e-mail, Lotus Notes, and many other nontraditional sources. Many companies are still collecting this information without fully exploiting its value. Multiprocessing is an ideal technique for searching these huge amounts of free-form corporate information.

First, a distinction needs to be made between multitasking and multiprocessing. *Multitasking* refers to the ability of a software package to manage multiple "concurrent" processes, thereby allowing simultaneous processing. OS/2 and Windows-NT are examples of this technology, but multitasking is found within all midrange and mainframe databases. *Multiprocessing* refers to the use of multiple CPUs within a distributed environment, where a master program directs parallel operations against numerous machines. There are two areas of multiprocessing: at the hardware level where arrays of CPUs are offered, and at the software level, where a single CPU can be partitioned into separate "logical" processors. The Prism software on the IBM mainframe environment is an example of this technology.

In any case, programming for multiprocessors is quite different from linear programming. Multiprocessing programming falls into two areas: data parallel and control parallel programming. In data parallel programming, the data is partitioned into discrete pieces and the same program is run in parallel against each piece. In control parallel programming, independent functions are identified and independent CPUs are used to simultaneously solve the independent functions (Figure 14.1).

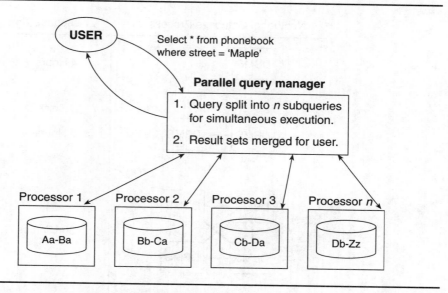

Figure 14.1   Multiprocessing with text searching.

Parallelism refers to the ability of a computer system to perform processing on many data sources at the same instant in time. Whereas many of the traditional database applications have been linear in nature, today's systems have many opportunities for parallel processing.

Parallelism is especially important to scientific applications that could benefit from having hundreds or even thousands of processors working together to solve a problem. But the same concept of parallelism applies to very large business databases. If a query can be split into subqueries and each subquery assigned to a processor, then the response time for the query can be reduced by a factor of thousands (Figure 14.2).

A review of the past 30 years makes it clear that there has been tremendous improvement in the speed of processors, while at the same time the prices of processors have steadily declined. However, this trend cannot continue forever. The physical nature of silicon processors has been pushed to its limit, and is now reaching a point of diminishing return. In order to continue to enjoy increases in performance, we need either to replace silicon as a medium or to devise ways to exploit parallelism in processing.

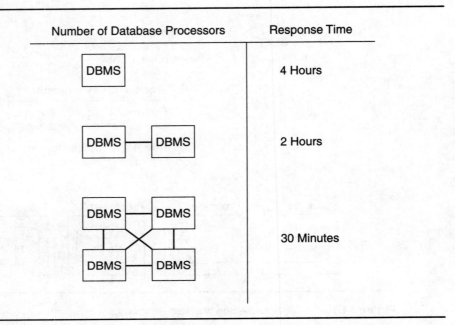

Number of Database Processors	Response Time
DBMS	4 Hours
DBMS — DBMS	2 Hours
DBMS — DBMS / DBMS — DBMS	30 Minutes

Figure 14.2   Performance improvements with multiple processors.

Parallelism is an issue of scale. Where a linear process may solve a problem in one hour, a parallel system with 60 processors should be able to solve the problem in one minute. However, only in situations where parallel processing is appropriate can the speed be improved, and traditional linear systems (where one process may not begin until the preceding one ends) will not benefit from parallel processing.

There are other facets to parallel processing. A query against a very large database can be dramatically improved if the data is partitioned. For example, if a query against a text database takes one minute to scan a terabyte, then partitioning the data and processing it in 60 pieces will result in a retrieval time of one second. There is also the issue of balancing the CPU processing with the I/O processing. In a traditional data processing environment, the systems are not computationally intensive, and most of the elapsed time is spent waiting on I/O. However, this does not automatically exclude business systems from taking advantage of multiprocessing.

There is a continuum of processing architecture for parallel processing. On one end of the spectrum we find a few powerful CPUs that are loosely connected, while on the other end we see a large number of small processors that are tightly coupled.

Parallelism can easily be identified in a distributed database environment. For the database administrator, routine maintenance tasks such as export/ import operations can be run in parallel, reducing the overall time required for system maintenance.

In an open systems environment, parallelism may be easily simulated by using a remote mount facility. With a remote mount, a data file may be directly addressed from another processor even though the data file physically resides on another machine. This can be an especially useful technique for speeding up table replication to remote sites (Figure 14.3).

To speed up the replication of two tables, a UNIX shell script directs CPU A to begin the copy of table A as a background task. The script then directs CPU B to issue a remote mount to table B, making table B addressable as if it were a local disk to CPU B. The script then issues a copy of table B, and the tables are copied simultaneously, reducing the overall processing time (Figure 14.4).

Of course, the overall elapsed time will be somewhat more than half of the time required for a linear process because the remote mount still requires the database on CPU A the manage the I/O against table B. The benefit lies in having the second processor, CPU B, handle all of the processing for the unload of table B.

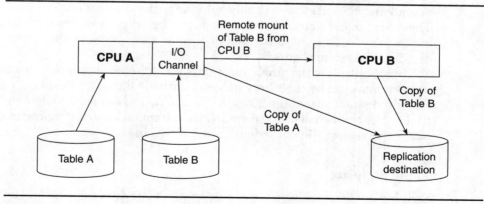

Figure 14.3   Parallelism in open systems.

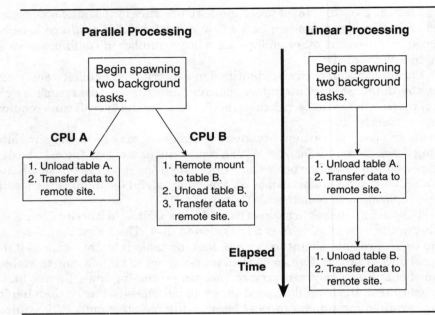

Figure 14.4 Comparison of parallel and linear processing.

14.3 I/O-BASED TUNING

In a distributed database environment it is important to understand that the overall distributed system is only going to perform as well as the weakest link. Therefore, most distributed database tuning treats each remote node as an independent database, individually tuning each one and thereby improving distributed system requests.

Input/output is the single most important factor in database tuning. Business systems are by their very nature relatively light on processing and heavy on their demands from the disks that make up the database. There are several tricks that can be used to reduce I/O time from disk, including cache memory, buffer expansion, file placement, and file striping.

Table Striping

Striping involves taking a very large or very busy data table and distributing it across many disks. When a performance problem occurs on a regular basis, it is most often the result of the disks waiting on I/O; by distributing the file across many physical devices, one can improve the overall system response time. Disk striping is generally done for tables that are larger than the size of a disk device, but striping can be equally effective for small, heavily accessed tables (Figure 14.5).

Note that the data file appears to the database management system as a single logical file and that there will be no I/O problem from within the database. As rows are requested from the table, the SQL I/O module will request physical data blocks from the disk, one at a time, unaware that the logically continuous table is actually composed of many physical data files.

An example of DMCL file allocation with IDMS might look like this:

```
ADD FILE BIG-FILE1
    ASSIGN TO FILE1
    DEVICE IS 3380.

ADD FILE BIG-FILE2
    ASSIGN TO FILE2
    DEVICE IS 3380.
```

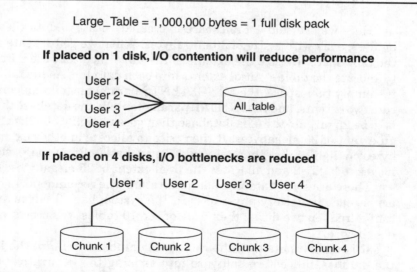

Large_Table = 1,000,000 bytes = 1 full disk pack

If placed on 1 disk, I/O contention will reduce performance

User 1
User 2
User 3
User 4
All_table

If placed on 4 disks, I/O bottlenecks are reduced

User 1   User 2   User 3   User 4

Chunk 1   Chunk 2   Chunk 3   Chunk 4

Figure 14.5   Table striping (splitting a tablespace into many physical files on many disks).

```
ADD AREA CUSTOMER-AREA
    PAGE RANGE IS 1    TO 1000 WITHIN FILE BIG-FILE1.
    PAGE RANGE IS 1001 TO 2000 WITHIN FILE BIG-FILE1.
```

The JCL that describes the files to the operating system would look like:

```
//FILE1 DD DSN-IDMS.BIGFILE1,DISP=SHR,VOL=SER=PACK01
//FILE2 DD DSN-IDMS.BIGFILE2,DISP=SHR,VOL=SER=PACK02
```

The device media control language (DMCL) insures that these data files map to a logically contiguous area within the database engine.

In a relational database, striping is done in a similar fashion. Consider the following Oracle syntax:

```
CREATE TABLESPACE TS1
    DATA FILE "/usr/disk1/bigfile1.dbf" SIZE=30M
    DATA FILE "/usr/disk2/bigfile2.dbf" SIZE=30M

CREATE TABLE BIG_TABLE (
    big_field1  char(8)
    big_field2  varchar(2000))
TABLESPACE TS1
(INITIAL 25M NEXT 1M MINEXTENTS 2 PCTINCREASE 0);
```

Here we see that a tablespace is created with two data files, bigfile1 and bigfile2, each with a size of 30 megabytes. When we go to create a table within the tablespace, we size the extents of the table such that the database is forced to allocate the table's initial extents into each data file. As the table is created in the empty tablespace, the MINEXTENTS parameter tells the database to allocate two extents, and the INITIAL parameter tells the database that each extent is to be 25 megabytes. The database then goes to bigfile1 on disk1 and allocates an extent of 25 megabytes. It then tries to allocate another extent of 25 megabytes on bigfile1, but there are only 5 megabytes of free space, so the database moves to bigfile2 and allocates the final extent of 25 megabytes (Figure 14.6).

There are some database administrators who recommend striping all tables across each and every physical disk. If a system has 10 tables and the CPU is configured for two disks, then each of the 10 tables would be striped into each disk device.

It is unfortunate that the relational databases require the DBA to "trick" the database allocation software into striping the files rather than allowing direct control over the file placement process. This lack of control can be a real problem when tables are "compressed."

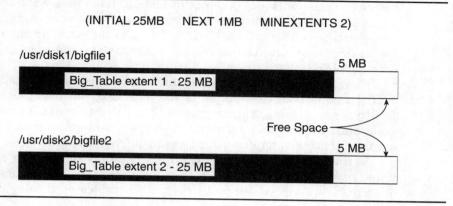

(INITIAL 25MB   NEXT 1MB   MINEXTENTS 2)

Figure 14.6   Table allocation within a striped tablespace. When the initial extents fill, future extents will be 1 megabyte each, and will fill the remaining free space at the end of the files. There will be space for 10 new extents.

There are several ways to insure that the tables are striped across the disks. Many databases with a sophisticated data dictionary allow queries that reveal the striping of the files. In Oracle, the following script is used:

```
SELECT DISTINCT file_name,
FROM    dba_data_files a, dba_extents b
WHERE
        a.file_id = b.file_id
AND
        segment_name = striped_table_name;
```

Other databases offer utilities that report on the physical file utilization for a specific table or database record type.

Data Fragmentation

Fragmentation occurs when the preallocated space for a data area or table has been exceeded. In relational databases, tables are allocated into tablespaces, and each table is given several storage parameters. The storage parameters include INITIAL, NEXT, and PCTINCREASE.

As tables grow, they automatically allocate "extents," or extra storage, at a size determined by the NEXT parameter. Most databases allow for 99 extents before the table fills and becomes locked up. Even before the data table fills, performance against the table will degrade as the number of extents increases. An operating system such as UNIX is forced to chase the "inode" chains to scan the entire table, and the increased I/O translates into performance delays (Figure 14.7).

There are several SQL queries that can be used to detect table fragmentation. These queries are unique to the database, but most databases have a facility for measuring table fragmentation. The fragmentation reports are generally incorporated into a periodic report, and those files that are fragmented are then scheduled for export/imports to unfragment the tables.

As the initial extents of a table fill, the database manager allocates additional spaces on the disk to allow the table to expand. These fragments eventually create a performance problem, and the tables need to be compressed to remove these extents:

1. Determine the level of fragmentation and determine the new table sizes.
2. Offload all table data using an export utility.
3. Drop the old tables.
4. Reallocate the new tables at their new sizes.
5. Import the data to repopulate the tables.

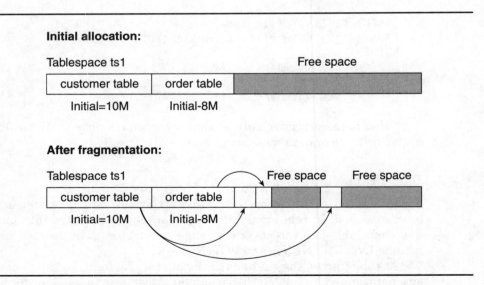

Figure 14.7   Space allocation into a tablespace.

Disk Issues Involving Other System Resources

There are other high-impact resources on most databases, such as recovery logs and transaction logs. Most systems have at least two recovery logs, and it is a good idea to locate these logs on different disk devices, and on devices that do not have any other high-impact data tables.

Memory-Based Tuning

Buffer Tuning As database blocks are retrieved from disk into the database, they are stored in RAM memory in an area called a *buffer*. The record remains in the buffer until it is overwritten by another database request. At read time, the database first checks to see if the data already resides in the buffer before incurring the overhead of a disk I/O (Figure 14.8).

The size of the buffer is determined by the database administrator. For some databases, separate buffers may be created for different tables.

The method for maximizing the use of buffers is to perform a check on the "buffer hit ratio"—the ratio of logical requests to physical disk reads. A logical

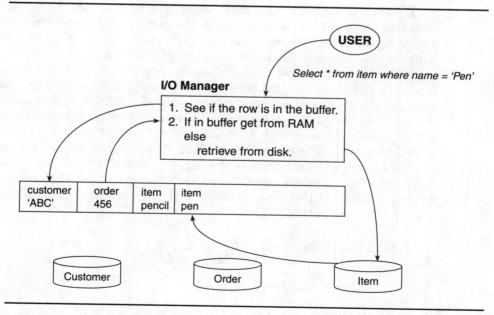

Figure 14.8   Buffer utilization.

read is a request from a program for a record, while a physical read is real I/O against a database. There is not always a one-to-one correspondence between logical and physical reads, since some records may have been fetched by a previous task, and still reside in the buffer. In other words, the buffer hit ratio is the probability of finding the desired record in the memory buffer.

$$\text{Hit Ratio} = \frac{\text{Logical Reads} - \text{Physical Reads}}{\text{Logical Reads}}$$

While some of the mainframe databases allow for individual buffers for each record type, midrange databases such as Oracle provide only one database-wide buffer for all of the database I/O. In general, the buffer hit ratio is a function of the application and of the size of the buffer pool. For example, an application with a very large customer table is not likely to benefit from an increase in buffers, since the I/O is widely distributed across the tables. However, smaller applications will often see an improvement as the buffer size is increased, as this increases the probability that frequently requested data remains in the buffer. For example, the high level nodes of an index are generally used by all applications, and response time can be improved if these blocks can be kept in the buffers at all times.

Databases like IDMS that allow segmented buffer pools can be configured such that small indexes will be kept in the buffer at all times. This is done by allocating an index to a separate area, and assigning the area to a separate buffer in the Device Media Control Language (DMCL).

If the hit ratio is less than 70 percent (e.g., two-thirds of data requests require a physical disk I/O), then you may want to increase the number of blocks in the buffer. In network databases such as IDMS, this is achieved by changing the DMCL to specify additional storage for the offending record type. In relational databases such as Oracle, a single buffer pool exists and is controlled by a parameter called DB_BLOCK_BUFFERS in the init.ora process.

Most databases provide ways to calculate the buffer hit ratios. Oracle uses a system table called sys.x$kcbrbh to track buffer hits. An SQL query can be formulated against this table to create a chart showing the size of the buffer pool and the expected buffer hits:

```
SELECT 250*TRUNC(indx/250)+1
       !!' to '!!250*(TRUNC(indx/250)+1)
       "interval",
       SUM(count) "Cache Hits"
FROM sys.x$kcbrbh
GROUP BY TRUNC(indx/250);
```

This SQL creates a result that shows the range of additional buffer blocks that may be added to the cache and the expected increase in cache hits:

Interval	Cache hits
1 to 250	9800
250 to 500	5023
501 to 750	823
751 to 1000	93

Here we see that we could expect an increase of 9800 hits by adding another 250 blocks to the DB_BLOCK_BUFFERS. As the number of buffer blocks increases, we see that the incremental benefit decreases. Additional buffer blocks increase the amount of required RAM memory for the database, and it is not always possible to "hog" all of the memory on a processor for the database management system. Therefore, the DBA will carefully review the buffer hits and determine an optimal amount of buffer blocks.

For more sophisticated databases, one can control not only the number of buffer blocks but also the block size for each buffer. For example, on an IBM mainframe, we might want to make the buffer blocks very large so that we can minimize I/O contention. An I/O for 32,000 bytes does not cost much more than an I/O for 12,000 bytes, and the database designer may choose to make the buffer blocks large to minimize I/O if the application "clusters" records on a database page. If a customer record is only 100 bytes, we will not gain by retrieving 32,000 bytes to get the 100 bytes that we need, but if we cluster the orders physically near the customer (e.g., on the same database page), and if I/O usually proceeds from customer to order, then we will not need further I/O to retrieve orders for the customer, since they will already reside in the initial read of 32,000 bytes (Figure 14.9).

Memory Caching When I/O contention becomes a performance problem, there are alternatives to disk striping. It is possible to make very small and high-impact data tables reside in RAM memory. The access time against RAM is 10,000 times faster than disk I/O, and this solution can often make a huge performance difference. There are two approaches to caching, the process of loading data from disk onto RAM. The first is a hardware solution that uses extra RAM memory to hold the data table (table caching), while the second approach uses software mechanisms to reserve buffer memory for the exclusive use of the data table. While not all databases support this feature, some allow the memory buffer to be "fenced" or partitioned for the exclusive use of specific tables.

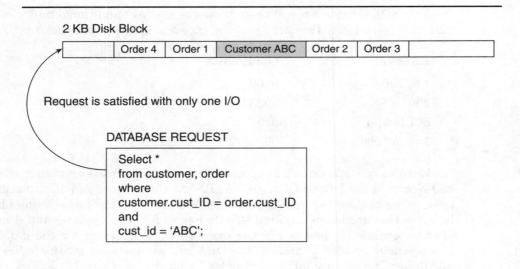

2 KB Disk Block

| | Order 4 | Order 1 | Customer ABC | Order 2 | Order 3 | |

Request is satisfied with only one I/O

DATABASE REQUEST

Select *
from customer, order
where
customer.cust_ID = order.cust_ID
and
cust_id = 'ABC';

Figure 14.9   Table clustering can reduce I/O (assume normal retrieval is from customer to order).

System-Based Tuning

Creating Batch-Window Instances   In some cases, widely differing types of systems may access the same tables. An excellent example of this scenario would be a banking application that processes fast, online transactions during the day, and is updated with long-running background tasks in the evening.

There is a fundamental difference between the database resources required for transaction processing and "batch" processing. Online transactions are usually small, and require few resources from the database lock manager. Batch processes are generally lock intensive, and sweep a table in a linear fashion.

Within a database there is a finite amount of RAM storage. This storage may be allocated to lock pools or buffer pools, but it is impossible to reallocate these resources as the applications change unless the system is brought down and then restarted with a new configuration (called "bouncing"). For online transaction processing systems with hundreds of concurrent users, the demands upon the database buffer pool are much more intensive than with systems that do not perform many online transactions. Conversely, batch updates make very little use of large buffers, but require a lot of room in the lock pools to hold row locks between commit checkpoints.

One simple way to meet the application-specific requirements is to create two database configurations of buffers and lock pools. At the end of the online transaction day, the online system may be brought down and a "batch" version of the database started with a different memory configuration.

Tuning Distributed SQL

While each dialect of SQL is different, there are general rules that can be used to keep database queries running efficiently. While there is no substitute for the SQL EXPLAIN PLAN facility, these guidelines can reduce the chances that a database query will consume large amounts of system resources. The tips for writing effective SQL are the same for distributed databases as for general tables:

- Never do a calculation on an indexed column (e.g., WHERE salary*5 > :myvalue).
- Use the UNION statement instead of OR.
- Avoid the use of NOT or HAVING in the WHERE clause.
- Always specify numeric values in numeric form, and character values in character form (e.g., do not state WHERE EMP_number = "565," or WHERE EMP_NAME = Jones).
- Avoid the LIKE parameter if = will suffice.
- Avoid subqueries when a JOIN will do the job.
- Always use table aliases when referencing columns.
- Specify multiple tables with the largest result set table specified first.

There are several steps to understanding how SQL is used in a distributed database. Distributed SQL queries function in the same way as queries within a single database with the exception that cross-database JOINs and updates may utilize indexes that reside on different databases. Regardless, a basic understanding of the behavior of SQL can lead to dramatic performance improvements.

It has always been a problem with SQL that a simple query can be written in many different ways. All the variants of the query will produce the same result, but with widely different access methods and query speeds.

For example, a simple query such as "What students received an 'A' last semester?" can be written in three ways, each returning an identical result—as a standard join:

```
SELECT *
FROM STUDENT, REGISTRATION
WHERE
     student.student_id = registration.student_id
AND
     registration.grade = "A";
```

a nested query:

```
SELECT *
FROM STUDENT
WHERE
     student_id =
     (SELECT student_id
          FROM registration
          WHERE
          grade = "A"
     );
```

or a correlated subquery:

```
SELECT *
FROM STUDENT
WHERE
     0 <
     (SELECT count(*)
          FROM registration
          WHERE
          grade = "A"
          AND
          student_id = student.student_id
     );
```

The following discussion will review the basic components of an SQL query, showing how to optimize a query for remote execution.

The Driving Table In some implementations of SQL the ordering of the table names in the FROM clause determines the "driving" table. The driving table is the first table to be retrieved, and "drives" all subsequent SQL processes. The driving table is important because it is retrieved first, and the rows from the second table are then merged into the result set from the first table. Therefore, it is important that the second table return the least amount of rows based on the WHERE clause. *This is not always the table with the least amount of rows* (i.e., the smallest cardinality).

For example, consider two emp_tables, one in London and another in New York:

	Rows	Dept 100	Dept 200
New York	1000	100	900
London	200	150	50

In this example, a total SELECT from the emp_table should specify the New York table first because London has the least amount of returned rows:

```
SELECT *
from emp@new_york, emp@london;
```

If the SQL specifies a WHERE condition to include only Department 100, then the order of table names should be reversed:

```
SELECT *
from emp@london, emp@new_york
WHERE
    DEPT = 100;
```

Since it is not always known what table will return the least amount of rows, procedural code can be used to interrogate the tables and specify the tables in their proper order. This type of SQL generation can be very useful for insuring optimal database performance:

```
Select count(*) into :my_london_dept
    from emp@london
    where dept = :my_dept;

Select count(*) into :my_ny_dept
    from emp@new_york
    where dept = :my_dept;

if my_london_dept >= my_ny_dept
{
    table_1 = emp@london
    table_2 = emp@new_york
else
    table_1 = emp@new_york
    table_2 = emp@london
}
```

```
/* Now we construct the SQL

select *
from :table_1, :table_2
where
      dept = :my_dept;
```

Index Usage As a general rule, indexes will increase the performance of a database query. In some cases where a query intends to "sweep" a table in the same sequence that the rows are physically stored, then indexes may actually hinder performance.

Index Predicates In order to use an index, the SQL optimizer must recognize that the column has a valid value for index use. This is called a *sargeable predicate*, and is used to determine the index access. The following have valid predicates:

```
SELECT * FROM EMPLOYEE WHERE emp_no = 123;

SELECT * FROM EMPLOYEE WHERE dept_no = 10;
```

The following have invalid predicates:

```
SELECT * FROM EMPLOYEE WHERE emp_no = "123";

SELECT * FROM EMPLOYEE WHERE salary * 2 < 50000;

SELECT * FROM EMPLOYEE WHERE dept_no != 10;
```

Whenever a transformation to a field value takes place, the system may not be able to use the index for that field.

Some databases such as DB2 will recognize a linear search and invoke a "sequential prefetch" to look ahead, reading the next data block while the previous data block is being fetched by the application. As a general rule, an SQL query that retrieves more than 15 percent of the table rows in a table will run faster if the optimizer chooses a full table scan than if it chooses an index.

For example, assume that a student table has 1000 rows, representing 900 undergraduate students and 100 graduate students. A nonunique index has been built on the STUDENT_LEVEL field that indicates UNDERGRAD or GRAD. The same query will benefit from different access methods depending upon the value of the literal in the WHERE clause:

```
SELECT * FROM STUDENT WHERE student_level = 'UNDERGRAD';
```

This query will retrieve 90 percent of the rows in the table, and will run faster with a full-table scan than it will if the SQL optimizer chooses to use an index.

```
SELECT * FROM STUDENT WHERE student_level = 'GRAD';
```

This query will only access 10 percent of the table rows and will run faster by using the index on the STUDENT_LEVEL field.

Unfortunately, databases cannot tell the number of expected rows that will be returned from a query, and many SQL optimizers will invoke an index access even though it may not always be the fastest access method.

To remedy this problem, some dialects of SQL allow the user to control the index access. This is a gross violation of the declarative nature of theoretical SQL, whereby the user does not control access paths, but in practice, these extensions can improve performance. Oracle, for example, allows the concatenation of a null string to the field name in the WHERE clause to suppress index access. The above query could be rewritten in Oracle SQL to bypass the STUDENT_LEVEL index as follows:

```
SELECT * FROM STUDENT WHERE student_level!!" = 'UNDERGRAD';
```

The concatenation (!!) of a null string to the field tells the Oracle SQL optimizer to bypass index processing for this field, instead invoking a full-table scan, which will run faster.

This is a very important point. While SQL optimizers are becoming more intelligent about their databases, they still cannot understand the structure of the data, and will not always choose the best access path.

Concatenated Indexes

A concatenated index is an index that is built on two fields. For example, a concatenated index could be created on STUDENT_LEVEL and MAJOR (in that order) to speed up queries that use both terms:

```
SELECT * FROM STUDENT
WHERE
    student_level = 'UNDERGRAD'
AND
    major = 'computer science';
```

However, some queries using MAJOR or STUDENT_LEVEL may not be able to use this concatenated index:

```
SELECT * FROM STUDENT
```

```
WHERE
    major = 'computer science';
```

Since MAJOR is not the leading field in the concatenated index, the index cannot be used.

```
SELECT * FROM STUDENT
WHERE
    student_level = 'PLEBE';
```

Since STUDENT_LEVEL is the first item in the index, the leading portion of the index can be read and the SQL optimizer will invoke an index scan.

The NOT (!) operator will cause an index to be bypassed, and the query "show all undergrads who are NOT computer_science majors" will cause a full-table scan.

```
SELECT * FROM STUDENT
WHERE
    student_level = 'UNDERGRAD'
AND
    major !='computer science';
```

Here, the "not" condition is not a sargeable predicate, and will cause a full-table scan.

Tracing SQL with EXPLAIN PLAN

There are tools within most implementations of SQL that allow the access path to be interrogated. Most relational databases use an "explain" utility that takes the SQL statement as input, runs the SQL optimizer, and outputs the access path to a PLAN_TABLE, which can then be interrogated to see the access methods. Let's run a query against the student database, showing all students who qualify for the honor roll with a grade average > 3.5:

```
EXPLAIN PLAN SET STATEMENT_ID = 'test1' FOR

SELECT student_name FROM STUDENT
WHERE
    student_id in
    (SELECT * from registration
        WHERE
        avg(grade_num) > 3.5);
```

This syntax is piped into the SQL optimizer, which will analyze the query and store the plan information in a row in the plan table identified by test1. The plan table contains the following fields:

OPERATION	The type of access being performed. Usually table access, table merge, sort, or index operation.
OPTIONS	Modifiers to the operation, specifying if there is a full table, a range table, or a join.
OBJECT_NAME	The name of the table being used by the query component.
Process ID	The identifier for the query component.
Parent ID	The parent of the query component. Note that several query components may have the same parent.

While the plan table is useful for determining the access path to the data, it does not tell the entire story. The configuration of the data is also a consideration. While the SQL optimizer is aware of the number of rows in each table (the cardinality) and the presence of indexes on fields, the SQL optimizer is not aware of data distribution factors such as the number of expected rows returned from each query component.

The other tool that is used with the plan table is an SQL trace facility. Most database management systems provide a trace facility that shows all of the resources consumed within each query component. The trace table will show the number of I/Os that were required to perform the SQL as well as the processor time for each query component.

Some databases such as DB2 allow the DBA to specify the physical sequence for storing the rows. Generally, this sequence will correspond to the column value that is most commonly used when the table is read sequentially by an application. If a customer table is frequently accessed in customer ID order, then the rows should be physically stored in customer ID sequence.

Database statistics packages can be made to capture this information, but they are very resource intensive, and it is a convention that SQL trace statistics should be turned on for a very short period of time during processing in order to gather a representative sample of the SQL access.

14.4 PLANNING FOR GROWTH

One of the biggest problems in performance and tuning is that of planning for growth and insuring that your distributed database continues to perform at an acceptable level. As we know, databases run within a well-defined domain of system resources, and a shortage of these system resources can lead to performance degradation. The trick is to design a database system with the ability to add resources on an as-needed basis without interrupting processing.

Growth can occur in several areas. As the physical size of the database increases, there is a greater need for disk storage. As the volume of users increases, there is a need for increased buffer and lock pool storage. As network traffic increases, there are increasing demands on the routers, and bandwidth may need to be increased.

Unlike the CODASYL databases, today's relational databases allow for tables to grow according to specified rules and procedures. In the relational model, one or more tables may reside in a tablespace. A tablespace is a predefined container for the tables that maps to fixed files of a finite size. Tables that are assigned to the tablespace may grow according to the growth rules that are specified, but the size of the tablespace supersedes the expansion rules, and data tables may fill, not because of a failure of the table expansion rules, but because of lack of space in the tablespace.

There are several allocation parameters that influence table growth:

INITIAL	The initial size of each extent
NEXT	The subsequent size of new extents
MINEXTENTS	The minimum number of initial extents (used for striping)
MAXEXTENTS	The maximum allowable number of extents
PCTINCREASE	The percentage by which each subsequent extent grows
PCTFREE	The percentage of space to be kept on each data block for future expansion

The PCTFREE parameter is used to reserve space on each data block for the future expansion of row values (via the SQL UPDATE command). Table columns may be defined as allowing NULL values that do not consume any space within the row, or with *varchar data types*. A varchar data type specifies the maximum allowable length for the column instance, but the acceptable range of values may be anywhere from four bytes (the size of the length holder) to the size of the field plus four bytes. Hence, a varchar(2000) may range in size from four bytes to 2004 bytes.

If an application initially stores rows with empty values, and later fills in the values, the PCTFREE parameter can dramatically reduce I/O contention. If a block of storage is filled by the addition of a row, subsequent updates to that

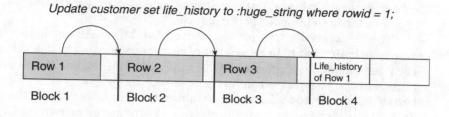

Update customer set life_history to :huge_string where rowid = 1;

Figure 14.10   Row fragmentation.

row to fill in column values will cause the row to fragment, usually onto the next available contiguous block.

In Figure 14.10, the next five blocks are filled with rows. When an SQL update adds 1500 bytes to row 1, the database chains to the next block and, finding no space, chains to the next block, and the next block, before finding 1500 bytes of free space on block 4. The fragment is stored in block 4 and a chain is established from the block header of block 1, to point to the next block header, and so on, until the fragment is located. Most databases have some type of "free list" at each block header to determine the total available space on each block.

Any subsequent retrieval of row 1 will require the database to perform four physical block I/Os in order to retrieve the entire row. Since I/O time is usually the largest component of overall response time, this type of row fragmentation can greatly reduce performance.

There are several preventive measures that can be taken to avoid this situation. If the row will eventually contain all of its column values, and the values are of fixed length, then the table could be defined with the parameter NOT NULL, thereby reserving space in the row when it is initially stored. If the row contains variable-length columns, then the PCTFREE parameter is used to reserve space on each block for row expansion. Most databases offer a utility that can be run periodically to check for row fragmentation, and if fragments are found, the data must be exported to a flat file, the table redefined with different storage parameters, and the table repopulated from the same flat file.

Table Normalization and Distributed Database Performance

Ever since E. F. Codd first published the rules of normalization, database designers have been attempting to find an optimum way of structuring tables for performance. Codd's rules create a table structure that is logically correct and contains no redundancy, but performance rules often dictate the reintroduction of redundancy to improve performance.

This is especially true for distributed databases. Any node in a distributed database may want to browse a list of customers at other nodes without having the need to establish connections to that node. The technological problems inherent in the two-phase commit necessitate the widespread replication of entire tables or selected columns from tables. But this does not give the distributed database designer free rein to introduce redundancy anywhere in the enterprise. There is always a cost for redundancy, whether it is the cost of the disk storage or the cost of maintaining a parallel update scheme. Figure 14.11 describes a strategy for analyzing the consequences of data redundancy.

Here we see a boundary line in a range between the size of a redundant data item and the frequency of update of the data item. The size of the data item relates to the disk costs associated with storing the item, and the frequency of update is associated with the cost of keeping the redundant data current,

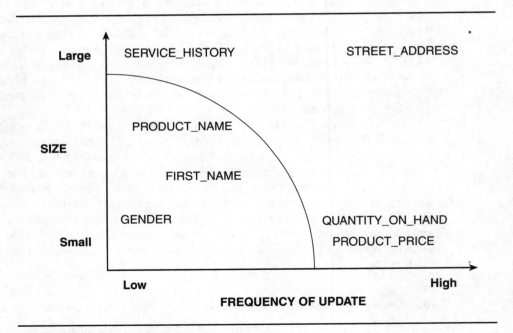

Figure 14.11   Redundancy boundary.

whether through replication techniques or by two-phase commit updates. Since the relative costs are different for each hardware configuration and for each application, this boundary may be quite different for different applications. With the rapid decrease in the costs of disk storage, we see that the size boundary is important only for very large-scale redundancy. Large items that change frequently (street_address) might not be good candidates for redundancy, while large items that never change (service_history) and small items that change frequently (item_price) may be acceptable for redundancy. Small items that never change (gender) are fine for redundancy.

14.5 DESIGNING EXPERT SYSTEMS FOR DISTRIBUTED DATABASE PERFORMANCE AND TUNING

When a centralized database is split into distributed systems, the overall maintenance requirements for each database do not decrease. While the overall costs for the system hardware will decline as companies abandon their mainframes, human resources will increase as redundant personnel are added to perform system and database administration tasks at each node.

Many distributed database shops are responding to this challenge by creating systems that automate the common performance tracking for each remote database, giving the DBA staff alerts when predefined thresholds are exceeded. This type of automation can be extended with statistical trend analysis tools such as the SAS product to give forecasts of database maintenance and performance trends.

While these systems can become very sophisticated, I recommend an evolutionary approach to the design of expert systems for performance and tuning. The work in 1981 by Robert Bonczeck on the theoretical structure of expert systems applies very well to performance and tuning applications. Bonczeck identifies a generalized framework for solving problems that consists of three components: states, operators, and goals. This approach assumes that the initial state is identified (namely a performance degradation), and a series of operators is applied to this state until the goal state is achieved (acceptable performance). This is called a "state-space" approach to problem solving.

The idea is to create a knowledge system to store relevant statistical information and periodically feed this knowledge system into a problem processing system. The problem processing system contains the decision rules that are used to analyze trends in usage and alert the DBA if a parameter has been exceeded (Figure 14.12).

This technique also relies on the knowledge that database performance and tuning do not require human intuition. While the decision rules applied to the

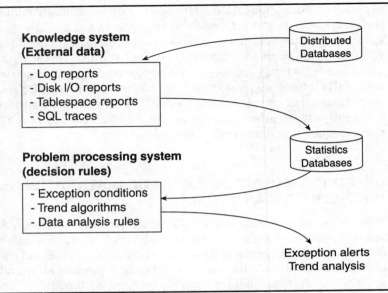

Figure 14.12 Expert system overview.

problem are very complex, performance analysis is nothing more than the application of well-structured rules to problem data. Therefore, an automated system can be devised to replicate the DBA's expertise in performance analysis.

The following steps can be used to create an expert system for performance and tuning:

1. *Identify the packaged utilities to be used.*

   These may include:

   SQL trace facility

   tablespace reports

   log analysis reports

   operating system–specific reports

   performance monitor reports

2. *Schedmule the reports to run on a periodic basis and direct the output to a file.*

3. *Write a summary program to interpret the reports and write summary statistics to a master file.*

4. *Create a problem processing system to read the knowledge system, generating trend reports and DBA alerts.*

There are many tools available for performance analysis. Reports can be run against the database logs to produce reports containing statistics about every task in the database. The SQL trace utility can be turned on for a few minutes each day to attempt to identify inefficient SQL statements. Operating system reports can be generated containing information on disk contention and I/O bottlenecks. Performance monitors can also be used to detect information about database deadlocks and incomplete transactions.

Scheduling can be performed to fire the reports at specific time intervals. UNIX utilities such as CRON can be used for time-dependent scheduling, but it is nice to have a gateway into the scheduler so that exception-based reporting can be conducted. For example, if a UNIX monitor detects excessive hardware contention against a disk, it could trigger a user-exit to start an SQL trace to obtain detailed information.

Most database reports contain a lot of irrelevant information, and a simple program written with C or even COBOL could be used to read the output from the reports, storing critical information into a table. This table would be used to feed the problem processing system to create the exception reports and trend analysis reports. While this may sound complex, the data from the knowledge system can be fed directly into a canned statistical package such as SAS or SPSS to produce trend reports.

Figure 14.13 shows a typical weekly exception report. All tasks for the day

Paychex
Weekly task exception report
for the week ending 11/25/94

Task Name	94306	94307	94308	94309	94310	94311	94312	Times invoked	Historical response	Variance
			Day of Week							
PC01	.55	.54	.68	.56	.54	.57	.00	21932	.55	
PC02	.05	.04	.08	.06	.04	.07	.00	3444	.01	slow 200%
PC03	.22	.23	.40	.21	.23	.21	.22	129342	.24	
PC04	.05	.08	.09	.02	.04	.01	.00	3444	.01	slow 183%
PC05	.35	.33	.42	.33	.32	.40	.31	3444	.31	

Figure 14.13   Typical weekly exception report.

are analyzed and compared with a running average for their historical response time. If the response time for the task exceeds 15 percent of the historical average, the variance is noted in the right-hand column.

This type of report can provide very useful information about the overall operation of the distributed databases. Note, for example, the performance degradation on Wednesday (94308). Wee see that all of the tasks in the system were running below their historical average on that day; there may have been some external influence that caused a system-wide response problem.

Other common reports can compare the buffer utilization for all of the distributed databases, comparing the ratio of blocks_requested to blocks_in_buffer. This can be used as a simple method of monitoring changes in buffer utilization over time.

DBAs who have implemented this type of system find that it removes the need for the tedious report analysis they used to do by hand, and it also provides a base for more sophisticated performance and tuning automation.

14.6 DISK ISSUES AND DISTRIBUTED DATABASE PERFORMANCE

The placement of the database files on the DASD (disk) devices can have a significant impact on the system performance.

On most disk devices, the volume table of contents (VTOC) can be placed anywhere on the disk device. While the VTOC placement is irrelevant if the database is not used for local mode processing (the database just locates it once at start-up time), the VTOC placement can become critical for local mode processing. A VTOC must be accessed each time a file is requested from disk storage, and it is the most frequently accessed file on the disk (Figure 14.14).

If one assumes that there is an equal probability of the read-write heads being under any given track, then it makes sense that all frequently accessed files, especially the VTOC, should be placed near the "middle" track on the disk. Since "seek time" (the time it takes for the read-write head to relocate) is the greatest component of disk delay, this strategy will minimize overall disk access time. Formally expressed, the probability of traveling an arbitrary distance across the disk (pdi) is:

$$pdi = \sum_{cyl=i+1}^{J} \frac{i}{J(J-1)} + \sum_{cyl=1}^{J} \frac{i}{J(J-1)} = 2\frac{J-i}{J(J-1)}$$

where J = number of cylinders.

Clearly, it follows that because I/O is the greatest contributor to database performance problems, and since seek time is the major component of disk

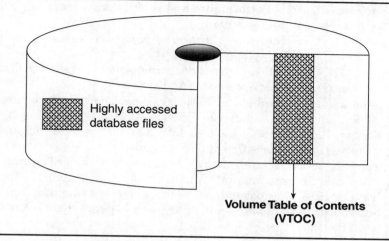

Figure 14.14   Cluster high-volume database files near the middle absolute track.

response, whatever can be done to reduce seek delay will result in a performance improvement for the overall database.

14.7   SUMMARY

With the myriad factors that contribute to system performance, it is not surprising that there is no magic formula that can be applied to distributed databases to insure acceptable performance. In a sense, performance and tuning are easier for distributed systems than for centralized systems because each remote site can be isolated and analyzed independently of the other remote sites. The complex nature of distributed processing insures that performance and tuning will remain a complex endeavor, and it is only with a complete understanding of the nature of performance that effective measurement methods can be devised.

REFERENCES

Bacon, J. 1993. *Concurrent systems, an integration approach to operating systems, database and distributed systems.* Addison-Wesley.
Bloomer, J. 1991. *Power programming with RPC.* O'Reilly & Associates.

Burleson, D. 1992. Performance and tuning for the very large database. *Database Programming & Design*.

———. 1993. *Practical application of object-oriented techniques to relational databases*. Wiley\QED.

Cattell, R. G. G. 1991. *Object data management: object-oriented and extended relational database systems*. Addison-Wesley.

Cellary, W., E. Gelenbe, and T. Morzy. 1988. *Concurrency control in distributed database systems*. Eslevier Science Publishing.

Demers, R. et al. 1992. Inside IBM's distributed data management architecture. *IBM Systems Journal*, September.

Franklin, M. 1993. *Local disk caching for client/server database systems*. Proceedings of the ninteenth VLDB Conference, Dublin, Ireland.

Gray, B. 1993. Database/file servers. *Computing Canada*, March.

Ricciuti, M. 1992. Terabytes of data—how to get at them? *Datamation*, August.

New Data Retrieval Methods

15.1 INTRODUCTION

We are entering a new era of data retrieval in which traditional database languages are giving way to free-form, nonprocedural database access. There is also a movement afoot to create "generic" database query languages that can be used against all database architectures, whether inverted list, network, hierarchical, relational, or object-oriented. At the same time, new techniques and tools are being developed for querying against non-database information sources such as e-mail and Lotus Notes repositories. Automatic speech recognition (ASR) is now beginning to be used as a front end for database access tools, and the next decade is certain to reshape the way that data is retrieved from database systems.

The following discussions explore the emerging data access methods and attempt to shed some light on how they may become players in the database arena.

15.2 SQL FOR OBJECT-ORIENTED DATABASES

Reproduced with permission of Objectivity Incorporated

Applying SQL to Object Databases

SQL is used for database access by a variety of types of applications. Developers directly building applications with traditional languages often program with

SQL as a database language that can be compiled and that provides portability. Many 4GLs use SQL for a similar reason, but usually hide the details of the SQL language to simplify application development. Report writers and query tools rely on SQL for *interoperability*, meaning flexibility at run time in accessing a variety of SQL-compliant databases. These uses of SQL are extremely common, and share an emphasis on portability and data independence.

As new applications are built using object technology and as object databases are introduced into these environments, the ability to use these same traditional non-object-oriented applications and tools to access information managed by object databases is very important. For users with a significant investment in SQL, the ability to use standard SQL to access objects reduces the learning curve because they can treat the object database as simply another database.

When users access information in an object database using SQL, they can benefit from object technology without additional investment. The application built with object technology and an object database can use its high performance and nontraditional functionality, while SQL users can transparently access the textual or numeric information they require. Objects that contain information appropriate to an application can be accessed through standard SQL, with results returned to the application exactly as they would be by any other SQL-compliant data source.

SQL3 takes this a step further by providing object extensions within the context of SQL. SQL3 object extensions can be used for invoking methods, navigating between objects, and accessing nested data structures. SQL tools and applications will then have the flexibility of optionally utilizing object database-specific functions through the SQL interface.

Mapping SQL to Objects

Although using SQL for access to an object database is an important innovation, using SQL for access to nonrelational database architectures is relatively common. Many network, hierarchical, inverted list, and other proprietary databases have offered SQL access by interpreting the semantics of SQL into the conceptual rules enforced by that particular database. Object database technology provides the same opportunity through mapping the semantics of tables, rows, and fields to object classes, objects, and data fields.

A complete mapping of SQL to an object database includes mapping the data definition language (DDL), used for defining tables, attributes, domains, and constraints, and the data manipulation language (DML), used for creating, querying, updating, and deleting data managed by the database.

The DML portion of the language includes query and modification of data. For SQL, the most basic operations are Select, Insert, Delete, and Update. Mapping these to an object database requires matching first the context of the data involved, then the semantics of the operation. The SQL engine maps relational tables to object classes, rows to objects, row identifiers to object identifiers, and columns to object data members. Table and attribute information to identify accessible table and column names is also available through SQL select operations.

In addition to standard SQL syntax, SQL3 includes object extensions for invoking object methods, navigating relationships between objects, and accessing nested structures. Extents and virtual object identifiers can also be supported (Figure 15.1).

A process architecture for implementing an SQL-to-object database interface is shown in Figure 15.2. Object-oriented applications can submit requests directly to the object database client or server system, while ODBC-compliant applications transfer their requests to an SQL mapping process that converts

Figure 15.1   Mapping of objects to SQL.

SQL Construct	Definition	Object Database Equivalent
Database	The scope of all stored data.	Database
Table	A two-dimensional array of data values referred to as rows and columns. A specific data value belongs to exactly one row and one column. All data values are of identical types. All rows have values for all columns.	Object class
Column	One unit of the vertical dimension of a table. All data values in a column have the same data attribute. A single column is associated with all rows in a table.	An object's data member. Field types include SQL-supported field types as well as embedded structures and dynamic arrays.
Row	One unit of the horizontal dimension of a table. A row contains data values from each column in the table. All columns are considered to be in the same order for all rows. Rows are analogous to records and are the smallest unit of data in the table.	Object
RowID	A unique reference to a single tuple.	Object identifier
Index	Defines the logical order of the rows of a table. A table may have one or more indexes, each defining a separate ordering. An index is internally maintained and used whenever an access is determined to be faster using the index than through sequential file search.	Index

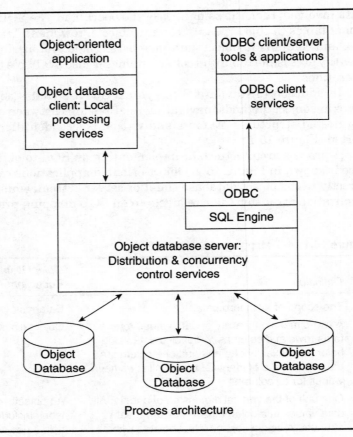

Figure 15.2   Mapping of objects to SQL.

the SQL constructs to appropriate object database requests. These are passed to the object database and results are passed back, using the same ODBC mechanisms.

Sample Query

To illustrate the use of SQL and object extensions with an object database, we will introduce a simple application and data model. This data model will be compared first to relational tables, and then to the object model that could be used to implement it. Next, several types of queries will be formulated against the object model using both standard SQL and SQL3 object extensions. One query will involve the same SQL statements that would be used with a standard relational model. Another query will demonstrate use of an SQL3 object extension.

This data model will involve relationships to provide specific use of an object extension. In fact, for the data model we will describe, the object model closely matches the data model, since it easily handles relationships, while the relational model requires additional constructs.

As our example of a simple SQL query against information managed by an object database, consider the following application and data model. The application models the organization of a company, combining traditional personnel information for company departments with the reporting structure. The data model used in the application captures employees, managers, departments, and their relationships. For this organization, an employee can report to one manager and belong to one department. A manager, on the other hand, can have many reports. For both managers and general employees, the database manages information about expertise, salary, address, and phone numbers (Figure 15.3).

The relational data model would be expressed using tables to define persons, employees, managers, and departments. Since the relationships between employees and managers cannot be directly expressed, these require an additional table (Figure 15.4).

These tables represent the same model described above. Relationships are implemented using ID keys managed by the tables. Using the IDs to access information in a related table requires a join operation.

This same data model can easily be represented as an object model. The object class "person" is defined as a class from which the "employee" class can inherit some generic attributes (Figure 15.5).

For this application, the object model looks very much like the data model as originally described. The class definitions define the possible relationships

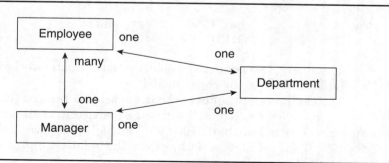

Figure 15.3   Employee data model.

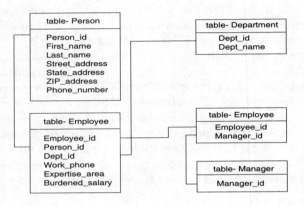

Figure 15.4 Addition of reports to table.

between employees, managers, and departments. Using related information involves direct navigation of that relationship (Figure 15.6).

A simple SQL query against this model would search for an employee with specific work phone extensions:

```
SELECT Last_name, FROM employee WHERE
     Work_phone LIKE '%-8037'
```

This query does not use any object extensions and works identically against a relational table or the object model.

The second sample query for our application returns the names of employees in the sales department with an expertise in SQL and whose burdened annual salary is less than $100,000. The SQL code given below to do this uses object extensions to directly navigate the relationship to a department and tests its value.

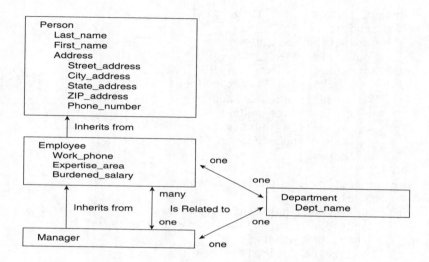

Figure 15.5   Inheritance with E/R model.

```
SELECT Last_name FROM employee WHERE
     traverse(oid, "employee", "department.Dept_name") =
'sales'
     AND
     Expertise_area = 'SQL'
     AND
     Burdened_salary < 100000;
```

The traversal operation uses the relationship between employees and departments to test the value of the department to which the employee belongs. In this case, the query directly navigates the relationship to acquire this value, without requiring any join operations. Submitting the same query against the relational model for this data would require a join, and most other queries would also require at least one join operation.

C++ code for the object model introduced in the query examples.

```
class person : public ooObj {
    public:
    ooVString Last_name;
    ooVString First_name;
    struct {
        ooVString Street_address;
        ooVString City_address ;
        char State_address [2];
        char ZIP_address [9];
        char Phone_number [10];
    } address;
};
class employee : public person {
    public:
    ooHandle(department) department <-> employees[];
    ooHandle(manager) manager <-> employees[];
    char Work_phone [10];
    ooVString Expertise_area ;
    ooSQLmoney Burdened_salary ;
};
class manager : public employee {
    public:
    ooHandle(employee) employees[] <-> manager;
};

class department : public ooObj {
    public:
    ooHandle(employee) employees[] <-> dept;
    ooVString Dept_name ;
};
```

Figure 15.6   Class descriptions.

The same query operation against relational tables would be formulated as follows. This SQL statement would also execute correctly against the object model if the key fields used to indicate the relationships were available.

```
SELECT Last_name FROM employee WHERE
    employee.Dept_id = department.Dept_id
    AND
```

SQL code for the relational model introduced in the query examples.

```
table Person(
    Person_id char(5),
    Last_name varchar(15),
    First_name varchar(10),
    Street_address varchar(30),
    City_address varchar(30),
    State_address char(2),
    ZIP_address char(9),
    Phone_number char(10),
)

table Employee (
    Employee_id char(5), //foreign key (1-1) to Person.Person_id
    Dept_id char(4),  //foreign key (1-1) to Department.Dept_id
    Work_phone char(5),
    Expertise_area char(4),
    Burdened_salary money,
)

table Manager (
    Manager_id char(5), //foreign key (1-1) to Employee.Employee_id
)

table Department (
    Dept_id char(4),
    Dept_name varchar(20)
)

//this table required to support employee/manager relationship
table Reports_to (
    Employee_id char(5), //foreign key (1-1) to Employee.Employee_id
    Manager_id char(5)   //foreign key (1-1) to Manager.Manager_id
)
```

Figure 15.6   *(Continued)*

```
            department.Dept_name='sales'
            AND
            employee.Expertise_area='SQL'
            AND
            employee.Burdened_salary < 100000;
```

The example demonstrates the natural use of an object model to capture information about relationships. These can be modeled directly, without requiring the developer to define keys and additional tables. Second, standard SQL can be used against the object model, returning the same results one would expect from a relational model. Last, SQL3 object extensions provide access to specific object-oriented attributes. In the case of relationships captured by the object model, this is accomplished without requiring costly join operations at run time.

15.3 AUTOMATIC SPEECH RECOGNITION (ASR)

Once confined to academic research laboratories, automatic speech recognition (ASR) is quickly becoming a mainstream technology. Due to the recent availability of commercial ASR products, including IBM's VoiceType 2, Kolvox's PowerTALK, and Dragon System's DragonDictate, many systems designers are beginning to incorporate voice technology into mission-critical systems. ASR is being used routinely to replace human transcription, and new products are being introduced that use ASR as the interface to word processing, spreadsheets, and databases.

ASR is being extended to allow the computer to be completely controlled by voice. Entire application systems may soon be driven by spoken words rather than entered commands (Figure 15.7). This new integration of voice with computers will soon make the keyboard as obsolete as Hollerith cards.

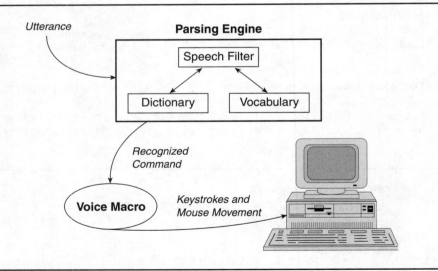

Figure 15.7   Architecture of automatic speech recognition.

ASR technology has borrowed heavily from artificial intelligence and research in natural language processing. Technically, one of the most formidable challenges of artificial intelligence is the parsing of human English. Before any meaning can be inferred from words, the spoken words must first be captured. For years, researchers have struggled with "context-sensitive" grammar ("Please write to Mr. Wright right now")—even the seemingly simple task of parsing spoken language into words, such that a system could recognize that "bus station" is two words even though it sounds like one. Programmers will soon be able to create ASR front ends for databases that accept the user's own slang and verbal shorthand. For example, if you tell your computer that all salespeople who have not met their quotas are "turkeys," you could then simply state "Show me the turkeys" to produce a list of poor salespeople.

There are many parallels between the development of the telephone and the development of ASR. Alexander Graham Bell designed the first telephone as a tool for his hearing impaired wife, but the telephone was so powerful that it grew into an indispensable communications tool. "ASR was originally developed to assist users who could not use a keyboard, and the technology has proven to be so powerful that ASR will soon become an integral component of computer systems," says Dan Thompson, a quadriplegic, and cofounder of Kolvox Incorporated in Toronto. "ASR provides a task-driven interface to the computer, and eliminates the need to memorize cumbersome keystrokes. However, programmers will need an entirely new set of skills to create systems that are friendly to users. In ASR, the brain power is kept in the voice interface, and programmers must possess expertise to make the system friendly. Once users are exposed to ASR interfaces, they are very enamored with it and often are reluctant to go back to the old-fashioned mouse and keyboard. The future demand for ASR will come from the end-users, and programmers must be ready to use a voice interface, just as they use a mouse and keyboard interface today."

All of the new products use a "vocabulary" of words, but the associations of words to events are done by the programmer. For example, the MedTalk product by Kolvox allows users to perform complex patient scheduling and patient records management, all with voice. While the MedTalk system appears extremely easy to the end-user, there is a great deal of sophisticated programming behind the "easy" voice interface.

While many of the new ASR systems are being developed for such specific applications, the generalized products such as DragonDictate and IBM's VoiceType 2 allow customized systems to be developed for nearly any data processing requirement.

Voice macro tools are commonly used to associate phrases with events, and some vendors include macro generators that allow programmers to associate up to 1000 keystrokes with a single "utterance." There are several voice interface toolkits on the market, including Dragon System's Voice Tools and IBM's ICCS toolkit.

All of the new ASR offerings run on PC platforms, and the ASR programmer needs to be PC literate, but the real skill comes when programming the voice interface. This generally involves building an "interface bridge" to the target system. The programmer defines a macro, which can be a C program or a macro language call to a database or word processing package. This macro is then associated with a "discrete utterance" that is trapped within the ASR engine.

The voice interface is very similar to the macro definition facility within MS-Windows. To define a macro, the user turns on the macro recorder, and all of the subsequent keystrokes are recorded until the recorder is turned off. At that point, the user "names" the sequence of keystrokes, usually to a function key such as F2. Similarly, to define a voice command, the user determines the keystroke sequence and assigns the sequence to an "utterance."

The assignment of keystrokes to utterances is relatively straightforward. The real skill for the programmer comes in configuring the utterances for the user. One of the biggest challenges is dealing with the intent of the user. While computers are very precise, the natural ambiguity of English makes it very easy for an end-user to assume that utterances do something that they are not intended for. For example, the user could utter "Copy Fred," intending to send a copy of a memo to a coworker named Fred. To the voice systems, the "Copy" utterance is used to send documents to destinations, and the system will attempt to locate a document called FRED and print it.

Another challenge is synonyms. A good implementation of ASR should include all utterances that possess a common meaning. For example, the EXIT function should be associated with the utterances of "clear," "leave," "bye," and "close."

The greatest challenge for the programmer is passing parameters. A parameter is a "keyword" that is expected to influence the sequence of events. For example, the "print" utterance can have a filename parameter, such that the utterance "print mydoc" will direct the system to take the MYDOC file and direct it to an output device.

Polymorphic parameters are especially challenging. Polymorphism occurs when a discrete utterance may be radically modified by the value of the parameter. For example, a "print" utterance will invoke vastly different procedures depending upon the destination of the print. "Print to fax" will have a very different behavior than will "print to printer."

While ASR is a nascent technology, it appears that it will become widely accepted within the next several years, and programmers will need to become proficient with the new voice interfaces. As keyboards and mice join glass TTYs and card punch machines, programmers will develop new and even more creative ways to allow ASR to exploit the power of the computer.

15.4   NEW TEXT RETRIEVAL TOOLS

Courtesy of ConQuest Incorporated

What is text retrieval? Until recently, industry experts defined text retrieval (or full-text retrieval) as the ability to search for and retrieve any single word, string of words, or words connected through logical or proximity operators within a document or collection of documents stored in electronic form. This definition encompassed the dominant environment of keyword and Boolean searching, which perceives words as strings of characters, and retrieves exact matches of those character strings.

Keywords and Boolean searching emerged from the world of structured, primarily numeric databases. While these have been useful technologies for over two decades, they are also very limited. A character string search cannot account for meaning, or context, or related, relevant terms or concepts. For example, a keyword search for the word "ground" cannot distinguish between the verb meanings of grounding an airplane or affixing something, or the noun meanings of an area of land or a rational motive for belief, or an electrical connection. Likewise, such a system cannot link "ground" to such related terms as anchor, earth, establish, evidence, garden, terra firma, and so on.

How can I measure text retrieval performance?

The limitations of keyword and Boolean searching have clouded the issue of how text retrieval software can and should perform. In fact, there are two fundamental metrics or measurements of text retrieval. They are: precision—the ability to retrieve only relevant documents (i.e., no false or "noisy" hits), and recall—the ability to retrieve all relevant documents in a given data collection. Together, precision and recall represent the overall accuracy of a text retrieval system.

How many times have you heard text retrieval vendors discuss accuracy, much less precision and recall? If the answer is "not very often," you shouldn't be surprised. The text retrieval community has skirted the issue of accuracy because today's systems are simply not very accurate.

Despite the fact that text retrieval has been around since the early 1970s, some experts still question its viability, even for such text-intensive applications as trial document management in the legal community. A recent article in *Law Office Computing* magazine (June/July 1993) points out, "text retrieval programs may only locate 20 percent of all relevant documents, hardly a percentage to bet a case on."

Twenty percent! That sobering figure derives from findings published in 1985 by academic researchers David Blair and M. E. Maron. Blair and Maron worked with a large litigation database of 40,000 documents, and used a Boolean search system.

Blair and Maron understood why Boolean yielded such low recall. They write, "full-text retrieval is difficult to use . . . because its design is based on the assumption that it is a simple matter for users to foresee the exact words and phrases that will be used in the documents." They give the example of a word such as "accident," which may also be described as an "event," "incident," "situation," etc. *Law Office Computing* also puts it well, commenting, "when searching . . . text . . . we are confronted with authors who use language in all its vague and colloquial richness."

Isn't there anything beyond Boolean?

Isn't there any system which can encompass the "colloquial richness" of language? Fortunately, the answer is Yes. Today, there is an alternative to pure character-string searching. Delphi Consulting Group, a leading research firm, now defines text retrieval as "a computer-based facility for the storage and retrieval of . . . documents that contain text, based on their explicit or implied content such as words, sentences, phrases, or concepts and ideas."

Concept or "idea" searching. True concept searching is an exceptionally important development in text retrieval. It has the capacity to break the accuracy barrier and stand the performance ratio of Boolean on its head. Not surprisingly, many players are jumping on the bandwagon. But what does a vendor mean when it claims to provide "concept searching"? Does this capability significantly improve the ability of a text retrieval system to be accurate and complete? Does it truly take into account word meanings, meaning-based relationships, and words in context? What must the customer do to set up and use concept capabilities? These are the questions you should ask of text retrieval vendors, and these are the questions they should be prepared to answer.

Vendors are using the term "concept searching" in three basic ways today:

1. Statistical "concept" searching
2. Concept building
3. Knowledge networked concept searching

1. Some vendors employ a statistical approach to text retrieval. When a user enters a query, the retrieval engine analyzes documents according to terms which occur frequently and/or in close proximity to the key terms in the query. The system then displays a list of words which, according to this statistical analysis, may be "conceptually related" to the query. For example, a query on

the word "bank" may retrieve words such as "money," "savings," etc. Yet, this approach still does not take into account the actual meaning of the query. For example, if the database happened to contain a number of articles about bank building and construction, the search might bring back words such as "window," "steel," etc. Such terms are statistically related, but not conceptually related. And, for the user, such terms are not helpful in his/her search for relevant information.

If you see a demonstration of this type of system, you should observe the list of concepts closely. If you find a "hit" which puzzles you, ask the vendor to explain why the hit was made. It will likely become clear that this is not "concept searching" in the sense of Delphi Consulting's definition of a search on actual content or ideas. Statistical searching is an important component in the text retrieval equation, but it alone cannot provide a concept capability.

2.   Other vendors employ a concept-building approach. With these systems, users have the opportunity to build groups or word relationships. For example, the user can take a word such as "space" and construct connections to words such as "rocket," "star," "astronomy," etc. After performing this task, subsequent searches for the word "space" will also bring back references to these related words.

Concept building does establish meaningful connections between words. However, it also has distinct drawbacks. Users must build and maintain all of these concept relationships themselves. This is a very time-consuming process, and one which does not necessarily encompass the full richness of words and their multiple definitions. "Space," for example, also refers to a room's volume or area. It can even be a verb, meaning to create a space. Unless concept building takes this into account, users who are interested in these alternative meanings are out of luck.

One of the easiest ways to understand the strengths and weaknesses of concept building is to ask the vendor of such a system to allow you to enter a query on any subject of your choosing. The chances are this will not be possible. The vendor may not have built concept relationships for the subject you are interested in. Even exploited to the fullest, concept-building systems allow for fewer than 10,000 concepts, a fraction of the number of words and word meanings in our language. Concept building cannot operate on unrestricted domains of documents and subjects.

3.   The third approach to concept searching is to build a knowledge network of word meanings and word relationships into the core intelligence of a text retrieval system. ConQuest has chosen this approach, and bases its knowledge network on actual, published dictionaries and thesauri. ConQuest has created a method of generating weighted links between all of the meanings of all of the words in dictionaries and thesauri, to deliver a concept-searching capability which is virtually unrestricted, out of the box.

The baseline knowledge network contains 340,000 concepts and 3 million word links. A ConQuest search draws upon this network, not simply on statistics or on user-defined concepts. A knowledge networked system reveals the conceptual reasons documents are selected as relevant. The user can "click" on any hit to display the dictionary definition which ties it to the terms in the query. A knowledge networked system is as rich as the dictionaries and thesauri on which it is based. Users are free to enter queries on any topic in the lexicon.

Another unique feature of the knowledge network approach is the ability to look up and select word meanings, just as you do with a dictionary. By selecting meanings, you tune your query precisely to your needs, and eliminate the false hits that other systems generate. A word like "stock" can mean anything from shares in a company to the liquid in which meat is simmered. It is important to have both meanings available, but the financial researcher does not want to know about the fine points of cooking, nor vice versa.

What about "natural language" searching?

"Natural language" is a phrase frequently heard in conjunction with concept-based searching. Vendors claim to utilize "natural language processing" so that users can enter their queries in plain English phrases and sentences, as opposed to rigid Boolean syntax.

However, there are widely recognized principles of natural language processing. If vendors are not adhering to these principles, it is likely that they are taking a plain English query and simply reducing it to a Boolean search. If you hear the term "natural language," you should be looking for the following:

1. Morphological analysis. Almost every text retrieval system on the market employs "suffix stripping," a relatively simple process which takes into account the common rules for recognizing inflected forms of words. For example, many words in the English language become plural with the addition of a final "s," e.g., "book" and "books." Suffix stripping is sufficient to recognize the singular root of such words. But what about the words which form plurals in an irregular fashion, such as "baby" and "babies"? What about words which end in "s" but are not plurals?

Morphology is a more powerful approach than simple suffix stripping. Morphology recognizes basic units of meaning and parts of speech. It recognizes the common roots of words which change their spelling in plural and other inflected forms. Morphology also recognizes when words are not plural nouns, but some other part of speech. An interesting example is the name of a certain jurist, Judge Evers. A suffix-stripping system would automatically remove the "s" from Evers, and then fail to retrieve references to this proper name. A morphological system would recognize that Evers is not the plural of "ever" (an adverb which does not have a plural form) and would index and search on it as a distinct word.

2. Syntactic analysis. Syntax gives insight into the relationships between words. Such relationships go well beyond the simple synonyms of a thesaurus, but include opposites, related words, contrasting words, parent/child, and even "part-of" relationships.

3. Semantic analysis. Semantics encompass the multiple meanings of a single word. For example, a "plant" may be a manufacturing facility or a member of the flora family.

4. Use of plain English to interact with the user. Plain English or natural language interfaces are inherent to natural language processing systems. But remember, plain English alone does not indicate a true natural language system. And in fact, a plain English system without true natural language may perform less accurately than a Boolean or statistical system at the hands of a trained user.

Many vendors today provide "relevance ranking." What exactly does that mean?

Relevancy ranking refers to the ability to present search results in ranked order, with the most relevant documents ranked highest and presented first. Ideally, relevancy ranking can help maximize search efficiency. It enables users to get at the most important information, without wading through many less relevant or even false hits. It may retrieve highly ranked documents while a query is still being processed, enabling users to start looking at information as they wait for full results.

However, there are important distinctions between the relevancy systems of various vendors. Typically, relevancy ranking is determined by a fairly straightforward statistical analysis of word frequency and/or proximity. That is, the software looks for the number of times a word occurs in a given document, and may also look for the proximity of that word to other words or concepts in the query.

ConQuest incorporates frequency and proximity factors into its relevancy ranking. Unlike any other software, however, it takes into account a number of additional factors bearing on word meaning and part of speech. In total, ConQuest uses seven distinct factors to determine relevancy:

1. Frequency of the concept within the document.
2. Closeness in the meaning of the concept in the document to the query.
3. Frequency of the concept in the remainder of the database.
4. Proximity of the terms of the concept within the document.

5. Importance based on syntactic role.
6. Importance based on the specificity of the term.
7. Position of the concept hits within the document.

As for the display of ranked documents, some vendors retrieve relevant documents with great speed because they divide their databases into segments or partitions. The search proceeds on a partition-by-partition basis, and brings back the most relevant documents in each. The problem with this approach is that the most relevant document in Partition A may not in fact be the most relevant document in the overall database. This can cause undue confusion when the list of documents and their rankings change as the query progresses.

I need quick answers. How fast can I expect a text retrieval system to be?

No one likes to wait for a computer. Text retrieval systems must execute queries rapidly, even over databases that are gigabytes or terabytes in size. However, query speed is only one element in an actual search for relevant information. Think about the time it takes to frame a query, especially if you must work in a structured language such as Boolean. Think about the time to create and maintain concept networks, if you are working with a concept-building system. Think about the time to reframe and refine your search, when you discover that the keywords you have selected do not yield useful results. Think about the time it takes to scroll through documents which are either not ranked, or which do not enable you to jump, hypertext fashion, from hit to hit. Think about the time it takes to take the information you've found, and move it into another application, such as a word processing document.

We urge you to think about "end-to-end" search time. Don't simply count the seconds as a query executes. Look at the whole process as an equation:

End-to-end search time = installation + database loading + indexing + training + (query construction/reconstruction + response time + browse time + think time + collection of results + export to other applications + maintenance) × number of queries required.

15.5 A CLOSER LOOK: PLATFORM COMPUTING'S LOAD-SHARING FACILITY

Courtesy of Dr. Songnian Zhou, President, Platform Computing

LSF is a distributed computing system that turns a cluster of UNIX computers from several vendors in a "virtual supercomputer." Platform Computing Corporation has formed strategic alliances with Digital Equipment Corporation and Convex Computer Corporation. Discussions with other major systems vendors are ongoing. LSF has been bundled with cluster products Alpha AXP Farm from Digital, and Meta Computer and HP Cluster from Convex. Digital and Convex are also distributing LSF on all supported systems worldwide and providing customer support. Platform has partnered with HP in its Cluster Computing Program. IBM is also a distributor of LSF.

Platform's LSF supports fully transparent load sharing across UNIX systems from different vendors. It is the enabling technology for the rapidly emerging cluster computing market. "There is a tremendous movement across the industries to downsize from mainframes and supercomputers to RISC-based open systems," said Songnian Zhou, President of Platform. "Users resources are transparently accessible to users. With LSF, we have seen interactive response time of key applications reduced by 30–40 percent and batch job throughput doubled at such large corporate sites as Bell Northern Research/Northern Telecom and Pratt & Whitney. In today's competitive and constrained business environment, sharing computing resources makes sound business sense and improves our customers' bottom line," Zhou said.

The performance of low-cost workstations has been improving rapidly, and a cluster of workstations represents a tremendous amount of computing power. Up to now, however, such computing resources have been scattered over the network, and harnessing them to run user jobs has proved to be difficult.

Platform's LSF automates cluster computing by hiding the network and heterogeneous computers from users. Instead of running all compute jobs on the local computers as is the case with most UNIX networks, LSF transparently distributes the jobs throughout the network, taking into consideration the architecture, the operating system, and the amount of resources required by the jobs, such as memory, disk space, and software licenses. LSF supports all types of applications—parallel and serial, submitted either interactively or in batch mode.

"LSF is an important technological advance towards single-system image for heterogeneous systems," said Phil Struve, Vice President of Convex Computer Corporation. "Every user wins when LSF is used to share cycles without sacrificing control. LSF is a natural evolution from time sharing of the '60s to resource sharing of the '90s. It's kind of full circle from a single system being shared by many users to many users sharing their systems. Convex views LFS as a strategic software technology that complements our high-performance systems product line. We have been receiving extremely enthusiastic responses from our customers. LSF allows us to provide more effective solutions [to our customers]."

LSF has an open system architecture with a network API supporting a wide variety of distributed applications and software packages, some of which are:

Isbatch:	a distributed batch queuing system with a powerful yet simple batch command interface, system-wide load balancing, configurable job queues, strong resource sharing control, partial NQS compatibility, and a GUI interface
Ismake:	parallel make fully compatible with GNU make
Istcsh:	load-sharing UNIX command shell fully compatible with tcsh
IsPVM:	load-sharing PVM for parallel computing fully compatible with PVM
Islogin:	load-sharing login to start a user session on the best host
Istools:	load-sharing toolkit for custom load-sharing applications built as shell scripts

LSF is currently supported on AIX, ConvexOS, DEC OSF/1, HP-UX, IRIX, Solaris, SunOS, and ULTRIX. Other ports are planned. Over the past three years, LSF has been used in many production sites ranging from several tens to over one thousand computers. The LSF technology is based on extensive research carried out at the Computer Systems Research Institute of the University of Toronto from 1988 through 1994.

Distributed computing has been gaining importance over the last decade as a preferred mode of computing compared to centralized computing. It has been widely observed that usage of computing resources in a distributed environment is usually bursty over time and uneven among the hosts. A user of a workstation may not use the machine all the time, but may need more than it can provide while actively working. Some hosts may be heavily loaded, whereas others remain idle. Along with the dramatic decrease in hardware costs, resource demands of applications have been increasing steadily, and new, resource-intensive applications are being introduced rapidly. It is, and will remain, too expensive to dedicate a sufficient amount of computing resource to each and every user.

Load sharing is the process of redistributing the system workload among the hosts to improve performance and accessibility to remote resources. Intuitively, avoiding the situation of load imbalances and exploiting powerful hosts may lead to better job response times and resource utilization. Numerous studies on load sharing in the 1980s have confirmed such an intuition. Most of the existing work, however, has been confined to the environment of a small cluster of homogeneous hosts, and has focused on the sharing of the processing power (CPU). With the proliferation of distributed systems supporting medium to large organizations, system scale has grown from a few time-sharing hosts to tens of workstations supported by a few server machines, and to hundreds and thousands of hosts. For effective load sharing, computing resources besides processing power, such as memory frames, disk storage, and I/O bandwidth, should also be considered.

Another important development in distributed systems is heterogeneity. Heterogeneity may take a number of forms. There may be configurational heterogeneity, whereby hosts may have different processing power, memory space, disk storage, execute the same code on different hosts. Finally, there may be operating system heterogeneity, thus the system facilities on different hosts vary and may be incompatible. Although heterogeneity imposes limitations on resource sharing, it also presents substantial opportunities. First, even if both a local workstation and a remote, more powerful host are idle, the performance of a job may still be better if executed on the remote host, rather than on the local workstation. Second, by providing transparent resource locating and remote execution mechanisms, any job can be initiated from any host without considering where the resources needed by the task are, thus a CAD package that can only be executed on a Sun host can now be initiated from an HP workstation.

There has been little research concerning issues related to large scale and heterogeneity in load sharing, yet they represent two of the most important research problems in load sharing in current and future distributed systems. As system scale for load sharing become inadequate, and new research issues emerge.

We study the problems of and algorithms for load sharing in large, heterogeneous distributed computer systems by discussing the design and performance issues in Utopia, a load sharing system developed at the University of Toronto over the past several years. Utopia employs scalable scheduling algorithms for load sharing in systems running various kinds of UNIX operating systems on multiple hardware platforms. The system has no restriction to the types of applications that can be remotely executed, and most applications are supported with no change. Computing resources in a distributed system are shared at two levels. First, monolithic applications can be transferred to remote hosts for execution. Second, applications can be divided into components and executed on multiple hosts simultaneously (i.e., parallel and distributed applications). Besides demonstrating the feasibility of a general-purpose load-sharing system for large heterogeneous distributed systems by building a system that is usable in diverse system and application environments, the two main contributions of our research to the field of resource sharing in distributed systems are (1) the algorithms for distributing load information in systems with thousands of hosts and for making task placements based on tasks' resource demands and hosts' load information, and (2) the collection of remote execution mechanisms that are highly flexible and efficient, thus enabling interactive tasks that require a high degree of transparency, as well as relatively fine-grained tasks of parallel applications, to be executed remotely efficiently.

15.6   A CLOSER LOOK: OBJECTIVITY/DB

Courtesy of Objectivity Incorporated

Objectivity Inc. was founded in 1988 to solve database management needs that were not being met by relational or other traditional database management systems (DBMSs). Our unique focus—to solve the *production needs* of applications in complex distributed environments—has defined our company mission and all aspects of our product design, including architecture, features, and future directions.

Objectivity evaluated applications that require complex data structures, highly interconnected data, complex operations, and distributed environments. Most of these applications could not use relational or traditional DBMSs due to limitations in functionality or performance. Some of these applications tried to use relational DBMSs, but quickly outgrew them because the DBMSs could not keep pace with increased data complexity and performance needs of the applications. Recognizing these needs, Objectivity set out to build a suite of products to solve the data management requirements of applications in distributed, full-production environments.

Objectivity identified the emerging field of object-oriented programming as the most promising technology to achieve these goals. Since then, object technology has been applied to a wide range of software engineering problems. The object-oriented approach has proven to be robust and reliable, and it has dramatically improved programming productivity through the reuse of code.

Our product suite is designed for application developers who want to use object technology to manage complex and highly interconnected data. Typical applications that have these characteristics are multimedia, engineering, software development, telecommunications, scientific, manufacturing, transportation, publishing, and financial applications. These applications also typically involve distributed, multidatabase, multiplatform, heterogeneous computing environments.

The Objectivity product suite consists of Objectivity/DB (a high-performance and flexible object database management system [ODBMS]), and a broad range of development tools and services to help developers move applications quickly from prototype to full production using object information management. The Objectivity/DB engine provides concurrent, high-performance access to complex and highly interconnected objects distributed over multiple databases on multiple heterogeneous machines.

The tools and services provided by Objectivity are delivered as a combination of direct products, third-party relationships, and integration services. These tools and services include ad hoc query and report tools, legacy application migration tools, legacy database connectivity solutions, database administration tools, object analysis and design tools, integration with third-party CASE environments, class libraries, and GUI and application builders. All Objectivity products are designed to be compatible with and complementary to other technologies, including traditional DBMSs.

Developers typically customize their environment using many related products, such as programming languages, compilers, design tools, CASE environments, and code debuggers. Objectivity has a complementary strategy, based on standards for compatibility with the broadest range of existing products, and on strategic alliances with vendors of such products and major users. This provides developers with the widest choice of solutions, and also allows tight integration and vendor cooperation for highly productive development environments.

Target Applications

Objectivity's technology has significant benefits for applications that share the following characteristics:

- Object-oriented (C++)
- Objects or data that are large or involve many relationships (C/C++)
- Objects or data that are distributed across multiple machines or databases (C/C++)

Major portions of the software industry are adopting object technology in order to improve productivity through better reuse of proven software and easier extensibility of systems. Object technology can make systems much easier to modify and enhance, can lower the cost of development once class libraries are in place, and can greatly increase the manageability of large systems, enabling major steps forward in the software industry. Developers working with object technology select languages and tools that match the object paradigm. An ODBMS is an important component of this environment because it makes sense for object applications to communicate to the DBMS using objects. This saves the overhead of translating from objects to the records or tuples required by RDBMSs and other DBMS technologies. Programmer efficiency, application run-time efficiency, and application integrity are all improved by using objects for both the application and the database. Objectivity supports the full object-oriented model, so the full benefits of object technology become available by using Objectivity/DB to support object-oriented applications. For complex applications, those that involve complex data structures, complex operations on those structures, and high performance for those operations, traditional DBMSs are generally cumbersome and too slow by orders of magnitude. RDBMS-based applications that involve traversal of highly interconnected data generally find themselves bogged down in DBMS operations such as joins that impact performance significantly.

Objectivity/DB provides a powerful mechanism to support not only complex objects with arbitrary structures and multiple varying-sized elements, but also high-speed direct inter-object references or associations. Composite objects can be built of any number of other objects, to any number of levels of depth, and any number of levels of breadth, with automatic propagation of operations.

As applications are moved from host-based systems to distributed computing environments, data distribution and application requirements can change significantly.

Whether data is centralized or distributed, applications need a DBMS that supports transparent access to objects from all the workstations. This full distribution capability, with access to objects on any platform from all other platforms, is a unique strength of Objectivity/DB. Heterogeneous mixtures of platforms are an integral feature of distributed computing environments because users want to choose the best combination of price and performance, regardless of the vendor. As a result, as applications interconnect data across departments and enterprises, the ability to transparently access objects across multiple databases throughout the distributed environment is critical.

Multiple databases may be under control of separate organizations, while composite objects span those databases. Applications should see only a logical view of objects connected to objects, with the ODBMS managing logistics such as data format translation, moving objects from remote disk into local cache, atomic transactions across databases, and propagation of methods.

Applications with these requirements are found in many areas, and many are now migrating to object technology. Objectivity has experience with: Multimedia CASE; Configuration Management; Telecommunications; Document Creation and Management; Transportation Design and Control; Manufacturing Design; Measurement, Control, and Automation; Office Automation and GroupWare Publishing; Service Management and Support; Economic and Financial Modeling; Scientific Research and Development; Imaging and Visualization; Medical Information; Geographic Information Systems; Network Management Systems; CAD; and CAM.

The Objectivity Product Suite

By integrating Objectivity products with third-party products (Figure 15.8), a broad range of object information management capabilities is addressed, pro-

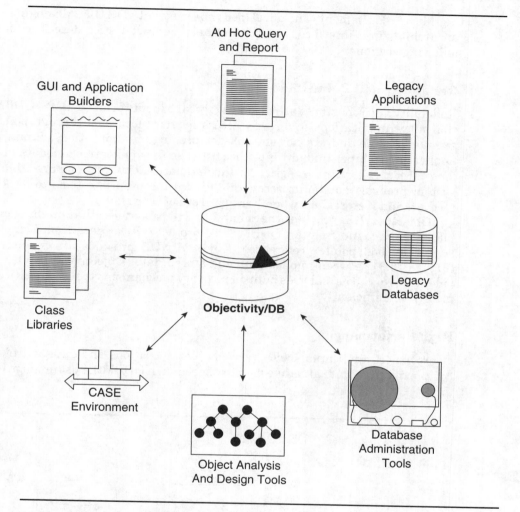

Figure 15.8   Objectivity Database Environment.

viding the largest variety of products to the users, and enabling them to take best advantage of the technology.

   Production must be considered early in the development cycle. Otherwise, an application prototype may fail under real-world conditions. Objectivity studied the requirements involved in moving applications through their development cycle from prototype to production deployment. We identified these high-level requirements and developed the Objectivity/DB ODBMS engine with an architecture, interface, and performance characteristics described in the following sections.

Reliability and Robustness

Reliability and robustness are the most critical benefits of an ODBMS. ODBMSs that allow applications to directly access memory locations through pointers are not reliable and are not suitable for production applications. Production applications require that any interface between the application and data insure long-term stability and integrity for the database. Robustness insures that the system provides maximum recoverability with appropriate tools to back up, recover, and restore data when hardware or software fails.

Objectivity/DB provides the reliability and robustness that production applications demand from an ODBMS. To protect critical data from being corrupted by bad pointer references, Objectivity/DB provides a safe interface (Figure 15.9) between applications and stored data. Objectivity/DB also provides recovery tools and uses built-in recovery mechanisms to restore data completely and efficiently.

High Performance

Users expect applications with very complex operations and data of arbitrary complexity to execute at native memory speeds. An ODBMS must manage these

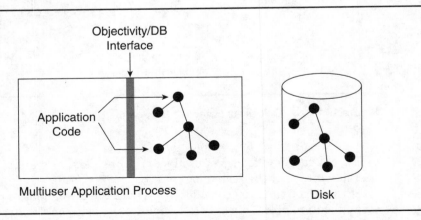

Figure 15.9   Safe Objectivity/DB interface between applications and stored data. Safe pointer access ensures data integrity.

situations for the application to provide high performance over a wide range of operating conditions. The key to judging performance is measuring how it scales under these conditions, even as the number of objects grows beyond memory, beyond swap space, beyond virtual memory, into multiple databases on multiple machines.

Objectivity/DB is a high-performance ODBMS engine that provides constant objects-per-second performance even as the amount of data grows in size to terabytes.

Multiuser Support

Virtual-memory architectures used by some ODBMSs can only work for limited-size databases or for single-user systems. A production ODBMS must allow concurrent access by distributed users from multiple machines to multiple databases. It is critical that the ODBMS maintain high performance as the number of applications and number of databases grow.

Objectivity/DB uses a distributed architecture to provide scalable high performance even as the number of users grows. We designed the architecture to provide direct connections between the distributed machines and the objects being accessed.

Distributed Databases and True Interoperability

In distributed computing environments, applications demand transparent access to objects distributed across multiple heterogeneous platforms and multiple databases. Some ODBMSs, because of their inflexible architectural design, are struggling to provide limited heterogeneous support.

The Objectivity/DB distributed architecture provides complete, transparent interoperability across all platforms, operating systems, and networks. Objectivity/DB insulates applications from the physical location and formats of objects in heterogeneous environments. The system transparently converts different byte ordering, floating point, and packing formats to provide full interoperability across heterogeneous systems, including UNIX, VMS, DOS, and Windows.

Capacity

What seems big today for storage and resources will seem small tomorrow. An ODBMS must be capable of supporting increasingly large and complex databases without sacrificing features or performance. Some ODBMSs are unable to meet these demands because they are capacity-limited by the 32-bit pointer addressing of virtual memory. Objectivity/DB is designed to support growth into the next generation of computing by directly managing object addressing using 64-bit object identifiers. This allows referencing over 1018 objects simultaneously, with individual objects up to many gigabytes. Objectivity complements this large capacity with tools especially for large project use, such as multiple schemas and schema encryption.

Standards and Open Development Environment

An ODBMS must support standards. Without standards, the ODBMS will not fit seamlessly with complementary products into a customer's environment, and will prevent the customer from taking advantage of new advances in technology as they emerge.

Objectivity actively participates in standard's organizations working on object technology and DBMS issues, including OMG, ODMG, OSF, ANSI DBTG (Database Task Group), PDES/STEP, and CFI.

Because of our commitment to standards, developers can create Objectivity/DB applications using completely standard languages, off-the-shelf compilers, debuggers, and CASE tools. Unlike other ODBMS architectures, Objectivity/DB does not require special compilers, preprocessors, or changes to development methodology.

Limitations of Central Server Architectures

A very different architecture approach is used for the centralized, mainframe-like design of RDBMSs and traditional DBMSs. These systems can, in some cases, manage very large amounts of data via direct DBMS memory and disk management. However, they support only simple structures, and completely lack support for dynamically varying sized structures, arbitrary structures, direct interobject connections, and composite objects.

These systems also isolate data buffers and database activity to a separate process and often a separate machine. For new distributed computing environments, this requires a slow interprocess interface to access each object. Typically milliseconds or tens of milliseconds are required for interprocess communication as compared to intraprocess operations, which run in a few cycles or a few tenths of a microsecond on a 10 MIP machine. Also, forcing all access to go through a central server creates a fundamental bottleneck when all users must wait in a queue at the server for all operations. This limits scalability for multiple users. Objectivity recognized that a full distribution of data and processing requires a fundamentally different approach.

Benefits of the Objectivity/DB Fully Distributed Architecture

Objectivity's solution was to design a new architecture incorporating the best features of virtual memory and central server architectures. It was possible to provide the arbitrary structure access and near-native performance of virtual memory by mapping objects directly into a cache in the application's address space and executing there. However, to allow the ODBMS to perform memory and disk management for high performance with more complex data, more users, multiple databases, and distributed users, application access to the objects in this cache is through one level of pointer indirection. The cost for this (several cycles to test and dereference) was shown to be negligible in production environments, where the greatest performance bottleneck was disk I/O.

The advantages were that the ODBMS could now provide an extra level of integrity, insuring that applications could never dereference a "stale" pointer due to commit or swapping, and subtly corrupt the database. The ODBMS could implement direct management of memory and disk, clustering, caching, multiple buffer management, and replacement algorithms for optimal application performance. The ODBMS could also provide a fully distributed approach, portable across all platforms, not limited by a single operating system's virtual memory limitations or restrictions.

In Figure 15.10 the traditional database client/server (actually a central server) architecture is shown. Figure 15.11 shows the Objectivity/DB new, fully distributed architecture. The network/process boundary in each figure shows

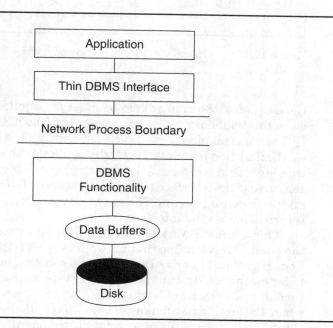

Figure 15.10   Traditional client/server architecture.

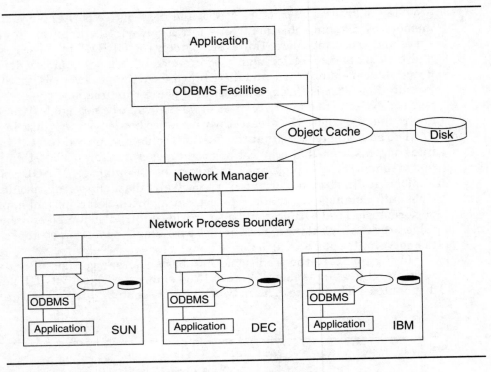

Figure 15.11   Objectivity/DB fully distributed architecture.

the position of the interprocess boundary is significant, because operations that cross this boundary suffer an overhead of 10,000X (ones or tens of milliseconds IPC versus submicrosecond cycle time within the process).

In traditional architectures, the application's address space contains a very thin layer that packages a database request. For example, a high-level query is sent across the interface to the server where all the buffers are maintained and all the processing occurs. The answer, typically a small number of bytes, is then returned across the interface.

This approach works well when the request and the answer are small, and the operation is long, so that network overhead is amortized over a long operation. High-level queries that can take seconds, or applications like automatic teller machines or airline reservation systems that are sequentially accessed by each user, can make efficient use of this architecture. However, it works poorly when the user must make repeated database requests, traversing from one object to another, performing complicated operations, all at interactive speeds.

To distribute processing and storage, the Objectivity/DB architecture moves the process interface boundary down, providing an object cache within the application address space. As objects are accessed, they are brought into the cache, and can then be accessed at native memory speeds. Traversal, creation, naming, indexing, method propagation, and other functions are all executed locally. When the application requests an object that is not in the cache, the ODBMS traps this request, and the network manager locates the database containing the object, the volume containing the database, obtains read/write locks if necessary, moves the object into the cache, performs heterogeneity transformations if necessary, and sets up the pointer indirection, so that later operations are at native speeds. This is all done transparently for the application.

In this way, virtual memory is used for local operations, while simultaneously providing transparent fully distributed access to multiple databases anywhere on the network of heterogeneous computers. The user may choose to localize objects in a single database or multiple databases, or on a single or multiple central servers. Processing and storage are provided according to the applications and the resources available. The result is full distribution.

- object distribution: objects can be located anywhere, and accessed from all platforms
- control distribution: objects can be distributed among multiple databases, each under separate administrative control
- Single logical view: regardless of location or format

Databases can be used for private use, by groups, or by departments; for example, for electrical design, packaging, test, manufacturing, finance. Each is under the administrative control of its owner, who determines when to back up, shut down, and how to control access. Yet composite objects and all database operations can extend across all databases. All of this occurs transparently. There is no need for the user or application developer to know which database an object is in, on which machine, or to manually move it to a private database or into memory.

The Objectivity/DB architecture transparently handles differences among heterogeneous machines and operating systems, including:

- byte ordering
- floating point formats
- compiler differences
- structure/class padding and alignment

All this is done at the object level, so it is not necessary to process more objects than actually requested. Further, this unique mechanism allows use of the exact binary representation of the native environment. Unlike approaches that change the representation by maximal padding for the worst-case architecture, this saves space and allows compatibility with preexisting binary libraries so a structure can be passed directly to an operating system routine.

The Objectivity/DB architecture also exploits distributed computing environment resources efficiently, for improved performance as networks grow. With traditional architectures, when additional capacity or performance is required, the only choice is to replace or upgrade the server. In this fully distributed architecture, a new machine adds its own processing resources to the network and can automatically access databases on other machines without reconfiguring a server. Of course databases may also be moved to the new machine to take advantage of additional storage, or to reduce network traffic. This allows maximum use of resources and provides the ability to take advantage of price and performance improvements in platforms while preserving the current hardware investment and not requiring changes to applications.

Objectivity/DB provides for a federation of databases and maintains a catalog of known databases and database schemas. Distributed schemas are managed by the federation, and databases can share schemas or have their own object definitions. Shared schemas reduce storage requirements and simplify schema evolution compared to systems that store a copy of the schema in each database. Cross-database object references are also managed by the federation for full referential integrity. Schemas and databases may be added, removed, secured, temporarily detached from or reattached to the federation with flexible administrative control. The Objectivity/DB architecture provides rich features for managing a distributed environment of multiple applications, databases, platforms.

Standard and Open Development Environment

The Objectivity/DB development environment provides high productivity for the developer. Standard C and C++ are easy to use as data definition and manipulation languages. Objectivity includes a rich interface with advanced modeling functions that make it simple to work with sophisticated objects, a query language that uses standard SQL and C++ for ad hoc query capabilities, as well as flexible object versioning and configuration tools.

The interface provides a simple logical view of objects independent of physical organization, and application migration tools that make it easy for C and C++ applications to use Objectivity/DB. The Objectivity tools environment enables very tight integration with third-party CASE tools for a rich and productive development environment.

Flexible Data Modeling

Objectivity/DB makes it easy to migrate existing C or C++ applications by using standard C++ for schema class definitions. C++ is used to define classes and to generate header and source files that are included with the run-time library for application development. The object technology approach for assigning and sharing behavior is through inheritance, so persistence is inherited with flexible run-time options to create either transient or persistent instances of the class. The user simply declares his or her class to inherit from the persistent class from ooObj and it becomes persistent-capable. Other classes, without such inheritance, have no overhead from the database and do not need to appear in the schema.

Objectivity/DB separates schema definition requirements from application development to simplify application development. Application build times and complexity are reduced, and different application development groups can share schema definitions as they build related applications. Objectivity/DB schema definition capabilities offer the full power needed for production applications, for customization and control, and for tuning.

Rich Programming Interface

For migrating pointer-based applications, pointers can simply be declared as references and the ODBMS will handle them correctly, with the benefit of integrity across the distributed environment. Associations can also be declared as uni- or bidirectional, one-to-one, one-to-many, or many-to-many. These associations can be annotated for behavior under versioning (copy, drop, move), and for propagating methods to create composite objects (networks of connected heterogeneous objects that act as a single object). As shown in Figure 15.12, such composite objects may cross databases, and the methods will propagate transparently throughout the fully distributed environment. The methods to manage these associations, such as those that create and delete them dynamically at run time, are automatically generated.

Objectivity/DB also provides varrays, dynamic varying-sized arrays of structures, with methods generated automatically. Both varrays and associations are fully dynamic: No space is allocated unless they are used. Other classes are provided, and because Objectivity/DB uses standard languages, and since the heterogeneity engine provides native in-memory packing layouts, the user can take advantage of many third-party class libraries. Users have successfully moved very large C-based systems to Objectivity/DB in only a couple of person-weeks with full DBMS functionality.

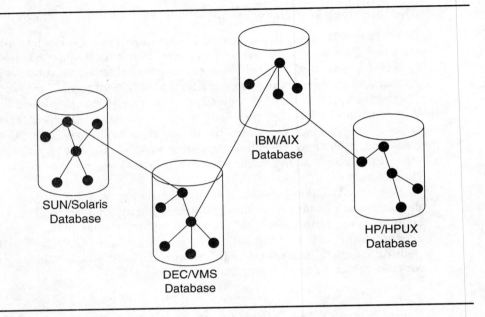

Figure 15.12   Composite object.

System Architecture

The architecture of Objectivity/DB has been designed to meet the needs of current ODBMS users, but is flexible enough to grow as the uses of ODBMSs grow. In order to accomplish this, Objectivity/DB is structured in a modular fashion, allowing easy replacement of major subsections of the system. This allows the rewriting of subsystems to incorporate new algorithms, new standards, or new hardware. The major subsystems are shown in Figure 15.13.

Programming Interface	The programming interface (C or C++) allows an application to communicate with Objectivity/DB. The programming language is not hard-coded into the system.
Type Manager	The Type Manager stores, retrieves, and maintains descriptions of all classes defined in the database. Types are defined as full objects.

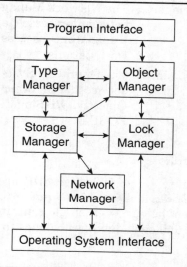

Figure 15.13   Objectivity/DB system architecture.

Object Manager	The Object Manager keeps track of and manipulates objects within the database. The Object Manager maintains the logical view of the data. Tasks handled by the Object Manager include propagation and versioning.
Storage Manager	The Storage Manager is responsible for the physical placement of data in virtual memory and physical storage.
Lock Server	The Lock Server is a process that coordinates access to all objects in the database, managing concurrent access to data among all application processes. The Lock Server supports concurrency management among multiple users, multiple hosts, multiple databases, and multiple networks.
Lock Manager	The Lock Manager communicates lock requests from an application process to the Lock Server. Each application process has its own Lock Manager.

| Network Manager | The Network Manager coordinates communication between processes, allowing local processes to transparently access data located on remote workstations. |
| Operating System Interface | The Operating System Interface provides basic services for all other software in the system. Objectivity/DB makes use of OS services through POSIX. |

Storage Hierarchy

As shown in Figure 15.14, Objectivity/DB uses four storage entities: *objects*, *containers*, *databases*, and *federated databases*. The fundamental storage is the *object*. Each object belongs to a single container, each container belongs to a single database, and each database belongs to a single federated database.

Objects

An *object* is the fundamental storage entity of Objectivity/DB. This is the entity that is accessed and manipulated by Objectivity/DB applications and stored on pages. When an object is first referenced in a transaction the object (not all objects on the page that contains the object) is converted to the proper machine format.

Containers

A *container* can hold a collection of pages. The container is the basic locking and clustering unit. A page is the unit of transfer from database storage to the application and back to storage. When an object that currently does reside in the Objectivity/DB in-memory cache is referenced, the disk page that contains that object is read and placed in the cache. Users have control over pages via the number of pages in the buffer cache, the initial number of pages in a container, and via the object cluster hints (put new object on the same page as the cluster object).

Databases

A *database* consists of a *default container* and can also contain user-defined containers. The default container holds objects that you have not explicitly put in user-defined containers. An application can simultaneously open and manipulate objects in multiple containers and multiple databases, which may be

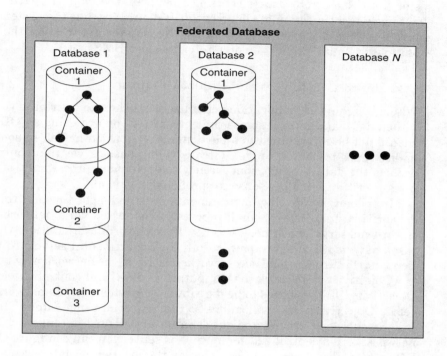

Figure 15.14   Objectivity/DB storage hierarchy.

distributed multiple network nodes. All databases in a federated database share the same schema(s). The database is the basic unit of distribution and administration.

Federated Database

A *federated database* contains user-defined databases. Each federated database maintains schemas that describe all of the publicly visible class definitions and catalogs of user databases—names and locations. Applications create objects of classes defined in these schemas.

Some administrative control is located at the federated database level, including configuration information (where Objectivity/DB files physically reside) and concurrent access control. Currently, the Objectivity/DB federated database is a collection of Objectivity/DB databases, but the system architecture has been designed to support the use of gateways to allow the federated database to man a collection of heterogeneous DBMSs.

Distribution of Objects and Object Databases

When designing an application you must decide how to distribute your computation, data, and control across the network. If you are using an ODBMS, you should not be constrained to a particular distribution model. In some cases it makes sense to have a single centralized database server that controls all aspects of the data (storage, concurrency control, query processing), but in many instances it makes more sense to spread out the load.

In modern computing environments, it is no longer the case that users of database systems are on small processors connected via a network to a large centralized server machine. Users now have powerful workstations that in some cases have more compute power than the departmental server. In this situation, distributing the load across workstations on the network may make sense.

Objectivity/DB allows the computation, data, and control associated with Objectivity/DB databases to be distributed anywhere on the network. You can set up Objectivity/DB applications so that the computing, administrative control, concurrency control, and data storage are all on different machines on the network, or if a centralized server makes sense, you can configure Objectivity/DB in that way. Later, you can change the location of databases and objects without affecting applications. In any case, Objectivity/DB applications access the data independent of its location. As shown in Figure 15.15, Objectivity/DB applications can run on any machine that can access the lock server and data files via the Objectivity/DB-supported network protocols (TCP/IP, DECNet for access to the lock server; NFS, AFS, HP diskless, DECNet, PC/NFS).

Support for Heterogeneous Environments

As new machines with greater performance or functionality appear on the market, many organizations end up with combinations of these new machines. A database management system should allow users to create data on any of the machines and retrieve that data on any of the other machines in a transparent manner.

Since different machines may store data in different formats (byte ordering: little-endian or big-endian; floating point format: IEEE, VAX) and compilers (even on the same machine) may align and pad structures differently, an ODBMS must be able to convert between a number of different formats.

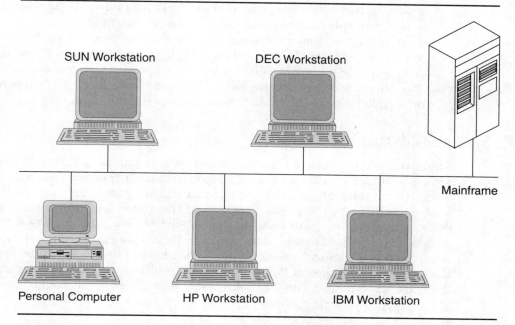

Figure 15.15   Objectivity/DB distributed network.

Objectivity/DB supports the transparent conversion of data between all machines and compilers that Objectivity/DB runs on. Data is stored in the format of the machine (and compiler) that created the data and conversion is only done when the formats or alignment/padding differs (some machines and compilers support the same physical representation of the data as others so no conversion is necessary).

There are three things to consider when evaluating the support of heterogeneity by an ODBMS:

- Is it fully supported? Some vendors claim heterogeneity because they run on different platforms or because they can convert between some small subset of machines that have the exact same format. Make sure that heterogeneity support means that they can fully convert between all of their supported platforms.
- How invasive is it? In order to support heterogeneity, some ODBMSs require you to change the definitions of any structures that you include in your persistent data to make sure that they are maximally padded. If you have to change a structure that is used by other libraries you will have to

recompile those libraries, and if that structure is used by the operating system, you will not be able to use it in the persistent structure.

- What is the performance? Some systems that support heterogeneity convert a large number of objects when a single object is accessed. If the data is being sparsely traversed, this can add a significant performance overhead. Only objects that are accessed should be converted. Also, if two machines (or compilers) have the same format, no conversion should take place.

Scalable High Performance

Applications must scale as the amount of data or number of users increases. This is a common problem in ODBMS use; the initial benchmark is small and easily understandable, but the performance characteristics for that small case bear no relation to the production uses of the system. An important design decision for Objectivity/DB was that the system be able to scale to large amounts of data and large numbers of users. As the problems get bigger, users should not see a significant change in performance or be required to use other interfaces to the system. A number of benchmarks and applications have shown that as database sizes increase, applications that access all of the data scale linearly.

Performance Tuning

Applications in different domains have their own performance characteristics and demands upon an ODBMS. It is important to be able to adjust the use of ODBMS to improve the performance of the application. Objectivity/DB provides the ability to adjust parameters, such as the number of buffers, clustering factors, and growth factors, to distribute the data and applications across the network, and provides a number of different access methods for use depending upon your particular requirements (speed vs. space trade-off, degree of fragmentation vs. performance).

Your ODBMS must provide for tuning based upon an analysis of the performance characteristics. Objectivity/DB provides run-time statistics, static analysis tools, documentation, and customer support to help in the tuning process.

Concurrency Controls

Concurrency is the ability of Objectivity/DB to allow simultaneous access to a database by multiple users and processes on a network. Concurrency control insures that the databases remain consistent under multiple concurrent accesses. Objectivity/DB provides three mechanisms that support concurrency control—locking, transactions, and the ability to support multiple readers and one writer on the same container at the same time. An important consideration in the evaluation of an ODBMS is to make sure that the performance of the ODBMS does not dramatically degrade as the number of concurrent users of the system increases.

Locking Facilities

Objectivity/DB is a multiprocessing system, allowing simultaneous multiple access to the data. To insure data consistency, database access is restricted through the use of locks. There are two types of locks: transient and persistent. A transient lock exists during a transaction or process; a persistent lock exists across transactions and processes. A process may obtain either a *read lock*, which allows other processes to read the data, or an *update lock*, which prevents all other processes from reading or modifying the data, as well as *shared* and *exclusive* locks, with support for upward escalation, and *propagation* across composites. For flexibility in controlling concurrent access to data, Objectivity/DB currently supports locking at the following levels of granularity:

> Container
>
> Database
>
> Federated Database

The programming interface and the architecture of Objectivity/DB support finer granularity of locking. Logically you can lock objects, but physically this is implemented as container locking. Currently, system data structures are locked at the object level, and support for finer physical locking granularity for user data will be available in future releases. Locks are granted automatically and transparently to an application. You can also explicitly set locks if you want to. For each federated database, locks are managed by a Lock Server, which is automatically started when Objectivity/DB is initialized. The Lock Server is a centralized resource; there is one Lock Server running per federated database. All applications accessing the federated database must request a lock for the data from this Lock Server.

Transaction Management

After an application accesses a database, any changes the application makes to the database are buffered by Objectivity/DB and not actually applied until specified by the application. Each buffered unit of work is a *transaction*. Transactions allow a collection of operations to appear as a single *atomic* operation to the database (that is, either all of the operations are performed, or none is). Once a transaction is *committed* (applied) to the database, the changes are permanent. However, an application may choose to *abort* a transaction at any time up to the commit point, leaving the database in its original state.

Check-In and Check-Out Capabilities

There are times when a user would like a database or container to be locked across a transaction boundary, for example, running a sequence of ECAD design tools on a design. Objectivity/DB provides a check-in/check-out mechanism allowing you to lock a container or database for an extended period of time, rather than for a single session.

Multiple Readers, One Writer (MROW) Facility

In order to increase the concurrency of the system, Objectivity/DB allows a container in a transaction to have multiple readers and one writer. One process can update a container while other processes are reading its original contents. This mechanism is known as MROW.

Dynamic Type Management

ODBMSs do not just store sequences of bytes, they store structured data, called objects. ODBMSs use type information to describe the structure of the data as presented to the user and stored in the database. The type information also describes how to convert data from one machine format to another (heterogeneity conversion). The type information for a related set of objects is called a schema.

Developing with Objectivity/DB

Objectivity/DB is clearly the market leader, providing developers the power and productivity features required for today's real-world applications. Objectivity/DB also provides clear gains in productivity, allowing developers easy access to the full power of an ODBMS, using standard languages, compilers, and development environments

Productivity Through Standards

A key to productivity is the ability to empower developers with new technology, without disrupting the existing development process, and Objectivity/DB is designed with this goal in mind. From start to finish, the process of developing an Objectivity/DB application fits naturally into virtually any existing object-oriented (or non-object-oriented) development environment. This is achieved by the following components:

- A standard C++ object-oriented interface. No proprietary language extensions mean that you control your development environment.
- A standard C (Pascal/Fortran) callable function interface.
- A Schema Processor.

Two distinct tasks exist in the development of application systems that deal with persistent data. One of the tasks is the definition of the schema, and the other is the development of applications that create and access data defined by the schema. These two tasks are usually performed by the schema designer and the application developer respectively. In an Objectivity/DB environment, the schema designer defines the schema using a superset of C++ in what is called a schema file. This file is run through the schema processor, which loads the schema into the database, producing a schema methods file (C++ only), and a schema header file (C++ and C). (See Figure 15.16.) Application developers need only include the schema header file in their own program source. The application source file and the schema methods file are then compiled and linked with the Objectivity/DB run-time library to produce an application. The entire process is a natural extension to the standard application development process.

Objectivity has a strong commitment to industry standards and trends, working with other vendors to provide a complete, state-of-the-art object-oriented development environment. Objectivity has agreements with vendors such as ParcPlace Systems, Centerline Software, Hewlett-Packard, IBM, and DEC to insure compatibility with all major CASE environments. This commitment not only gives you the freedom to choose your development environment, but it also preserves your current investment in tools and training.

Powerful Data Modeling

One of the benefits of object-oriented systems is the ability for developers to closely match the application data model to the problem at hand, and Objectivity/DB fully realizes this potential. By providing a full range of data modeling constructs, Objectivity/DB gives the developer the freedom to store and access ODBMS data in the most efficient and logical manner.

Flexible Modeling Language

The schema for an Objectivity/DB database is specified using the objectivity data definition language (DDL), a high-level data modeling language that is a superset of the standard C++ language, with extensions for associations. Methods for using associations are automatically generated by the objectivity schema processor.

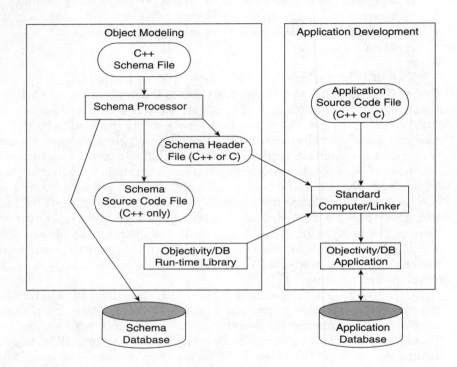

Figure 15.16   Objectivity/DB development process.

Associations and Referential Integrity

Objectivity/DB fully supports *entity-relationship* data models through the use of *associations*. An association is a logical link used to indicate that a relationship exists between two persistent objects. Associations can indicate 1:1, 1:N, and N:M relationships. Objectivity/DB also allows objects spanning multiple remote databases to participate in an association. Virtually any relationship between object classes can be modeled using Objectivity/DB associations.

Associations are type safe, and are declared as part of an object class. They also have standard object-oriented semantics in regard to class compatibility, e.g., if the developer declares an association to a class, instances of that class or any subclass may be associated to the object. This allows the developer to freely trade off between run-time flexibility and strong compile-time type checking.

Associations can be declared on both object classes involved in the relation. This kind of association is called *bidirectional* and allows you to traverse freely between related objects. The bidirectional associations also allow Objectivity/DB to maintain *referential integrity*. This means that Objectivity/DB will ensure the validity and integrity of the association, e.g., if an object participating in an association is deleted, the association is automatically removed from the related object. A primary benefit of referential integrity is that it is not possible to have a dangling object reference in the ODBMS.

For cases where efficiency is the primary concern, Objectivity/DB also allows you to define an association on only one of the object classes involved in the relationship, and this is called a *unidirectional* association. This type of association has semantics very similar to a simple object pointer.

Although associations are defined at schema definition time, their behavior is completely dynamic. No overhead is incurred in an object unless an association is actually used, and associations may be added and removed from objects at run time.

As Figure 15.17 demonstrates, associations allow the developer to create a

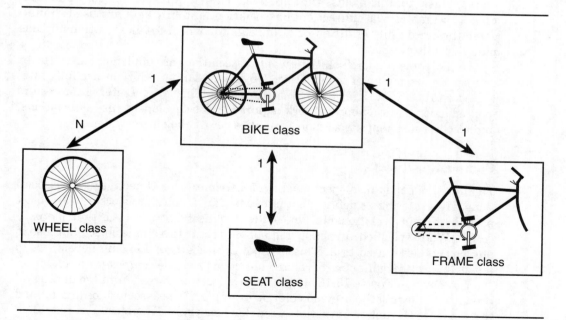

Figure 15.17   Data modeling with associations.

data model that naturally reflects the physical relationships involved. The declarations for class BIKE and class WHEEL defining the associations in Figure 15.17 look like this:

```
class WHEEL : public ooObj {
 public:
  ooHandle(BIKE) wheel_to_bike <-> bike_to_wheel[];  // bidirectional N:1

} ;
class BIKE : public ooObj {
 public:
  ooHandle(WHEEL) bike_to_wheel[] <-> wheel_to_bike; // bidirectional 1:N

  ooHandle(SEAT) bike_to_seat <-> seat_to_bike;       // bidirectional 1:1

  ooHandle(FRAME) bike_to_frame <-> frame_to_bike;    // bidirectional 1:1

} ;
```

Associations are represented as a member field in a class declaration, with the type represented by the macro *ooHandle(className)*. This macro defines a *handle* class, that is, a class that provides persistent object access. Double arrows (<->) indicate a bidirectional association, and brackets are used to indicated the cardinality of the association; e.g., the wheel-to-bike relationship has many wheels per bike.

Unlike some vendors' solutions where associations are implemented as a layer or class library on top of the ODBMS, Objectivity/DB associations are fully integrated into the ODBMS at the architecture level. This level of integration results in a reduction of the amount of work required by the developer to use associations, and also in consistent association semantics across the entire system.

Composite Objects

The developer may also specify behavior attributes for Objectivity/DB associations. These attributes define what happens if an action should occur to an object participating in a relationship. One of the most useful attributes is that of *propagation*. When specified, an action will not only occur to a single object, but also to any objects associated to it. This is a powerful feature, allowing developers to model an arbitrary number of related objects as a single *composite object*.

As shown in Figure 15.18, a composite object may have unlimited depth and breadth. Following the previous bicycle example, if the associations are defined to propagate the delete operation, then deleting the BIKE object also results in

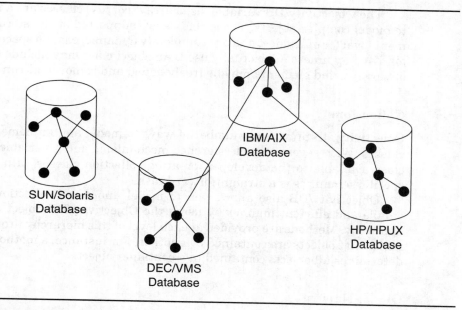

Figure 15.18   Composite object.

the deletion of any associated WHEEL, SEAT, and FRAME objects. Only the definition of class BIKE need be modified.

```
class BIKE : public ooObj {
    public:
    ooHandle(WHEEL) bike_to_wheel[] <-> wheel_to_bike : prop(delete);
    ooHandle(SEAT) bike_to_seat <-> seat_to_bike : prop(delete);
    ooHandle(FRAME) bike
to_frame <-> frame_to_bike : prop(delete);
} ;
```

Complex Objects

Objectivity/DB allows the developer to create and manage *complex objects* in the ODBMS. These objects vary in size dynamically, and tend to have many relationships with other objects in other databases. Typical objects of this category include multimedia (sound, video, animation), telecommunications, and design data.

The Objectivity/DB variable-sized array (*varray*) classes are a natural way to model complex objects. These classes are supported at the storage management level for efficiency, and are completely dynamic, e.g., no space is allocated for a varray unless it is actually used. An object class may include any number of varrays, and elements may be freely added and removed at run time.

Collections

Objectivity/DB provides a number of ways to model and implement collection classes. With several object reference mechanisms and a variable-sized array class available to the developer, creating collection classes with application-specific semantics is a straightforward task.

Objectivity/DB also allows you to model unordered collections in a very simple and efficient manner by using the Objectivity/DB object containment hierarchy. Methods are provided at each level of this hierarchy to quickly determine what objects are contained by another. For instance, a method exists that determines all objects contained in a container object.

Object Names

Another mechanism that the developer can use to model data is object *naming*. Objects in an Objectivity/DB database may be given a name within a *name scope* defined by the user. Any object can be used to define a name scope, and an object may be given a name in several name scopes. The semantics of additional names are determined by the application. For example, they may be aliases or they may be related to the design structure of a product.

A Complete ODBMS Interface

Objectivity/DB provides full-featured interfaces that allow the developer to fully realize the benefits of ODBMS technology. For those working in non-object development environments, a standard C (Pascal, Fortran) call-compatible library is available. For those working within an object development environment, a standard C++ library interface is available. In both cases, all the features of Objectivity/DB are readily available to the developer.

A programming interface, like most user interfaces, must cater to a wide audience ranging from novices to expert users. The key to designing a successful interface is the principle of *progressive disclosure*. This means an interface where basic tasks are made simple, and more power and complexity are made available to the user as he or she requires it. The Objectivity/DB C and C++ library interfaces both follow this principle, offering easy-to-learn base functionality, and a rich set of sophisticated features that allow the developer to tune application performance and function according to need.

The ideal interface between a C++ application and an ODBMS is C++, and Objectivity/DB offers the most intuitive native C++ library interface of any ODBMS. From coding to debugging, the developer stays entirely within the realm of the standard C++ language, taking full advantage of the benefits of object-oriented programming.

The C++ language is very extensible, allowing customizing of operations and classes via overloading and subclassing. The Objectivity/DB C++ library interface uses these standard features to their maximum benefit, resulting in a comprehensive ODBMS interface that fits naturally into the realm of C++ applications development. By using the features of the standard language rather than a proprietary compiler approach, the Objectivity/DB C++ programming interface insures that the developer won't encounter any unpleasant "surprises" with the language. All the features of the C++ language behave exactly as one would expect.

At the root of any ODBMS is the behavior that allows an object to be persistent. One of the basic tenets of object-oriented programming is that behaviors should be inherited from base functional classes. This principle promotes code reuse, and allows the system to provide strong type checking to insure that only allowed operations may be performed on an object. As such, in an Objectivity/DB application, the behavior of persistence is inherited from one of several system classes (Figure 15.19). The exact persistent behavior is determined by the base class used.

With the Objectivity/DB C++ library interface, it is the ability to be persistent which is inherited. Whether or not an object is actually created persistent is determined at object creation time by the developer.

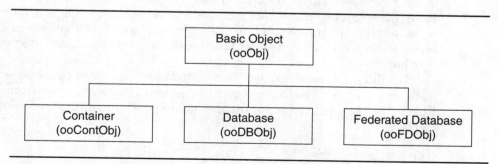

Figure 15.19   Objectivity/DB persistent base classes.

A Logical Interface

The programming interface to Objectivity/DB presents the developer with a consistent *logical view* of the entire system, encompassing such concepts as associations, versioning, and objects. The logical view isolates the developer from the complexity of the physical view of the ODBMS, which covers such issues as files, network hosts, and clustering. This allows the developer to work entirely in the realm of the logical model, independent of such issues as actual network location of databases. In fact, physical relocation of a database at a later time does not affect the application's view of the data.

Easy Migration to Full ODBMS

Beyond the behavior of persistence, an ODBMS should be capable of offering full database functionality to the developer at object-level granularity. These features might include security, heterogeneous data conversion, and concurrency control. At the architecture level, the only way to provide full database functionality on a per-object basis is by *handle-based object management*.

This means that a level of indirection to persistent objects is provided by the ODBMS to allow full object-level database functionality, including physical object management and validation of object references. Objectivity/DB uses this architecture, and the C++ library interface supports it in a language-transparent manner.

A memory-mapped ODBMS architecture is simply incapable of delivering full DBMS functionality to the developer at object-level granularity, and in many cases a performance penalty is incurred because an operation intended for a single object must be performed on all other objects located on the same physical page.

In an Objectivity/DB application, objects are primarily accessed through *object references*. These are system-defined classes that are type safe and behave like pointers, but provide persistent object reference. Objects may also be accessed through *handles*. Handles are type-compatible with object references; however they also have member functions that relate specifically to persistent attributes.

The following code samples demonstrate the ease with which object references are used. This example shows the declaration for a nonpersistent simple linked list element, including the method to count the number of elements in the list.

```
class list {
        public:
        list(){
```

```
        next = 0;
    } ;
    list *next;
    int count(){
        lnt i;
        list *elem;
        for (i = 1, elem = next; elem; elem = elem->next);
            return(i);
    }
}
```

The following example is the declaration for the same class, only made persistent. The differences are highlighted in the example.

```
class list : public ooObj {
        public:
        list(){
            next = 0;
    } ;
    ooRef(list) next;
    int count(){
        int i; ooRef(list) elem;
        for (i = 1, elem = next; elem; elem = elem->next);
            return(i);
        }
}
```

Note that in the persistent class, objects are referenced using the arrow operator (->) like a standard C++ pointer. Object references and handles are *smartpointers*, a type that is defined to behave like a pointer, but also allows Objectivity/DB to provide full database functionality at object-level granularity.

Because of this ease of conversion from C or C++ applications to full ODBMS applications, several users have successfully converted large C software systems to Objectivity/DB, and received the full benefits of integrity, address space, and scalable performance. In one case a half-million-line mostly C-based ECAD system was converted in two person-weeks. In another a PL/1-based MCAD/CAM system of several million lines was converted in a similar time. A very large, complex technical application in C was in process of conversion from memory-based C structures to virtual-memory-based persistent objects. After several weeks and over 8000 lines of new code to manage the pointers among all those objects, the user tried Objectivity/DB, and had it running in only three days, with full DBMS capability, not just persistent objects. A large telecommunications application was moved from another object DBMS to Objectivity/DB in a week with 10X improvement in performance, and substantial code simplification.

Object Traversal and Iterators

As shown in the previous example, Objectivity/DB supports traversal of objects in a traditional navigational (pointer chasing) fashion. However, a general drawback of this style of object traversal is the relative complexity involved. One of the benefits of object-oriented programming is data and control abstraction, and a common abstraction for the traversal of a collection of elements is the *iterator*. An iterator hides the details involved in object traversal, and merely returns the current element of the collection. Iterator is a subclass of handle, so object reference from an iterator is performed in a standard manner. The Objectivity/DB library interfaces provide full and consistent support of iterators.

Integrated Tools and Interfaces for ODB Development

We work with leading technology suppliers to bring you the best technologies available through strategic development partnerships and technology licensing agreements. An example of this commitment is our use of Motif technology from the Open Software Foundation in our graphical tools. Objectivity was one of the first licensees of OSF Motif and is active in working with OSF to determine future requirements and directions.

More recently, Objectivity announced that it has licensed the SoftBench Broadcast Message Server (BMS) from Hewlett-Packard Company. The HP BMS is also licensed by IBM for its AIX CASE workbench.

Our commitment to provide the best integrated tools and interfaces also means working with leading solution providers through our Partners Program to identify the best third-party tools and interfaces and to insure a high level of compatibility with our products. Our adherence to standards already ensures that Objectivity's products are compatible with the widest range of tools and interfaces, including those from CASE and 4GL tool companies, gateway suppliers, and language and library vendors. We provide these third-party solutions to our customers through joint sales and marketing activities with our partners. These solutions include, among others, HP SoftBench, CenterLine ObjectCenter, ADT PTech, ProtoSoft, IDE, and Persistence. Objectivity has also announced plans with Sun DOE/DOMF, Tooltalk, DEC Cohesion/Fuse, IBM AIX/Workbench, SGI CaseVision, and ParcPlace.

In the Objectivity Open Tools model (Figure 15.20), applications communicate by sending generic messages that other tools can receive and act on. This kind of message is called a *notification*. As an example, if a certain object is deleted in one tool, the tool sends a Delete(object) notification through the

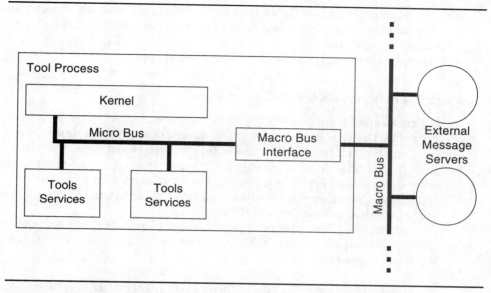

Figure 15.20   Objectivity Open Tools architecture.

backplane to indicate which object was deleted. Any other tool interested in that event can receive the message and perform some action based on which object was deleted.

The other kind of message in the Objectivity Open Tools model allows a tool to send a generic *request* for a service without being concerned with what other tool will provide that service. For example, if one tool needs to show the methods associated with a selected object, the tool sends a ShowMethods(object) request through the backplane. If another tool is running that can show object methods, it responds by showing the methods for the selected object. If no tool is running, the framework starts a tool that can provide the service, then delivers the request.

The Objectivity Open Tools integration model is very flexible because it allows other tools to be added later on that can perform new functions and provide new services based on a standard set of messages. By using standard notification and request messages, Objectivity/DB tools can perform actions based on messages sent by other development tools as well as using existing tools where appropriate to perform Objectivity/DB-specific functions. The Objectivity Open Tools model allows you to continue using all of your familiar tools even when working with Objectivity/DB-specific data.

Objectivity's Open Tools architecture insures that each Objectivity/DB tool can be easily integrated into today's popular tool integration frameworks and message sets, and that the full functionality of all tool services is available through standard framework message interfaces.

Integration with CASE Environments

Integration of database development tools is an important issue because such a large part of developing a database application involves developing software applications that create and access data in a database. Objectivity/DB provides integration with several leading CASE environments, with other integrations in progress. Because Objectivity/DB is available on such a wide variety of computing platforms, our objective is to be integrated with the CASE environments our customers use on those platforms.

In studying how programmers use database and other software development tools, we found that there are four important levels of integration in a CASE environment.

Compatibility Level. Compatibility-level integration allows you to design, develop, debug, and test database applications using standard tools and language processors from the CASE environment or third-party tool vendors, together with database-specific tools provided by the database vendor. The integration should not require you to discard existing tools such as debuggers in favor of ones supplied by the database vendor, or to change language interfaces to use standard CASE tools. Finally, the integration should be a fully documented and supported part of the database vendor's product.

Language Level. Language-level integration includes all of the aspects of compatibility-level integration, plus the customization of existing CASE tools to support schema design, processing, and language extensions for the vendor's data definition language (DDL). All editors, build managers, debuggers, and static analyzers should be able to work with DDL language files, and allow generated standard language files to be viewed and processed in terms of the original DDL language files. If the CASE environment performs operations based on file type, it should perform appropriate operations for DDL or other database-specific file types.

Tool Level. Tool-level integration includes all aspects of language-level integration, plus the ability to start specific database tools from the CASE environment based on the current selection within a CASE tool or on a user-supplied value. In the same way, it should be possible to start specific CASE tools from within individual database tools. If possible, the status of the tool that was started should be reported when it exits.

Operation Level. Operation-level integration includes all aspects of tool-level integration, plus the ability to register new notification and service request messages for database tools with the CASE framework. In operation-level integration, new actions occur across the entire toolset based on new notifications and requests that are registered as part of the integration. Unlike tool-level integration, the benefits of operation-level integration extend to both existing tools and new tools that are added later. Operation-level integration is only possible for ECMA-style CASE integration frameworks and database tools.

Integration with HP SoftBench Environment

Objectivity/DB is fully integrated with HP SoftBench for C and C++ at the operation level. Database application developers can use SoftBench to design Objectivity/DB databases and develop applications that use Objectivity/DB. Objectivity/DB-specific file operations, database schema browsing, syntax checking, application development procedures, and other information are provided in a highly integrated environment.

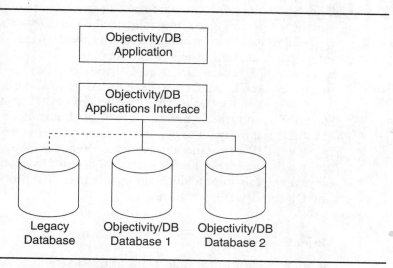

Figure 15.21   Objectivity/DB gateway to RDB and other legacy databases.

Gateways

Gateways allow applications to use both Objectivity/DB databases and relational or other types of databases. One use of gateways is to enable an Objectivity/DB application developer to access legacy data from a relational database from within an Objectivity/DB application. As an example, a mechanical design application could present parts, cost, and inventory information drawn from a relational database, allowing the designer to specify parts that are the most cost effective or readily available.

Today, Objectivity/DB application developers can access both Objectivity/DB and legacy databases within the same application. Since Objectivity/DB develops standard C and C++ languages and development tools, accessing legacy data requires only adding the appropriate procedure calls to the legacy database system from within an Objectivity/DB application. Also, through partnership with Persistence, a C++ Class Library interface is available to Oracle and Sybase.

Objectivity/DB is uniquely designed to allow for future expansion by providing access to relational or other kinds of databases through the Objectivity/DB federated database. As shown in Figure 15.22, the Objectivity/DB Federated Database architecture allows an application to access multiple Objectivity/DB databases. Other legacy databases can be included in a federation through a common Objectivity/DB programming interface, with command access to both Objectivity/DB and legacy databases controlled by a distributed transaction manager that supports a two-phase commit protocol.

Gateways can also allow relational database applications to access Objectivity/DB data. As an example, a 4GL application can show parts and inventory information about a mechanical assembly and its components that is stored in a relational database, and also provide access to the design information and images created by an Objectivity/DB mechanical design application.

An OpenRDB gateway that supports RDA/SQL protocol can accept requests from a 4GL application and retrieve object information from an Objectivity/DB database and return it to the application, either in terms of an existing relation from the RDB's data dictionary, or as a reference that can be stored in a table and used to retrieve the data later. A distributed transaction manager again plays a key role in providing common transaction processing between the RDB and Objectivity/DB databases.

Objectivity/SQL++

Both 4GL applications and Objectivity/DB applications require the ability to query for objects based on types, scopes, and content. Objectivity/DB supports a

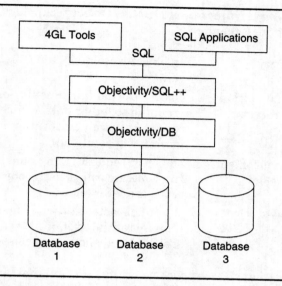

Figure 15.22   SQL gateway from RDBMs.

subset of the ANSI standard SQL that enables applications to make queries against an Objectivity/DB database. Objectivity/SQL++ is unique because it allows queries to be made using standard ANSI SQL syntax, standard C++ syntax, or a mixture of syntaxes. This makes it possible to apply SQL where-clause query strings to an Objectivity/DB database from an SQL gateway, and also to embed queries that use C++ language features within an Objectivity/DB application.

As standard object-oriented extensions to SQL evolve, Objectivity/SQL++ is uniquely positioned to provide new object database capabilities to 4GL and other kinds of applications through enhanced gateways. At the same time, Objectivity/DB developers will be able to take advantage of object-oriented SQL features provided by relational databases through a common federated database and programming interface that can pass more object-oriented SQL queries directly to RDB query engines.

Object and DBMS Technology

The following sections provide a brief introduction to object and DBMS technology.

Technology: Object and DBMS. Object technology, in brief, consists of the following ingredients:

identity	an object is uniquely identifiable independent of value(s)
encapsulation/ abstraction	object internal implementation is hidden by grouping together data (which may be hidden) with code (whose implementation may be hidden, while interface is available)
polymorphism	an object request is implemented by code chosen at run time according to the object type, even when new types are later added
classes	object characteristics may be defined in a class, and then instantiated Inheritance behaviors may be assigned and shared via classes composition

These capabilities become critical for building large, complex systems, allowing reuse of code and allowing the system to be extended easily. Database technology, in brief, consists of the following ingredients:

persistence	data is available beyond the lifetime of processes (programs)
recovery	following hardware or software failure, data is restored to a consistent state
language and query	multiple language and interfaces are available, including programmatic (procedural), ad hoc query (declarative), and graphical
concurrency	multiple users may simultaneously access the same data
distribution	transparent access is provided to data on multiple heterogeneous platforms
versioning	multiple alternative states of objects are accessible and are tracked
security	control over access to objects according to privileges is provided
administration	ability is provided to manage administrative tasks such as data collection and backup

These capabilities become critical for applications that require multiuser access to shared data, very large amounts of data, and high reliability.

Objectivity/DB provides full ODBMS capability by supporting object technology capabilities within a full DBMS. Inheritance provides persistence within the object paradigm, allowing fully flexible use of classes, extensibility, composition, etc., with full availability of all DBMS functionality, flexibility at run time to instantiate objects of any capability, and without the restriction of modified languages or hard-coded non-object persistence.

Technology: Object and Relational. Traditional, including relational, DBMS products provide effective solutions for simple fixed-size data that fits easily into tables, has little structure and little interconnection. Sample uses include order entry systems, reservations systems, accounting, inventory, and automatic teller machines.

However, applications with complex, interconnected data and high-performance requirements have not been able to use traditional databases. Translating such complex models into simple tuples and records is overwhelming, and the resulting performance is often two orders of magnitude slower than needed or available through native language implementations. Examples include CAD, CASE telecommunications, multimedia, and financial modeling and simulation, all of which, until now, have had to use flat files to achieve their required modeling and performance capabilities.

Traditional and object DBMSs will continue to coexist, with the traditional continuing to meet the needs of simple applications. As these older technology DBMSs add object layers, they will add some improved capabilities in interface, but the performance overhead of translating from objects to tuples/records will mean they still cannot meet the needs of complex applications. They will, however, integrate more and more naturally with ODBMSs.

User applications are becoming more complex and approaching enterprise integration by combining separate tasks (order entry with inventory and project management, engineering with manufacturing and finance). The more complex the application, the greater the need for the modeling and performance capability of Objectivity/DB. More complex environments need to work across multiple databases controlled by different departments. The full distribution capability of Objectivity/DB meets this need.

REFERENCES

Bloor, R. 1993. The patterns of change: are you ready for the third major computer technology wave? *DBMS Magazine* 6:1 (January).

Burleson, D. 1993. *Practical application of object-oriented techniques to relational databases.* Wiley\QED.

Comaford, C. 1993. At long last, a true query tool for end users. *PC Week*, March.

De Troyer, O., J. Keustermans and R. Meersman. 1986. *How helpful is object-oriented language for an object-oriented database model?* Proceedings of the International Workshop on Object-Oriented Database Systems. IEEE Computer Society Press.

Kersten, M. and F. Schippers. 1986. *Towards an object-centered database language.* Proceedings of the International Workshop on Object-Oriented Database Systems. IEEE Computer Society Press.

Scholl, M., C. Laasch, and M. Tresch. 1990. *Updateable views in object-oriented databases.* Proceedings of the International Workshop on Object-Oriented Database Systems. IEEE Computer Society Press.

Psychological Issues— Dealing with Resistance

16.1 THE BUSINESS REVOLUTION IN THE 1990s

Historically, corporate managers have had a schizophrenic attitude about their information systems areas. On one hand, they recognize that their companies would not be able to compete without computerized access to their information, and that many mission-critical functions are under the control of the information systems staff. On the other hand, top management often fails to see the direct benefit from their expenditures in computerized systems. They complain that the information system's staff is unresponsive to the needs of their end-users, and that systems are seldom delivered on time and within budget. They view the spiraling expenses of computer equipment and wonder if the investment is really worth the benefit.

Much of this perception dates from the earliest times of computing. Since the first mainframes were installed, managers have struggled with how they might exploit these very expensive resources. Once a need was identified, a staff of highly paid programmers often took months to deliver even the most basic functionality. Then many end-users felt that they were hostages to their computer staff, who controlled their information as well as their access to the information.

This tension has run in both directions. The information systems management perceives that top management does not understand the issues involved in the development of complex computer systems, and that they have been blinded by the media hype that computers are far more powerful than they are in reality. The movie *2001* and its HAL computer fostered this misconception. People naturally believe, and want to believe, that computers are highly intelligent, and they have a great deal of trouble understanding why it takes weeks to develop a simple report, and why the programmers charge their department thousands of dollars for very simple changes.

With the introduction of IMS, the first mainframe database, in the mid-1960s, the attitude of companies about their information changed radically. Prior to this time information systems were not seen by management as a resource, but as a burden that had to be controlled and maintained. The early adopters of the database system soon proved that it could be exploited and used to react faster to changing market conditions. Soon, all companies rushed to adopt database technology so that they could also exploit their information resources. The new databases promised information at their fingertips, and data processing has not been the same since.

The advent of decision support systems in the 1970s promised that information systems would be able to fulfill their mission of allowing companies full access to their information. This distribution of information takes many forms; lower-level managers require highly structured information, mid-level managers require semistructured information, and top-level managers require unstructured information (Figure 16.1).

There was also the issue of the source of information. While lower-level and mid-level management rely on internal information, top management required a significant amount of external information that did not reside in the company's databases. In fact, some 20 years after the advent of the decision support system, few top-level managers have a computer on their desks.

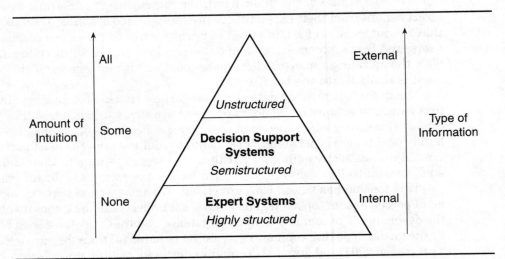

Figure 16.1   Problem structure hierarchy.

Part of the answer is due to a real failure on the part of the information systems staff. The end-users put forth a very simple request: "Deliver all of the information and allow me to summarize and control my information without interference." Management of the end-user departments was also under pressure to capitalize on the corporate information resource in order to make better decisions. The information systems management delivered systems that were far from this wish. Management reports were often "core dumps," long unintelligible listings that either did not contain the information that the manager wanted, or did not have it in a form that the manager could use.

Computer systems were also touted as being excellent tools for forecasting. Lower-level managers required forecasts for periods ranging from one week to six months, mid-level managers required forecasts that could go for six months to two years, and top-level managers required planning and forecasting for periods that could be measured in decades.

What these managers failed to recognize was the inherent failure of their data. While sophisticated computerized forecasting techniques such as triple exponential smoothing can be applied to data, no amount of computer modeling can compensate for bad data. As a forecast moves out on the time line, it becomes less valid, to the point that it becomes essentially meaningless. This widening confidence interval has been referred to as the "trumpet of doom" (Figure 16.2).

Some large companies, fed up with endless backlog and undelivered systems, have taken to outsourcing as an alternative to their information processing needs. Advocates of outsourcing argue that a large outsourcer can deliver systems more cheaply than an in-house staff because they can draw from a large pool of talent. Also, human resources are committed only for the duration of the project (Figure 16.3). Critics of the outsourcing approach argue that the company puts itself at great risk by trusting its mission-critical operations to an outside company. They also state that the company can no longer gain a competitive advantage because the technology that it has purchased from the outsourcing company is also available to its competitors. The verdict has not yet been reached about the overall benefits of outsourcing, but major corporations, such as Kodak and Xerox, are attempting to leverage outsourcing to control their spiraling computer costs. Those who have been most successful with outsourcing adopt a phased approach whereby the outsourcer is contracted at first to develop a small noncritical system. After this system has been delivered, the outsourcer moves on to a larger and more critical system. Companies that have a "whole-hog" approach to outsourcing have met with phenomenal problems, and many have returned to their in-house data processing.

Another undesirable side effect of the tension between data processing and management occurs when top management decides technology direction independently. IBM has practiced targeting top management for years in the hopes

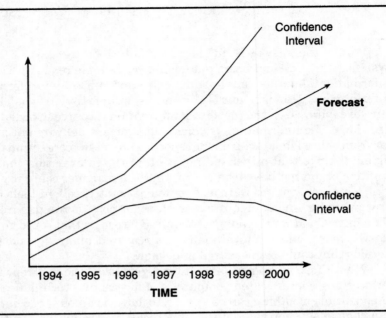

Figure 16.2   The trumpet of doom.

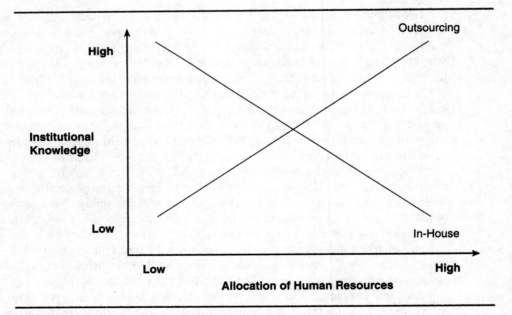

Figure 16.3   Outsourcing vs. in-house data processing.

Figure 16.4   "Mrs. Burleson, we must have an object-oriented database in order to remain competitive. Please find out what an object-oriented database is."

that the executive, who has no training in computer systems, will mandate the adoption of IBM systems and hardware. While this practice may seem ludicrous, it remains a common occurrence within many companies. Many top executives have been known to mandate downsizing of their IS organizations, stating "you have two years to get rid of the mainframe" or "I understand that we need client/server" (Figure 16.4).

When directives like these come in from top management, the information systems manager is compelled to comply regardless of the consequences. This practice is especially dangerous when an executive is led to believe that a technology such as downsizing will result in dramatic savings.

16.2   REINVENTING THE CORPORATION

There is a trend in the 1990s that has grown from the theories of Dr. Michael Hammer, whose basic tenet is that organizations must continually reinvent themselves in order to compete in the marketplace. This type of reinvention takes many forms; organizations are encouraged to toss out all preconceived notions about how they do business and take a fresh look at how their work processes can be changed.

This procedure also involves information systems. As the divisions within a company reinvent the way that they do business, information systems must adapt to meet changed requirements. The old days of large-scale information systems development are gone. Management can no longer wait for a period of years to see a new system develop from the initial concept to completion. Computer systems that take more than a few months to develop are guaranteed to be obsolete, and business needs are constantly changing. Information systems managers also no longer have the luxury of creating static systems. That is, they can no longer design systems around a strict architecture that cannot easily be modified. Organizations are no longer willing to be locked into a technology, and they are demanding that their computer systems be able to change as quickly as the business changes.

One of the most important factors in the ongoing success of any company is its ability to react quickly to changing market conditions. This ability to react extends to all areas of the organization, including the data processing staff. Within large corporate infrastructures it is not uncommon to see changes in reporting structures, workflows, and internal accounting on an almost constant basis. At times these internal changes can hinder reaction times. It has been suggested that the Japanese type of management, one where decisions are carefully crafted with input from many sources, has made the Japanese less able to respond quickly to changes in the marketplace. On the other hand, the Japanese style of management insures that all affected areas are aware of changes and the ramifications in their areas of responsibility.

One of the most embarrassing failures of data processing departments has been their inability to deliver fast, seamless access to information that will allow their end-users to improve their productivity. The idea of empowering the end-user has been around for many years, but we have failed dismally in efforts to allow end-users control over their information.

16.3   OBJECTIONS TO DISTRIBUTED SYSTEMS

There are many reasons data processing managers cite for not venturing into distributed databases. Upon first observation, many of their reasons appear grounded in conservative thought; after all, no manager wants to be seen as too radical. However, a closer look reveals that many of these managers have come to understand that distributed, open databases are a proven technology and they know about competitors that have been very successful with distributed database architectures. The managers also know that these successes have not come without a cost. Those shops that are successful with distributed architectures must have a financial commitment from top management, and they must be able to show that the companies will have a tangible benefit from distributed databases.

All companies tend to have a corporate philosophy about risk that falls somewhere between conservative and progressive (Figure 16.5). Where a company falls along this continuum is a reflection of the culture of the organization and the nature of its business. Up until about 1985, many companies did not need to venture into the high-cost, high-risk area of database systems because their existing technology was satisfactory and they would not have benefited greatly from state-of-the-art computer systems. As the market environment became more competitive, even the most stodgy companies began to realize that their information systems had to become more flexible; those companies that remained risk-averse were finding themselves being swallowed alive by their competition.

Today, managers who are honest about why they have failed to enter the distributed database world will cite fear as their roadblock. Managers who are responsible for millions of dollars in legacy systems must be very conservative, and they feel this means that they are compelled to remain "late adopters"

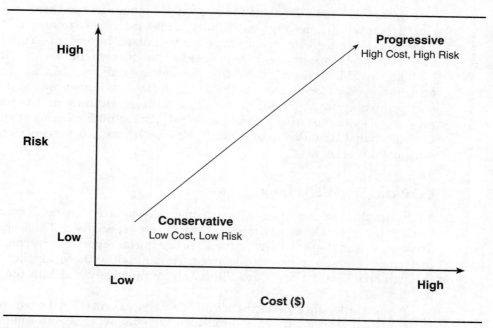

Figure 16.5   Cost vs. risk.

of technology, especially when the functionality of mission-critical systems is at risk.

Risk

Many managers state that the newest technology offerings are too "bleeding-edge" and risky for their shops. The perception of risk is especially prevalent in centralized, mainframe environments. When confronted with the prospect of abandoning their comfortable MVS operating systems and time-tested COBOL and IMS databases, many managers shudder with horror at the prospect of retraining their staffs in UNIX, C++, and PC-based GUIs. Equally disconcerting is the prospect of managing multiple databases instead of only a single database.

While horror stories abound from companies that have failed in their efforts to smoothly enter distributed database environments, many credit the success of their information systems, and even their entire companies, to their new computer architectures.

Lack of Security

Managers joke that "they call them 'open' systems because there is no security." In the mainframe days, one simply purchased a package such as RACF or ACF2 and let this prewritten package manage all of the system security. However, in an open environment, each package has its own unique security facility, and these facilities often fail to communicate well together. For example, on a single processor, entry onto the operating system is governed by a user ID and password, but entry into a database package running on the processor may require another user ID and password. This situation becomes amplified tenfold when distributed networks are used, with dozens of servers running on multiple processors.

Performance and Tuning

Many people from mainframe environments recognize that performance and tuning in a centralized environment can be an especially difficult challenge. They must work backward, starting from the initial report of a response delay, and track through a maze of sources, starting with the operating system, through the VTAM lines, onto the database manager, and into the specific application.

While challenging, performance and tuning in a centralized environment is relatively simple compared to tuning open systems. When a performance problem is encountered in an open environment, it can often be a nightmare to identify the offending component. A response problem could be due to an over-loaded processor, a buffer problem on a database server, a bottleneck in the LAN, or any number of other sources.

Staff Retraining

"My staff has been programming with COBOL for 20 years. They say C++ looks stupid, and that object-technology is only a fad." This is a very common complaint among experienced programmers. Any manager who plans to implement client/server systems should be prepared for this resistance, especially if the implementation is to be object-oriented. Fortunately, many of the GUI tools are very easy to learn, but the design of the interface to the database servers is another matter. The interface from the GUI to the server is very complicated, involving an understanding of remote procedure calls (RPCs), application programming interfaces (APIs), and the programming of the database server.

Programmers are forced not only to deal with a whole new conceptual framework, but with new programming languages. The C language is very common among client/server and distributed applications, and any successful effort must involve a programming staff that is capable of programming with C. The terse syntax of C, combined with the different ways of handling strings and arrays, often scares traditional programmers.

There are many approaches that are used to induce acceptance among the programming staff. The most effective approaches emphasize that the company is going to adopt the new technology regardless of the resistance, and that the staff will be given adequate training in the new technology. One manager put his request as "We will carry the wounded and shoot the stragglers."

Another effective approach is to salt the programming staff with junior-level programmers who already are familiar with the technology. Many universities offer internships for C++ experts who can be hired for as little as $10/hour. It is amazing what a difference the introduction of junior programmers has on the attitude of a resistant staff. It becomes clear to the elder programmers that they are going to be required to learn the skills or be displaced by junior programmers who earn less than one-half of their salary. Also, many experienced programmers become more willing to learn the new technology when they see a youngster in college who has mastered the cryptic new skills. "If this kid can lean C++, then so can I" is another motivating force.

Economic Payback

While many early client/server migrations could be justified from an economic perspective, this economic incentive is rapidly eroding. One of the economic benefits of client/server systems is the ability to offload processing onto the client, but managers are finding that implementing a client/server system can become more expensive after they factor in the additional costs for the client and server software. For example, a typical relational server can cost more than $50,000, and many vendors price the client software on a per-client basis. The client software costs can range from $200 for a simple client interface to more than $1000 for a multidatabase client package. These additional costs are becoming a major problem for systems managers on a limited budget.

Many savvy managers assume that client/server is going to be a more expensive proposition, and they justify the client/server system by emphasizing the intangible benefits of increased productivity for the end-users. In fact, this productivity increase can be very dramatic for some types of systems. Text-processing systems, for example, allow the end-users to "check out" text from the server database and edit the text locally on a powerful word processor. The edited text can then be reloaded into the server at a later date. This relieves the database server of a tremendous processing burden because all of the text editing is performed on a local PC, and the end-users are happy because they can use a state-of-the-art word processor.

In many cases, the illusion of productivity can be enough to justify the adoption of client/server. End-users are enamored with the futuristic look and feel of the GUI front ends, and they are often willing to fund a client/server conversion solely on the basis of a perceived productivity increase. This parallels the early adoption of mainframe computers by corporations in the 1950s for the status of having a computer. Regardless of the reasons for getting client/server, systems managers have had great success in introducing the technology by staging "gee-whiz" demonstrations of visual front ends such as PowerBuilder and Visual Basic. Once the end-users agree to get the new technology, applications for client/server begin to emerge.

While it seems backward to choose a technology before a legitimate use has been identified, this approach has been very effective. After the users begin to play with a client/server GUI, they often get ideas for productive uses that they would never have been able to identify if they had not had access to an initial tool. The moral is simple: Encourage your end-users to attend as many of the GUI vendor presentations as possible, and strive to get the users to implement a GUI, however simple it may be, in the hopes that it will serve as a catalyst for new application ideas.

New Human Roles in Distributed Databases Systems

17.1 INTRODUCTION

As data processing enters a new era of open, distributed systems, many of the traditional job roles are going to change dramatically. The duties of the system administrator and database administrator will undergo a huge turnabout and new roles will begin to emerge, especially in the area of object administration.

17.2 NEW ROLES FOR THE 1990s

The next decade will herald a revolution in the way computer professionals define their jobs. The days of the centralized database are gone forever, and data processing professionals must understand how new job roles are defined within the "open systems" paradigm. Thousands of businesses have undertaken "rightsizing" projects, and the widespread acceptance of C++ has made object-oriented technology ingrained into their delivery mechanisms.

The marriage of these technologies, distributed object technology (DOT), is being used successfully by major vendors in client/server systems. The Object Management Group (OMG) has been very successful with its Common Object Request Broker Architecture (CORBA), and IBM, Hewlett-Packard, and DEC have adopted CORBA for distributed object-oriented systems. "This technology will provide an evolutionary approach to the development of this much-needed solution," says Chris Stone, president of the Object Management Group. DOT will become an integral part of all new operating systems, and it seems clear that object-oriented technology will become ingrained in mainstream systems development in the late 1990s.

With DOT systems, the traditional roles of the database administrator (DBA) and data administrator (DA) will become obsolete. In the past, the DBA and DA were responsible for managing the information resource and insuring that all corporate information was controlled and distributed to all areas of the corporation. With distributed object technology, both data and behavior may be encapsulated within a persistent object or "pointed to" within the object.

This radical new approach to information processing will bring about many changes in job functions, but few will be more critical to the overall success of the corporation than the role of the object administrator (OA). The OA will perform the traditional duties of the DBA, but with an added dimension. The OA must be expert in object-oriented programming and distributed systems as well as database administration. The OA will perform a quality control function, and must oversee all systems development projects to insure that the objects "behave" properly. The OA will be responsible for the maintenance of the object class hierarchies and for insuring that all objects properly access the data repository. Object-oriented features such as inheritance and polymorphism add another dimension of complexity to the task.

The greatest challenge to the OA is the management of behaviors; object-oriented databases store both data and behavior, and the OA will be responsible for the management of the complex interactions between data and behavior, as well as the management of persistent storage.

Persistent storage for DOT systems can be achieved either by writing an internal database manager or by utilizing an object-oriented database package. In either case, the objects will be "composed," or assembled from some type of data repository (Figure 17.1). The OA will be responsible for managing the repository.

Data management techniques will also change dramatically. The OA must be able to track the usage of items by objects and to provide impact analysis for any data or behavior changes. In addition, the OA must be able to track context-sensitive data usage, such that the item LAST_NAME may be used as EMPLOYEE_NAME in one context and PAYEE_NAME in another. Behaviors must also be managed, and the OA must know the locations, names, functions, inheritance, and polymorphism of all behaviors that are stored within the objects.

Many companies are already establishing object administration groups to prepare for these changes in job responsibilities, and the successful professionals will be those who are willing to adapt to the changes that are mandated by these new paradigms. Only those companies that have the foresight to adapt to the changing technology will harvest the benefits of distributed object technology.

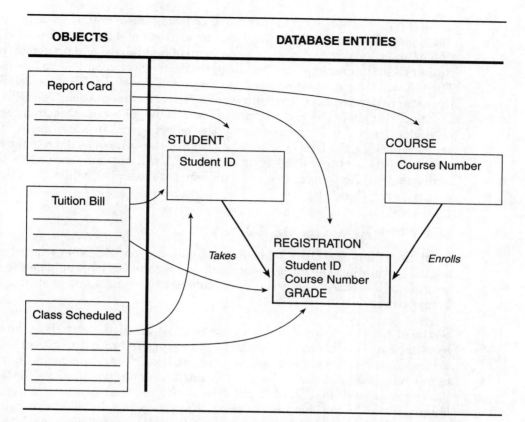

Figure 17.1   Objects are composed of many database entities.

How Object Administration Is Different from Database Administration

As the roles evolve, the OA and DBA will each have very separate responsibilities, although small shops may have one person performing both duties. The DBA will continue to be responsible for performance and tuning, security administration, database recovery, and database schema changes, but the OA will take over the responsibility for application migration and documentation of the database design. The OA will be much more visible to the programmers than the DBA, because they will rely on the documentation from the OA to give them the road map that they require to perform programming.

The biggest change for the DBA will be losing the overall responsibility for the system. Whereas a traditional system consists of a database and a collection of programs, an OT system is made up of a database and an object layer. Rather than the database driving the system, an object layer will be the driver. The OA will thus assume some of the responsibility of the DBA, especially in the areas of performance and tuning and system documentation. The DBA will no longer document the architecture of the database, because this architecture is hidden from the programmers by the object layer. In sum, much of the prestige of being the DBA will be taken over by the OA, who will have far more responsibility for the overall system. The DBA will now only manage a small component of the system (e.g., the hidden data storage), while the OA will manage everything else.

Who Will Step into the OA Role?

Even more than the DBA, the OA must be a person with very sophisticated technical training. The most likely candidate for the OA job would be the DBA because of the DBA's understanding of database engines and overall system architecture.

Skills of the OA. The OA must understand the detailed internals of the database engine. This is true even when the developers are not using an OODB. Today, most developers are building "object layers" and interfacing to traditional relational databases, so the OA must understand relational database internals. In addition, the OA must be very proficient in the programming language used by the object layer, and if the system uses distributed databases, the OA must understand the Common Object Request Broker Architecture (CORBA), which is becoming the de facto industry standard for distributed object systems. The OA is also the chief technician, and must have excellent interpersonal skills in addition to technical knowledge, because the OA will be the first person that the programmers will contact when they are having a problem.

The OA must also possess excellent planning skills. Careful object analysis is critical to the success of an OO system, because a poorly designed OO system is much harder to fix than a poorly designed relational system. The OA must be expert at object-oriented analysis (OOA), and must be able to act as teacher and mentor to the programming staff.

One very important point: Most new object-oriented systems development efforts are *not* using an object-oriented database. Instead, they are building an "object layer," usually in C++ or SmallTalk, and interfacing this to a traditional relational database. This means that the traditional role of the relational DBA does not change, but that the OA must understand the object layer as well as the internal structure of the relational database.

The New Job Responsibilities

The roles of the DA and DBA will change because of the introduction of object technology (OT). DBAs will continue to perform their present functions, while the OA will take over the new responsibilities of managing the object layer.

Responsibilities of the DBA. In the future, the DBA's responsibilities will include:

- Overall responsibility for the database.
- System performance and tuning; monitoring of the database system.
- Maintenance of system security (systems access, user ID administration).
- Migrations of applications from test to production.
- Database schema changes, database restructuring.
- Technical oversight for all database problems.
- Recovery (restores, roll-back, roll-forward).
- Reviewing and documenting of all database designs.

Responsibilities of the DA. The DA is often a nontechnical position, and is sometimes performed by nonprogrammers. Responsibilities might be listed as:

- Review of database design and cross-referencing all data elements (e.g., If the ZIP-CODE field changes in size from 5 digits to 9 digits, what programs use the ZIP-CODE field?).
- Maintenance of corporate data dictionary (e.g., standard word abbreviations, definition of data items).
- Maintenance of "roles" for data items. For example, the database field called PERSON-NAME could be used in the role of PAYEE-NAME by a payroll system, as EMPLOYEE-NAME by a personnel system, or as CUSTOMER-NAME by a marketing system.

The Role of the Object Administrator (OA). Object administration combines some the responsibilities of the DBA and DA with new responsibilities that are germane only to distributed object technology.

The OA must manage all of the behavior class libraries. For example, a change to a method in a base class may impact the behaviors of objects in many subclasses. The OA must analyze the impact of these changes and devise a way to insure that unintended results are avoided.

The OA must also document the interfaces to all objects. In OT, all objects can be accessed only via their methods, and the OA must document all of the methods that are encapsulated within each object. The OA must also document the "messages" that activate all of the methods in the application. In short, the OA documents the "road map" for the application, so that the programmers understand the interactions between objects.

The OA must manage distributed object systems. Distributed object technology (DOT) requires that all protocols (the "standard" way to talk to objects) be defined between systems. The software that manages this protocol is called an ORB (object request broker). The OA is responsible for defining the protocols for the ORB and insuring that all distributed data requests follow the standard interface method.

The most difficult management problems for the OA are the control of polymorphism and multiple inheritance. Polymorphism occurs when a method performs a different function because of the message used to activate the method. For example, in the BASIC language, the "+" sign is used to specify addition when it is used with numbers (x=1+1), or concatenation when it is used with character data (x="hello" + " there."). All of the polymorphism must be documented, usually in a matrix form, maintained, and distributed to the programming staff. Another problem is multiple inheritance, which occurs when a subclass inherits objects from more than one superclass.

Just as a change to a data item may affect many programs, changes to a method may affect lower-level classes that inherit the changed method. Whenever a change is made to a high-level method (called a base class), all of the lower-level methods must be checked to insure that unintended consequences do not occur. For example, a change to a ComputeDiscount method within a base class called INSURANCE may be inherited by the subclasses AutoCollisionPolicy and HomeownersPolicy, and all other subclasses of INSURANCE. These subclasses must be tested to insure that ComputeDiscount does not have any unintentional side effects.

What distinguishes a DOT system from a traditional distributed database is that all of the interdatabase communication is handled with "messages" instead of SQL calls. The messages are forwarded to an object request broker (ORB), and the ORB passes the messages along to the appropriate object layer. It is the management of the ORB that is the responsibility of the OA. The ORB insures that all objects, regardless of their home database, communicate with each other in a standard way.

In sum, the OA must take an OO system that is very complex and three-dimensional, and create two-dimensional documentation. This is one of the most challenging tasks for the OA, as well as one of the most time consuming and tedious.

Unlike traditional systems in which the database interacts with independent computer programs, object-oriented systems couple the data with the programs that manipulate the data. When pure object-oriented databases become robust enough to support mission-critical applications, companies will shift from using object layers on top of relational databases to a pure object-oriented approach. When the relational databases disappear, the OA will assume full responsibility for the entire object architecture, and the DBA role will become completely obsolete.

REFERENCES

Burleson, D. 1993. *Practical application of object-oriented techniques to relational databases.* Wiley\QED.

———. 1994. Objects, objects, everywhere: the role of object administrator. *Computerworld*, March 14.

Appendix: Distributed Object Environments

There are numerous projects to create object-oriented distributed systems to herald the introduction to this new architecture. Some of the major efforts include:

The "Pink" system by Taligent Incorporated

NeXTSTEP by Next Incorporated

The Borland Object Component Architecture (BOCA)

The Distributed Systems Object Model (DSOM) by IBM

Cairo/Chocago by Microsoft Incorporated

DOMF by Hewlett-Packard and Sunsoft

Distributed Objects Everywhere (DOE) by Sunsoft Inc.

Each of these products is described on the following pages. Because all of these products are currently under development, it is very difficult to accurately access the features of each product. The descriptions are based on vendor presentations and product announcements, and while some descriptions are vague, they provide a general overview of the direction of distributed object-oriented technology.

The players in this market will continue to jockey for position and align their products to capture market share. However, some vendors may be able to "force" their products on the market with massive marketing campaigns or by bundling their software with other system components. The good news for the user community is that each of the products will comply with the CORBA standard, and a new type of interoperability will become widely available.

PINK BY TALIGENT INCORPORATED

In 1992, IBM and Apple Inc. entered a joint venture to develop a revolutionary object-oriented operating system. Apple had been developing its own object-oriented operating system, code-named the "Pink" project, and the joint venture established a new company, Taligent Inc. Taligent also is using the highly regarded microkernel product called Mach 3, which was developed at Carnegie-Mellon University. The Mach kernel will also be incorporated into later releases of OS/2 and AIX.

The 125 developers on the Pink project moved to Taligent, which now employs more than 250 developers. Taligent has formed three primary business groups. The Development Environment Group (DEG) is responsible for soliciting third-party vendors to develop tools, such as utilities, for Pink. The Native Systems Group (NSG) is working on versions of Pink for various hardware, including Intel and Motorola chips. The Complementary Products Group (CPG) will be a remarketing group and is developing standard class libraries for Pink.

Pink promises to be a complete operating environment and tools set. It will have full object-oriented architecture, and is being created from the hardware level, meaning that all system operations, including basic input and output, will be governed by the environment.

This bottom-up approach promises to make Pink a processor-independent and portable product. Conventional operating systems such as DOS are constrained by their own architectures, and even small enhancements to the base operating system are very hard to assimilate. By using an object-oriented framework, Pink hopes to be easily extensible and simple to enhance and reconfigure. The ability to adapt quickly to changes in technology could give Pink a major advantage in the marketplace.

Pink is being marketed as a "vertical" product, focusing on value-added resellers and developers who specialize in system integration. Taligent is totally committed to the object-oriented approach in its operating system, and it foresees that object technology will become a necessity for all operating systems in the future.

Numerous third-party vendors are already developing tools for Pink. Borland, Novell, and WordPerfect Corp. have all expressed support for Taligent's efforts. Pink is being developed in a secret environment, and few developers have seen the working code.

Backward compatibility is also an issue for Pink. Objects must be created for existing applications to run under the new object environment. Compatibility with existing file structures is critical to the success of Pink. No matter how revolutionary, the Pink system must be able to support legacy applications. One of the major problems with IBM's OS/2 is that it was not compatible with existing operating systems such as MS-DOS. The inability of OS/2 to read MS-DOS files has been a primary reason for the slow acceptance of OS/2, even though OS/2 is considered to be technically superior to MS-DOS. IBM and Apple are currently working on software adapters that will allow Pink users to run existing Macintosh and OS/2 applications.

The greatest promise of Pink is the ability of developers to create cross-platform programs. This is very important to value-added resellers, who could use Pink to create custom systems that could be embedded in other system components. For example, a developer could use Pink objects to create a spreadsheet system that could be coupled with a database.

Parts of the Pink system began appearing in IBM's OS/2 and AIX systems in 1993. The incorporation of object-oriented layers to OS/2 should improve the overall functionality of OS/2, and will work with the System Object Model (SOM). Pink will probably provide objects for dealing with system tasks such as graphics. Objects will allow OS/2 to be more portable, and even to run multi-platform applications. In theory, OS/2 could utilize the Pink objects to run simultaneously on a PC and UNIX. At this time, Apple has no plans to incorporate Pink code into its System 7 operating system.

Pink is competing with several other object-oriented operating systems developments, namely NeXTSTEP from Next, Inc., and Windows NT (Cairo) from Microsoft. Pink is scheduled to ship in 1996, after the scheduled delivery of Cairo.

NEXTSTEP FROM NEXT INCORPORATED

NeXT is promising to deliver a remarkable product for client/server development in an object-oriented environment. Like Pink from Taligent Inc., NeXTSTEP is based on the Mach 3 microkernel from Carnegie-Mellon University. NeXTSTEP has been shipping for some time, and recently a NeXTSTEP for Intel Processors was introduced. The NeXT corporation hopes to compete directly with other object-oriented operating systems offerings, namely Windows NT (Cairo) and Pink. With end-users having become accustomed to delays in delivery from software vendors, the early introduction of NeXTSTEP may prove to be a major market advantage, provided that NeXTSTEP is relatively bug-free and offers all of the promised functionality.

This PC-based client/server tool allows users to develop systems that communicate seamlessly by using objects, and includes a library of objects. For example, NeXTSTEP has a set of database objects that allow the user to connect to a database by choosing and dragging the desired database icon. The icon contains all of the code required to connect to the SQL server for the database.

NeXTSTEP promises a complete object-oriented operating environment, with all of the robust features that are inherent in an object-oriented system.

NeXTSTEP has also announced a tool called Portable Distributed Objects (PDO), which will enhance the client/server capabilities of its product. PDO allows systems running on client/server machines to access objects from high-speed network servers.

THE BORLAND OBJECT COMPONENT ARCHITECTURE (BOCA)

BOCA is the method Borland has chosen to integrate all of the products within the Borland family. In theory, BOCA will allow common communications between Paradox, Quattro Pro, dBASE, C++, and Object Pascal.

The framework for BOCA is the Borland Desktop. Desktop functions as an all-purpose environment and, much like Microsoft Windows, acts as a container for "User-Friendly Objects" or UFOs. Desktop claims to provide a complete object-oriented environment that allows the user to access and customize any object within the framework. For example, a user could enter the "object inspector" and review all of the data attributes and behaviors for a UFO. The data and behaviors could then be modified to dynamically create a new UFO. Example of UFOs are graphic interfaces, print managers, and all of the customizable screen icons, including push buttons, spinners, radio buttons, and data fields.

BOCA is designed to integrate all Borland tools, but it is only used within the context of a single workstation. Client/server and remote workstation connections are not directly supported by BOCA. These functions are delivered with Borland's Integrated Database API (IDAPI), which uses the Borland InterBase Engine. The InterBase engine will also support remote database drivers and the "object layer," Borland is also developing the Borland Object Exchange Architecture (OBEX). Through OBEX, Borland hopes to extend the single-machine BOCA system to multiple platforms in a fully functional peer-to-peer distributed architecture.

A delivery date for the IDAPI has not yet been set, and the detailed functionality of IDAPI has not been published. However, some assumptions can be made based on the promises from Borland. To truly integrate all Borland databases, the IDAPI must be able to access nonstandard SQL databases such as dBASE and Paradox, in addition to a standard SQL interface for relational databases. In fact, any "open" connectivity package will need to deal with non-SQL databases. The most reasonable approach to this problem is to have the tool create a logical request that could then be parsed into the appropriate access language for the database. Under this scenario, a request could be translated into the SQL dialect for Paradox, and into a record-oriented syntax for non-SQL databases. This "dual access" strategy has been successfully implemented in the IDMS database. IDMS release 12.0 supports both relational and network data architectures under a single database engine, and requests are translated into the appropriate syntax depending on the target database. Borland has announced that this dual access will be handled with virtual tables. A virtual table is a common view of a database table, and this common view may be composed of data from different databases. In order to join tables from different databases, the InterBase engine must be able to join a relational table with a nonrelational table in a single query, and pass this data to the user by using a virtual table.

In order to compete with the huge Windows market, IDAPI developers also plan to establish bridges to allow Borland components to interface with Windows as well as OS/2 and the AIX operating system. Conversely, Microsoft has delivered its Open Database Connectivity (ODBC) product, which will allow Windows applications to communicate with Borland products. Being "first to market" is critical to both Microsoft and Borland, because the company that delivers a truly "open" connectivity tool will enjoy a tremendous market advantage. Because the InterBase engine is already a mature product on the UNIX platform, Borland has a much better chance of bringing the product to the marketplace than Microsoft.

The InterBase engine uses a peer-to-peer architecture, which means that any instance of InterBase can serve as either a client or a server. For example, the InterBase engine on a PC could be the client, while another instance of InterBase on UNIX could be the server.

Unlike Microsoft, Borland has chosen to implement object communications with dynamic link libraries (DLLs). Because the DLLs are precompiled, the BOCA architecture runs far faster than Microsoft's object linking and embedding (OLE), but it will not support dynamic binding of objects.

Borland has also introduced a visual programming tool for end-user development. The tool, called ObjectVision, allows the end-user to use "forms" to create screens and reports. ObjectVision is designed to run in a Windows shell, and allows the end-users to create applications that access both relational databases and ASCII files. ObjectVision will access Paradox and dBASE databases on the PC, and will also allow client/server connections to Sybase and DB2. This means that an end-user could create a Windows application that could access data from three platforms simultaneously: Windows, a UNIX database, and an IBM mainframe.

THE DISTRIBUTED SYSTEMS OBJECT MODEL (DSOM) BY IBM

IBM has made a commitment to object technology with its long-term plans for the OS/2 operating system environment. The Distributed Systems Object Model (DSOM) is an extension of the Systems Object Model (SOM), which currently exists within IBM's OS/2 operating system. SOM is designed to provide a language-independent method for defining class libraries and managing communications between objects, and DSOM adds a distributed component to this architecture.

Because DSOM will provide a language-independent standard interface, IBM is currently working on compiler enhancements that will allow DSOM statements to be embedded within standard third- and fourth-generation languages. Other third-party compiler vendors have also committed to delivering languages that support SOM, including Borland's C++ and Mircofocus COBOL. Digitalk Inc. has also announced support for SOM in its family of Smalltalk language products.

It is important to understand that SOM is a tightly integrated component of the OS/2 operating system, and not just an implementation of an object-oriented operating system. In other words, the base object classes that are created within OS/2 become a part of the OS/2 system, and are dynamically bound to programs at execution time. At run time, SOM currently acts as an object-oriented messaging system, whereby the sending object acts as a client, sending messages to the receiving object, which acts as a server. This type of architecture, combined with the language-independent feature, suggests that DSOM will not require that the client and server software be written in the same language. As an object-oriented tool, SOM has some shortcomings such as a lack of support for multiple inheritance; a new upgrade to SOM, SOM-2, is planned to address multiple inheritance and support for C++.

DSOM development is closely tied to the Taligent Inc. "Pink" system, and components from Pink are being incorporated into DSOM. Because IBM and Apple have undertaken a joint effort to create the Pink operating system, it is not clear if OS/2 and Pink will be competitors, or if Pink will eventually replace OS/2. Regardless, DSOM and Taligent's Pink will share a large portion of their base architecture. IBM has announced that all future releases of OS/2 will incorporate many of the object-oriented features of the Taligent product, and IBM also states that Taligent is not a successor to OS/2. At this time it is not clear how future releases of OS/2 will fare in the marketplace after the introduction of Taligent's Pink, and IBM appears to be unwilling to abandon OS/2 in favor of the Taligent effort.

IBM has committed to implementing DSOM in accordance with the CORBA standard of the Object Management Group. This will insure that DSOM systems will be compatible with other CORBA systems on different platforms.

IBM plans to incorporate DSOM into many different platforms, including midrange and mainframe systems, and IBM is currently collaborating with Novell to create a cross-platform system standard based on DSOM, to be called the Distributed Computing Environment (DCE). DCE, an environment for open systems, is currently in beta testing.

Many professional evaluators consider SOM to be more robust than other object-oriented development environments such as ObjectVision and Visual Basic. The future implementation of DSOM will contain complete APIs, message systems, and database servers.

CAIRO/CHICAGO BY MICROSOFT INCORPORATED

Cairo is the code word to describe the next major release of Microsoft Windows NT operating system. Cairo claims to offer a fully distributed object-oriented operating system. While Microsoft has been very vague about the details of Cairo, some features can be inferred by examining the current release of Windows NT. Clearly, Microsoft intends to capitalize on its huge Windows market to become the dominant object-oriented development system for personal computers. The team leader for Cairo is James Allchin, who has a proven track record at Banyan Incorporated, where he developed a well-received distributed computer environment. Microsoft has announced that Cairo will also support multimedia and pen-based computing.

Cairo is being designed as a low-level operating system, with management of the system at the physical storage level, and on up to the object level. In addition to the management of distributed tasks, Cairo will also manage system security and integrity. While Microsoft has not announced details about the database engine for this system, it will probably be an all-encompassing database manager with an object request broker for the front end. Object management will probably take the form of an extended release of OLE. OLE is used as an integration tool within most of the Microsoft product line, and adopts a simple object-oriented method.

While Microsoft has not yet expressed a full commitment to support the CORBA standard for distributed object technology, Chris Stone, president of the Object Management Group, has stated that he expects Cairo to "closely" follow the CORBA standard. Regardless of the quality of Cairo, it is probably going to capture a large share of the distributed market, especially if the current releases of Windows NT are well received.

DOMF BY HEWLETT-PACKARD AND SUNSOFT

Hewlett-Packard has made a commitment to the development of object-oriented technology with the creation of its Distributed Object Computing Program (DOCP), which will function as a superset of HP's Distributed Application Architecture (DAA).

In a very interesting turn of events, Hewlett-Packard entered into a joint effort with its major competitor, Sun Microsystems. In a joint submission to the Object Management Group (OMG), Sun and HP delivered the Distributed Object Management Facility (DOMF), which allows for the creation of distributed systems. DOMF will be fully compliant with the CORBA standard, and includes a complete object broker that allows multiplatform systems development. HP has always been committed to development standards for object-oriented systems, and was a founding member of the Object Management Group. HP and Sun hope that DOMF will allow users to take advantage of object-oriented distributed systems without having to adopt a new operating system.

The data storage engine behind DOMF will be the HP database, OpenODB. Unlike other object-oriented databases, OpenODB has support for relational architectures with its object-oriented structured query language (OSQL).

The HP efforts with DOCP will integrate many of the HP products, including OpenODB, HP visual user environment (HP-VUE), C++/SoftBench (HP's version of C++), and the HP line of OpenView products. HP also plans to take existing products and enhance their functionality by incorporating DOMF utilities. Especially important will be the enhancements to HP's NewWave. NewWave version 4 will be an enhancement to allow the object-oriented facilities of NewWave to function in a distributed environment. Version 4 of NewWave also supports Microsoft's Windows DLLs and Microsoft's object linking and embedding (OLE) tool. Most users of NewWave version 4 will probably choose to use the OLE API rather than the NewWave API, since HP has indicated that it plans to get out of the desktop API business.

The heart of DOMF is an object-oriented class definition facility, and includes a location broker. The HP location broker governs the behavior of three key services:

- The Manager of Objects Region Experts (MORE)
- The Object Region Expert (ORE)
- The Manager of Objects Manager (MOM)

The Manager of Objects Manager (MOM) stores information about several object managers, allowing distributed processing. MOM works with an Object Region Expert (ORE), which stores information about the storage domains for each MOM. At the highest level, the Manager of Object Region Experts (MORE) stores information about each MOM within the ORE.

HP and Sun are developing their own separate implementations of DOMF. Unfortunately, even though the implementations share a common architecture, Sun's DOMF will not handle naming conventions and binding in the same way as the HP version of DOMF.

DISTRIBUTED OBJECTS EVERYWHERE (DOE) BY SUNSOFT INC.

SunSoft Inc., the software development division of Sun Microsystems, has recently completed project DOE, an object-oriented distributed environment intended to compete with other object-oriented distributed systems. Project DOE has become a part of SunSoft's OpenStep environment, and SunSoft has contracted with Object Design Inc., the creators of the highly regarded ObjectStore database, to develop a Persistent Storage Manager Engine (PSME) to serve as the heart of DOE. PSME will use a subset of the ObjectStore database to allow DOE to store basic object information. Of course, DOE will comply with the CORBA standard.

Bibliography

Database Systems

Bacon, J. *Concurrent systems — an integration approach to operating systems, database and distributed systems.* Addison-Wesley, 1993.

Batelle, J., et al. Planning for 1995: the future is now. *Corporate Computing,* December 1992.

Baum, D. Middleware: Unearthing the software treasure trove. *InfoWorld,* March 1993

Bell, D. *Distributed database systems.* Addison-Wesley, 1992.

Beech, D. *Collections of object in SQL3.* Proceedings of the ninteenth VLDB Conference, Dublin, Ireland, 1993.

Blaser, A., ed. *Database systems of the 90s.* Berlin: International Symposium, 1990.

Bloomer, J. *Power programming with RPC.* O'Reilly & Associates, 1991.

Bobak, A. *Distributed and multidatabase systems.* Bantam Books, 1993.

Cellary, W., E. Gelenbe, and T. Morzy. *Concurrency control in distributed database systems.* Elsevier Science Publishing, 1988.

Chivvis, A. and J. Geyer. Think again: face the facts. These misconceptions about downsizing are just lame excuses for procrastination. *Corporate Computing,* March 1993.

Chorafas, D. *Handbook of database management and distributed relational databases.* TAB Books, 1989.

Chu, W., ed. *Distributed database systems.* Books on Demand, 1986.

Date, C. What is a distributed database? *InfoDB* 2:7 (1987).

Demers, R., et al. Inside IBM's distributed data management architecture. *IBM Systems Journal*, September 1992.

Fiorio, T. Managing distributed applications. *DEC Professional*, December 1992.

Franklin, M. *Local disk caching for client-server database systems*. Proceedings of the ninteenth VLDB Conference, Dublin, Ireland, 1993.

Goulde, M. Open systems: analysis, issues and opinions. *Open Information Systems*, December 1992.

Gray, B. Database/file servers. *Computing Canada*, March 1993.

Hackathorn, R. *Enterprise Database Connectivity*. Wiley, 1993.

Katzan, H. *Distributed Information Systems*. Petrocelli Books, 1991.

Korzeniowski, P. Gateways link legacy, distributed databases. *Software Magazine*, November 1992.

Lawton, G. Protecting integrity of distributed data. *Software Magazine*, January 1993.

McFadden, F. *Modern database management*, 4th edition. Benjamin Cummings Publishing Company, 1994.

Mulqueen, J. Distributed Database: a dream? *Communications Week*, March 1993.

Ozsu, M. and P. Valduriez. *Principles of distributed database systems*. Prentice-Hall, 1993.

Ozsu M. and P. Valdurez. Distributed database systems, where are we now? *Database Programming & Design*, March 1992.

Ricciuti, M. Terabytes of data—how to get at them? *Datamation*, August 1992.

Rymer, J. Will the RDBMS vendors dominate distributed computing? *Distributed Computing Monitor*, December 1992.

Shinhyalov, I. and P. Bourne. The shape of database to come. *DEC Professional*, November 1992.

Stein, J. Distributed databases: what they are, what are they good for? *Journal of Object-oriented Programming*, July–August 1992.

Stodder, D. Return of the process: client/server computing forces us to reexamine the data-centric approach. *Database Programming & Design*, March 1992.

Watt, P. and J. Celko. Hewlett-Packard's relational/object paradigm. *DBMS*, February 1993.

Weitz, L. Desperately seeking database independence: options for accessing diverse corporate data. *Software Magazine*, December 1992.

Object Technology

Abiteoul, S., P. Kanellkis, and E. Waller. *Method schemas*. Communications of the ACM, 1990.

Accredited Standards Committee X3/SPARC/DBSSG/OODBTG final report of the object-oriented database task group. September 1991.

Ahad, R. and D. Dedo. OpenODB from Hewlett-Packard: a commercial object-oriented database system. *Journal of Object-Oriented Programming* 4:9 (February 1992).

Alagic. *Object-oriented database programming.* Springer Verlag, 1988.

Ahmed, S., A. Wong, D. Sriram, and R. Logcher. *A comparison of object-oriented database management systems for engineering applications.* MIT Technical Report IESL-90-03, 1990.

Atkinson, et al. *The object-oriented database systems manifesto.* Deductive and object-oriented databases. Elsevier Science Publishers, 1990.

Atwood, T. and J. Orenstein. Notes toward a standard object-oriented DDL and DML. *Computer Standards & Interfaces* 13 (1991).

Babcock, C. Object lessons. *Computerworld*, May 3, 1993.

Banciinon, F. *Building an object-oriented database system: the story of O2.* Morgan Kaufman Publishers, 1992.

Banerjee, J., *Data model issues for object-oriented applications.* ACM Transactions on Office Information Systems, 5(1):3-26, 1987.

Beech, D. Collections of objects in SQL3. Proceedings of the Very Large Database Conference, Dublin, Ireland, 1993.

Bloor, R. The patterns of change: are you ready for the third major computer technology wave? *DBMS Magazine* 6:1 (January 1993).

Bradley, J. An object-relationship diagrammatic technique for object-oriented database definitions. *Journal of Database Administration* 3:2 (Spring 1992).

Brathwaite, K. *Object-oriented database design: concepts and applications.* Academic, 1993.

Bratsberg, S. E. *FOOD: Supporting explicit relations in a fully object-oriented database.* Proceedings of the IFIP TC2/WG 2.6 Working Conference, 1991.

Brown, A. W. *Object-oriented database and their applications to software engineering.* McGraw-Hill, 1991.

Burleson, D. Building your own SQL generator. *Database Programming and Design*, January 1994.

———. C neophytes. *Computerworld*, February 14, 1994.

———. Can you cope? Voice recognition technology. *Computerworld*, February 21, 1994.

———. Distributed object technology. *First Class Magazine*, October 1993.

———. Getting the GOOD GOOP on OOP. *Computerworld* April 1993.

———. Managing distributed databases—an enterprise view. *Database Programming & Design*, June 1994.

———. Mapping object-oriented applications to relational databases. *Object Magazine*, January 1994.

———. Objects, objects, everywhere: the role of object administrator. *Computerworld*, March 14, 1994.

———. Performance and tuning for the very large database. *Database Programming and Design*, 1992.

————. Performance and tuning strategies for the very large database. *Database Programming and Design*, October 1989.

————. *Practical application of object-oriented techniques to relational databases*. Wiley\QED, 1993.

————. An update on object-oriented databases. *Software Magazine*, November 1994.

Burleson, D. and S. Kassicieh. *A decision support system for scheduling*. Proceedings of the International Conference, Operations Research Society of America, Chicago, IL, 1983.

Burleson, D., S. Kassicieh, and R. Lievano. Design and implementation of a decision support system for academic scheduling. *Information and Management* 2:2 (September 1986).

Cattell, R. G. G. *Object data management: object-oriented and extended relational database systems*. Addison-Wesley, 1991.

Cattell, R. G. G. and T. Rogers. *Combining object-oriented and relational models of data*. Proceedings of the International Workshop on Object-Oriented Database Systems. IEEE Computer Society Press, 1986.

Chung, Y. and G. Fischer. Illustration of object-oriented databases for the structure of a bill of materials. *Computers in Industry* 19 (June 1992).

Codd, E. F. *The relational model for database management*, version 2. Addison-Wesley, 1990.

Comaford, C. At long last, a true query tool for end users. *PC Week*, March 1993.

Date, C. J. *An introduction to database systems*. Addison-Wesley, 1990.

Deductive and object-oriented databases. Proceedings of the First International Conference on Deductive and Object-Oriented Database. Elsevier Science Publishing, 1990.

Deductive and object-oriented databases. Proceedings of the Second International Conference on Deductive and Object-Oriented Database. Elsevier Science Publishing, 1991.

De Troyer, O., J. Keustermans, and R. Meersman. *How helpful is object-oriented language for an object-oriented database model?* Proceedings of the International Workshop on Object-Oriented Database Systems. IEEE Computer Society Press, 1986.

Dittrich, K. *Object-oriented database systems: the notions and the issues*. Proceedings of the International Workshop on Object-Oriented Database Systems. IEEE Computer Society Press, 1986.

Dittrich, Dayal, Buchmann, *On object-oriented database systems*. Springer Verlag Publishers, 1991.

Franklin, M., M. Carey, and M. Linvey. *Local disk caching for client/server database systems*. Proceedings of the Very Large Database Conference, Dublin, Ireland, 1993.

Gidman, J. Practical applications of distributed object technology. *Object Magazine*, March–April 1994.

Gorman, K. and J. Choobineh. *An overview of the object-oriented entity relationship model (OOERM)*. Proceedings of the Twenty-Third Annual Hawaii International Conference on Information Systems, Vol. 3, 336–345.

Goutas, S., P. Soupos, and D. Christodoulakis. Formalization of object-oriented database model with rules. *Information and Software Technology* 33 (December 1991).

Gray, P. *Object-oriented databases: a semantic data model approach*. Prentice-Hall, 1992.

Implementing persistent object bases : principles and practice. International Workshop on Persistent Object Systems. Morgan Kaufman Publishers, 1991.

Kersten, M. and F. Schippers. *Towards an object-centered database language*. Proceedings of the International Workshop on Object-Oriented Database Systems. IEEE Computer Society Press, 1986.

Kim, W. *Introduction to object-oriented databases*. MIT Press, 1990.

———. *Issues of object-oriented database schemas*. Doctoral thesis, University of Texas at Austin, 1988.

———. Object-oriented database systems: promises, reality, and future. Proceedings of the Very Large Database Conference, Dublin, Ireland, 1993.

———. *Research directions in object-oriented database systems*. Communications of the ACM, 1990.

Lampson, B. and D. Lomet. A new commit optimization for two-phase commit. Proceedings of the Very Large Database Conference, Dublin, Ireland, 1993.

Larson, J. and R. Saeed. Five-schema architecture extends DBMS to distributed applications. *Electronic Design*, March 18, 1982.

Liu, L. and E. Horowitz. *Object database support for CASE*. Prentice-Hall, 1991.

Lomet, D. Key range locking strategies for improved concurrency. Proceedings of the Very Large Database Conference, Dublin, Ireland, 1993.

Loomis, M. Integrating objects with relational technology. *Object Magazine*, July/August 1991.

———. Object and relational technology—can they cooperate? *Object Magazine*, July/August 1991.

Loomis, M., T. Atwood, R. Cattel, J. Duhi, G. Ferran, and D. Wade. The ODMG object model. *Journal of Object-Oriented Programming*, June 1993.

Lyngbaek, P. and W. Kent. *A data modeling methodology for the design and implementation of information systems*. Proceedings of the International Workshop on Object-Oriented Database Systems. IEEE Computer Society Press, 1986.

Magedson, Building OT from the bottom up. *Object Magazine*, July/August 1991.

Martin, J. and J. Odell. *Object-oriented analysis and design*. Prentice-Hall, 1992.

McFadden, F. Conceptual design of object-oriented databases. *Journal of Object-Oriented Programming* 4 (September 1991).

McFadden, F. and Hoffer. *Database management*. Benjamin Cummings Publishing Company, 1987.

Meyer, *Object-oriented software construction*. Prentice-Hall, 1988.

Morgan, J. Ingres for DB2 users. *Relational Database Journal*, May–July 1993.

Roy, M. and A. Ewald. Locating and managing ORB objects. *Object Magazine*, March–April 1994.

Rowe, L. *A shared object hierarchy*. Proceedings of the International Workshop on Object-Oriented Database Systems. IEEE Computer Society Press, 1986.

Ruben, K. and A. Goldberg. *Object behavior analysis*. Communications of the ACM (September 1992).

Schek, H. and M. Scholl. *Evolution of data models*. Proceedings of the International Workshop on Object-Oriented Database Systems. IEEE Computer Society Press, 1990.

Scholl, M., C. Laasch, and M. Tresch. *Updateable views in object-oriented databases*. International Workshop on Object-Oriented Database Systems. IEEE Computer Society Press, 1990.

Soloviev, V. An overview of three commercial object-oriented database management systems: ONTOS, ObjectStore, and O/sub 2/. *SIGMOD Record* 21 (March 1992).

Stileleather, J. Why distributed object computing is inevitable. *Object Magazine*, March–April 1994.

Stone, C. The rise of object databases: can the Object Management Group get database vendors to agree on object standards? *DBMS*, July 1992.

Stonebraker, M. and E. Neuhold. *A distributed data base version of Ingres*. Berkeley Workshop on Distributed Data Management and Computer Networks, 1977.

Thalhiem, B. *Extending the entity-relationship model for a high-level, theory-based database design*. Proceedings of the International Workshop on Object-Oriented Database Systems. IEEE Computer Society Press, 1990.

Unland, R. and G. Schlageter. *Object-oriented database systems: concepts and perspectives*. Proceedings of the International Workshop on Object-Oriented Database Systems. IEEE Computer Society Press, 1990.

Yourdon, E. The marriage of relational and object-oriented design. *Relational Journal* 3:6 (January 1992).

Varma, S. Object-oriented databases: where are we now? *Database Programming & Design*, May 1993.

Vasan, Relational databases and objects: a hybrid solution. *Object Magazine*, July/August 1991.

Index

A

Access database, 3, 8, 88
Access control facility (ACF2), 213, 336
ACF2. *See* Access Control Facility
ad hoc queries, 41
ADS/Online, 4
ANSI, 133
API. *See* Application Programming Interface
application objects (AO), 143
application programming interfaces (API), 81, 133, 149–153, 192
architectural distribution, 71
automatic speech recognition (ASR), 269, 278–280

B

Bachman, Charles, 34
Bachman diagram, 34–35
BDAM, 28, 35
bill-of-materials (BOM) relationships, 21

Bonczeck, Robert, 263
Borland's Integrated Database API (IDAPI), 350
Boyce-Codd third normal form, 18

C

C language, 4, 9, 216, 265, 311, 324
C++ language, 8, 117, 123, 143, 160, 291, 311, 316–317, 324–325, 337, 350–352
CAD, 132
cascading revokes, 222
CASE, 291, 322
Chelko, Joe, 75
Chen, Dr. Peter, 18
CICS, 4
client/server, 87, 129, 179
COBOL, 3, 4, 6, 10, 72, 93, 175, 216, 265, 336–337
CODASYL, 15, 23, 32–39, 131, 182, 199, 208, 260
Codd, Dr. E. F., 18, 38–39, 262
commit, 188